THE
SHORTEST WAY
TO THE ESSAY

THE
SHORTEST WAY
TO THE ESSAY

Rhetorical Strategies

———————

M A Y F. M c M I L L A N

MERCER

ISBN 0-86554-132-9

Library of Congress Cataloging in Publication Data

McMillan, May F. (May Flewellen), 1921-
    The shortest way to the essay.

    Includes index.
    1. English language—Rhetoric.   I. Title.
PE1408.M3955   1984   808.4   84-20567
ISBN 0-86554-132-9 (alk. paper)

CONTENTS

Foreword xv

Acknowledgments xix

Chapter I
   Introduction 1

Chapter II
   Inquiring 7
      Thinking through a Topic: Search, Sort, Select 7
      Relating Parts to the Whole: Outline Form 18

Chapter III
   Shaping the Deductive Essay 29
      Audience and Voice 29
      Outline to Essay 39
      Student Essay: "Violence and the Young" 51
      Paragraph to Sentence 58
      Word to Punctuation 79

Chapter IV

Shaping the Inductive Essay 89

Establishing Perspective 89

Student Essays:

"What is Objectivity" 95

"Beware: Chicken Crossing" 103

"A Childhood of Pegasus" 111

"The Braves' Chances in 1982" 121

Structuring the Essay 132

Chapter V

Shaping the Familiar Essay 145

Establishing Perspective 145

Student Essays:

"Procrastination" 153

"The 1960s" 157

"On the Persuasiveness of Print
        or Why I Appear Schizophrenic" 161

"O Christmas Tree, O Christmas Tree!" 167

Structuring the Essay 171

Chapter VI

Variations and Applications 181

Structural Variations 182

Essay: "My Wood," by E. M. Forster 185

Voice Variations 189

Essay: "Who Killed King Kong," by X. J. Kennedy 193

Variations in Subject Treatment 197

The Persuasive Essay 198

Essay: "Bid a sad farewell to the landscape
plotted and pieced," by Ted Walker 203

Selected Essays for Reading and Analysis 215

"Needed: Full Partnership for Women"
        by Margaret Mead 217

"Crane and Hemingway: Anatomy of Trauma"
        by Earle Labor 221

"The Music of *This* Sphere"
    by Lewis Thomas 231
"Reflections on Gandhi"
    by George Orwell 237
"Preface to a Book of Statistics"
    by Don Marquis...................................... 245
"Which"
    by James Thurber 249
"What's a Mother For But to Suffer?"
    by Erma Bombeck 251
"Old China"
    by Charles Lamb..................................... 257
"Once More to the Lake"
    by E. B. White.. 263

EXTENDED TABLE
OF CONTENTS

Foreword xv

Acknowledgments xix

Chapter I
   Introduction 1

Chapter II
   Inquiring 7
      Thinking Through a Topic: Search, Sort, Select 7
        Search 1 7
          Assignment 1: Search 1 9
        Sort 1 10
          Assignment 2: Sort 1 12
        Select 1 12
          Assignment 3: Select 1 12
        Search 2 13
          Assignment 4: Search 2 13
        Sort 2 14

Assignment 5: Sort 2 15

Select 2 15

Illustration—The Search, Sort, Select Process 16

Assignment 6: Select 2 18

Relating Parts to the Whole: Outline Form 18

Inductive Topic Outline 19

Assignment 7: Inductive Topic Outline 22

Inductive Sentence Outline.................................... 23

Assignment 8: Inductive Sentence Outline............. 24

Checklist for Inductive Sentence Outline 24

Deductive Sentence Outline................................... 25

Assignment 9: Deductive Sentence Outline............ 26

Chapter III

Shaping the Deductive Essay 29

Audience and Voice... 29

Identifying the Audience 30

Assignment 1: Describing Your Audience 31

Assignment 2: Discovering Magazine Audiences 32

Creating the Voice 33

Chart: The Personal, Conversational, and Objective
Voices 35

Assignment 3: The Voice and the Reader 36

Assignment 4: The Voice and the Writer............... 37

Illustration—Voice: A Few Writer-Subject-Reader
Relationships 38

Outline to Essay... 39

The Introduction... 40

Illustration—Deductive Pattern for Essay of Medium
Length 41

Assignment 5: Rough Draft of the Introduction 44

The Body 45

Assignment 6: Rough Draft of the Body 46

The Conclusion 46

Assignment 7: Rough Draft of the Conclusion 47

Polishing the Rough Draft................................... 47

Checklist for the Rough Draft 48
Assignment 8: Polishing the Rough Draft.............. 49
Student Essay: "Violence and the Young" 51
The Typed Essay 57
Assignment 9: Typing the Revised Essay.............. 57

Paragraph to Sentence 58
Deductive Paragraphs 58
Assignment 10: Analyzing Paragraphs 1 61
Assignment 11: Analyzing Paragraphs 2 67
Assignment 12: Checking the Paragraph 69
Checklist for Paragraph Development.................. 69
Assignment 13: Deductive Essay #2 70
Sentence Variety and Emphasis 71
Checklist for Sentence Variety and Emphasis.......... 78
Assignment 14: Deductive Essay #3................... 79
Word to Punctuation 79
Word Choice.. 79
Checklist for Word Choice........................... 84
Assignment 15: Revising the Word Choice 84
Punctuation 85
Assignment 16: Deductive Essay #4................... 87

Chapter IV
Shaping the Inductive Essay 89
Establishing Perspective 89
Characteristics 89
Creating the Reader 90
Achieving Closeness 91
Choosing a Subject................................... 92
Student Essays: "What is Objectivity" 95
"Beware: Chicken Crossing"....................... 103
"A Childhood of Pegasus" 111
"The Braves' Chances in 1982"..................... 121

Structuring the Essay 132
The Inductive Outline 132
Assignment 1: Inductive Sentence Outline........... 133

The Introduction... 133
    Assignment 2: Rough Draft of Introduction 137
The Body 137
    Illustration—Abbreviated Inductive Pattern
         for Essay of Medium Length 138
The Conclusion 141
    Assignment 3: Rough Draft of Body
and Conclusion 142
    Assignment 4: Revising and Typing the Essay 142
    Assignment 5: Inductive Essay #2....................143
    Assignment 6: Inductive Essay #3....................143

Chapter V
Shaping the Familiar Essay 145
Establishing Perspective 145
  Characteristics 145
  Assuming a Stance 146
  Other Elements 148
  Choosing a Subject 149
    Student Essays: "Procrastination" 153
    "The 1960s" 157
    "On the Persuasiveness of Print
        or Why I Appear Schizophrenic" 161
    "O Christmas Tree, O Christmas Tree!" 167
Structuring the Essay 171
  The Preliminary Steps......................................171
  The Introduction...172
  The Body 175
  The Conclusion 176
  The Total Effect on the Reader 177
    Assignment 1: The Familiar Essay 178
    Checklist for the Familiar Essay......................178
    Assignment 2: Familiar Essay #2....................179

Chapter VI
Variations and Applications 181

Structural Variations 182
    Assignment 1: Analysis of Structure 183
    Essay: "My Wood" by E. M. Forster 185
Voice Variations 189
    Essay: "Who Killed King Kong?"
        by X. J. Kennedy 193
Variations in Subject Treatment 197
    Assignment 2: Choice Essay #1 197
    Assignment 3: Choice Essay #2 198
The Persuasive Essay 198
    Essay: "Bid a sad farewell to the landscape
        plotted and pieced" by Ted Walker 203
    Assignment 4: Persuasive Essay #1 214
    Assignment 5: Persuasive Essay #2 214
Selected Essays for Reading Pleasure and Analysis 215
    "Needed: Full Partnership for Women"
        by Margaret Mead 217
    "Crane and Hemingway: Anatomy of Trauma"
        by Earle Labor 221
    "The Music of This Sphere"
        by Lewis Thomas 231
    "Reflections on Gandhi"
        by George Orwell 237
    "Preface to a Book of Statistics"
        by Don Marquis 245
    "Which"
        by James Thurber 249
    "What's a Mother For But to Suffer"
        by Erma Bombeck 251
    "Old China"
        by Charles Lamb 257
    "Once More to the Lake"
        by E. B. White 263

to my students

FOREWORD

The Shortest Way to the Essay: Rhetorical Strategies is a unique college writing text designed for intermediate levels. It combines both traditional and innovative rhetorical strategies to teach mastery of three essay forms—the deductive, the inductive, and the familiar essay. In small steps, with plenty of examples, it leads students through the process of thinking, drafting, and polishing.

The author is an experienced classroom teacher whose methods have evolved over twenty years of practice with students of all backgrounds, personalities, and interests. She has learned ways to lead students through thinking processes that focus on exploring topics, arranging ideas, and presenting them to readers. Informed by recent rhetorical theory and firmly grounded in practice, this model/process approach develops mastery of important essay skills. The book includes three modes of thought (association, deduction, and induction), three voices (objective, conversational, and personal), and three essay forms (deductive, inductive, and familiar). The last chapter, which adds sample essays written by professionals, extends the basics of the preceding chapters to variations of the voices and thought arrangements and to the persuasive essay. The text deliberately limits assignments to those absolutely necessary to the method, thereby allowing instructors to add assignments appropriate to their use of the book. The sequence of assignments needs to be followed because it is a carefully structured process; however, topic choices are left up to individual students or teachers.

Teachers and students may use this book in many ways. On the intermediate level it can be used for a single course; for less advanced classes it can be divided into two courses (one course: first three chapters; second course: last three chapters). English teachers will find that handbooks dovetail very nicely with the book—as do books of readings or literature if they wish to use them to provide common experience for the class to write about. They may also add assignments directed especially toward essays of illustration, classification, cause and effect, comparison and contrast, and extended definition. Teachers in other disciplines who are trying to share with English departments the task of teaching writing can refer to *The Shortest Way* for helpful guidelines in the writing process and in the finished product. The text can provide the foundation for a cross-curricular writing program because the essays provide basic understandings that can be supplemented by other kinds of academic writings like lab reports or journals. Moreover, students who have forgotten how to write essays can turn to the book for aid, and adults who are reentering the academic world can use it for a refresher course in college writing. In other words, the three essay forms explained in this book provide an appropriate set of rhetorical models that, when mastered, give the student powerful tools of expression that can be used in any kind of writing task.

In addition to its flexibility, another advantage of the text is its emphasis on process. For far too long, teachers have marked the final products of students without giving them any direction about how to achieve the desired products. Recent rhetorical theory has begun to emphasize the process. This text provides a complete, clear, efficient method for invention or prewriting based on Search, Sort, Select procedures; it progresses through thought verification and planning, considers the writer's distance and audience roles, discusses moving from outline to essay, shows how to evolve paragraphs and produce varied and effective sentences, and also provides procedures for critical review of what one has written.

The process is designed around models of student writing. Students gain confidence by having a peer model to follow, and their sense of participation in the evaluation adds immeasurably to their competence in judging good writing. This process-oriented, model-based approach to teaching writing is useful for students at all levels: those students who cannot handle abstractions well; more advanced students who can write one kind of essay but not others; returning adult students who may have been away from academic writing for a while and lack confidence in how to proceed or knowledge about what "essays" really are.

Besides having these obvious advantages for students, the text offers considerable advantages to teachers. A beginning teacher of composition will find it useful because it takes the lead in speaking directly to the student about how to work. An experienced teacher will appreciate the flexibility the three-essay and three-voice model offers as he or she builds the kind of course desired. For any teacher, three clear advantages emerge. First, the text functions as a stand-in for the teacher outside of class when a student, locked in the process, needs a helping hand. Second, the clarity of the goals and objectives makes grading much easier and feedback more helpful. Because the expectations about writing are explained and illustrated, a student can see how the essay measures up. There is no mystery about why a teacher calls one essay good and another one poor. If a teacher uses peer critiques in class, the evaluations are made even clearer. Finally, the method has this outstanding advantage: it really works. Both experienced and inexperienced teachers who have used the method report with enthusiasm their success and their joy in watching a wide range of students grow enormously in skills, confidence, and understanding. And they are even more pleased when former students tell them that the course based on this method was the most valuable course they had in college.

Those who use this text will come to see the significance of the title. *The Shortest Way to the Essay* is a path through good thinking, careful planning, and thoughtful revisions. The author points the way.

Marjorie T. Davis
Associate Professor of English
Director of the Writing Program
Mercer University

ACKNOWLEDGMENTS

Books are not created alone—although an author may feel that way as she labors at the typewriter. I had the help of students, colleagues, typists, administrative officers, editors, designers, friends, and family. I thank them all.

I learned from my students as I taught. They gave me their loyalty and enthusiasm and willingly furnished me with examples for this book. Except for one example I could not identify, I have, where appropriate, credited the selected examples by name. I regret being unable to credit that one writer, having removed her name from the paragraph "Reading Informs" when I first used it for class work. Other teachers who taught from my manuscript also contributed three essays by their students, students whom I like to think of as partly my own.

I began this book many years ago, but put it aside when the perceptual approach to writing was popular. Then came the time when rhetoric was once more revered. After Marj Davis used my technique in her own Advanced Composition class, she insisted that I bring my chapters forth and complete the book. She bolstered, cajoled, and directed me over a long period, critiquing each part as I wrote. Without her this book would not exist.

Other colleagues added their support. George Espy, Dale Mathews, Loxley Nichols, and Remington Rose-Crossley taught from my manuscript and offered valuable insights. Never too busy to help, Margaret Engelhart warmed me with her interest and her beneficial counsel. When I needed it, Ken Hammond came to my aid—whether to advise, to suggest revisions in wording, or, as Chairman of the English Department, to rearrange a schedule. Rollin Armour, Dean of the College of Liberal Arts, took a friendly personal interest in my project. Through his office came approval for leaves of absence and financial support provided by the Faculty Research and Development Fund. Isabella DeWitt, former secretary of the English Department, and Karen Cheshire, our present secretary, tallied many hours in typing and xeroxing. Bessie Killebrew, Livonia Howard, and Vivian J. Lewis also helped with manuscript preparation.

In addition, I had the assistance of those who interpreted ideas for me. Martha Hutcherson, friend and neighbor, created the Search-Sort-Select and Voice illustrations which were later prepared for the press by Sam Hutto of the Mercer Art Department, and my nephew Charlton McMillan took the photograph that appears on the cover.

The manuscript was shaped into a printed text by the staff of Mercer University Press. Their patience with me and their expertise speak for themselves.

Mercer University   *May F. McMillan*
Macon, Georgia
February 2, 1984

True ease in writing comes from art, not chance,
As those move easiest who have learned to dance.

Alexander Pope

Honey, 'tain't nuthin' hard ter do—
hit's jes th' dreadin' uv it.

Folk saying

CHAPTER I

Introduction

This textbook cannot teach you everything about writing—no textbook can. Nor can you learn everything about writing in one or two writing courses—or even in four years of college. Just as education is an ongoing process that does not end when you grasp your diploma, so writing, a part of that process, does not end when you have closed your notebooks. Long after you graduate, you will continue to communicate in your personal and professional lives, and, if you practice the art, you will continue to grow as a writer.

Even when you recognize that writing is an essential part of education, you still may not enjoy writing or look forward to weekly writing assignments. In fact, many of you face a writing course with an uncertainty and a dread not shared by the happy spirits who hit it on the first draft. This book is for those who find writing a difficult and disagreeable task as well as for those who find writing a pleasure. One of its aims is to take the chore out of writing so that everyone can find gratification in shaping language to convey ideas. It will give all, including those who write intuitively, the opportunity of learning how to apply some principles of the art of writing, thereby freeing many from the dread of writing and others from depending on chance inspiration.

This text uses the essay form to demonstrate basic principles of communication both for aesthetic and for practical reasons. Aesthetically, knowing the essay as a literary genre can lead you to delight in its creation and to appreciate the accomplishments of other essayists. Practically, knowing how to write an essay can help you succeed in college. Instructors require essay writing for assignments and exams to determine if a student can select, organize, and interpret salient facts so that the ideas are clear to readers unfamiliar with the subject. This ability is expected of the educated person.

Of course, ideas are conveyed in prose forms other than essays, and that is why this book presents some basic principles that are valid for written communication whether you are writing essays for college credit now or business reports for your boss after graduation. The overall aim of this book is to prepare you not just to write an essay but to adapt to almost any writing situation—personal, educational, or professional. And, as a bonus, you should acquire a few thinking devices and problem-solving techniques whose application can be extended beyond writing to situations in everyday life.

These are big aims, big for so small a book, and only you can achieve them. You will have to be willing to work and to work patiently. You will have to be willing to set aside your own way of doing things and follow the directions given in the book even when you do not perceive where they are leading. Many of you will be frustrated, some will feel restricted and worry about losing what creativity you possess, and most of you will decide that the book has been titled incorrectly since the shortest way to the essay seems like a very long journey. At the end of the road, if you have done your part, you can look back and see that the way was really a short, direct one and that the freedom you thought you were losing has been multiplied many times. You can then claim freedom to write without fear, freedom to write on demand without having to wait for an inspired moment (though a bit of help from the Muse is always welcome), freedom to think clearly and to express ideas easily, and freedom to be creative and still communicate to the reader.

Although the details of this book's procedure will become clear only after you have studied all the chapters, a survey of the tables of contents will give you some clues. Note that the second chapter begins with the problems of how to think through a topic and generate ideas. Then, once you have gained some thoughts, you arrange them so that the relationships among the ideas are clear. By showing you how to use your mind to bring a subject into focus, these steps, a necessary prelude to writing, will relieve you of much frustration. Yet the steps are simple ones, so simple that you will not realize what is occurring, for in this process of thinking and arranging you will use the three modes of thought—the inductive, the deductive, and the movement-by-association—that shape the structures of this text's three major essay forms. Chapter 2, therefore, is a very important one because it forms the foundation of the remaining chapters.

To the second chapter's techniques of thinking clearly and organizing thoughts, chapter 3 adds other basic principles of communication. Unless you are recording notes or impressions for yourself, your purpose in writing is always to communicate to someone else. Consequently, you should never try to write unless you know who your reading audience will be. This chapter shows you how to project that audience and explains why you need to be aware of the reader with every word you write. In addition, you cannot write without establishing a particular relationship with your subject and your reader, a relationship that is reflected by the voice you assume. In clarifying the meaning of *voice*, this chapter describes in detail the objective, the conversational, and the personal voices, the three voices you will use with the three major essay forms of the text. After understanding audience and voice, you then employ objective voice in writing a deductive essay based on the deductive thought arrangement you made in chapter 2. Additional deductive essay assignments, each with its own goal, help you to achieve better communication as you learn to evolve paragraphs, vary your sentence structure, and select and place words with care.

In chapter 4 you will use the inductive thought arrangement and the conversational voice for the inductive essay, and in chapter 5, the movement-by-association and the personal voice for the familiar essay. Finally after you have developed your skills in using the three voices and the three modes of thinking to produce the three essay forms, in chapter 6 you will add new forms to your essay repertoire by experimenting with variations of the basic thought arrangements and voices. In this last chapter you will also gain greater audience awareness by writing a persuasive essay. A number of essays are placed at the end of this chapter as additional illustrations of varying types.

Do all of these expectations sound overwhelming? If so, remember the childhood story of Grandfather Clock who stopped running when he thought of all the ticks he had to make—but started again when he realized that he was given one moment to each tick. You, too, will be given a moment to make each tick, for the book proceeds very slowly on the assumption that no can learn composition all at once. In fact, learning essay writing from this text is like learning figure skating. An ice skater must first know how to skate forwards, backwards, and in curves before he can attempt the skating patterns called *figures*, and then he must practice his body positions and the figure eight, the loops, and other figures until he has control of his movements. After practicing until he can execute these figures precisely, he can advance to free skating in which he adds leaps and spins in choreographing the various parts of the movements that make up the figures. At last, after constant effort, he performs his program to music. And when the audience applauds with enthusiasm, he knows the exaltation that justifies a commitment to art. This same sense of achievement will be yours, too, when your reading audience responds to you as an essayist.

Before you begin your work in this book, make a few preparations. First set up your writing tools in a place where you can work without too many interruptions. Check to see that you have scratch paper, pen and pencils, typing paper, typewriter, type correctors, scissors, transparent tape, ruler, paper clips, stapler, essay folders, dictionary, handbook, and thesaurus. Having a place where you can write in comfort is important; habitually writing in this same place helps psychologically. Arrange your tools within reach so that you will not lose a thought by having to cross the room for a dictionary or other necessities. In other words, be professional. Carpenters, plumbers, doctors, or dentists would never try to perform their jobs without their equipment at hand.

Your tools are there to be used—not ignored. But use them imaginatively. If you find that you must constantly refer to your handbook for rules of the semicolon or a list of transitional expressions, save yourself time by typing this information on sheets that can be clipped inside the cover of your dictionary where they will be accessible. Use the scissors and tape for rearranging thoughts: a paragraph can be cut out and taped in another place faster than a page can be copied. To keep from repeating a word unnecessarily, look up the word in the thesaurus, select a similar one, and verify its shade of meaning and its usage with the dictionary.

Particularly as a means of germinating topics for the familiar essay, form the habit of carrying a small, pocket-size notebook for jotting down your thoughts. A loose-leaf one is preferable since it lends itself to rearranging ideas more readily. Be observant and put down a thought of some kind every day, especially one that is concerned with the relationships of human beings to each other, to objects, and to situations. Take note of the obvious as well as the strange and foolish. For example, you might notice on "M*A*S*H" that Hawkeye sniffs his food before he eats. You jot that down, perhaps with the notations, "Dogs also sniff their food, Why? B. J. finds the habit annoying. Why?" Later from this beginning you may be able to evolve a familiar essay about instinctive behavior that annoys the fastidious. Or you may record a joke you have heard, a quotation you liked, an interpretation that occurred to you, a new word you discovered, or an idea you conceived. Any one of these notes, perhaps some of them combined, may later give you a subject for an essay (or, at least, a topic for a bull session).

In addition to jotting down interesting thoughts or observations in your small notebook, plan also to write every day. For instance, write a paragraph explaining some idea being discussed in another course (a good study technique), describe something you saw or heard or tasted or touched, write a letter, or simply play with words. Even a few sentences about some topic will help. If you wish, buy a spiral notebook just for this purpose and date the entries to keep tabs on yourself. Just as you exercise daily to keep your muscles in tone, your circulation stimulated, and your body in shape, you write daily to keep your vocabulary supple, your style flexible, and your mind alert.

One more point: good writing takes time. You need to allow yourself plenty of time to reflect on an essay topic, to shape it on paper, to put the paper aside and then come back to it for revisions, to alter it and reread and alter it again, and finally to type it and correct the typographical errors. Be good to yourself by allowing plenty of time for a writing assignment so that you may do justice to your abilities. Make yourself begin early. Then follow the shortest way to the essay.

CHAPTER II

Inquiring

Long before an essay assumes a recognizable shape and even longer before it develops an independent life of its own, it is initiated in the mind through a process of inquiry. This process of inquiry is a quest for information, a careful examination of what the writer's mind contains. The mind itself is both a live computer and a storehouse of impressions and knowledge. The computing ability of the mind is used to assemble, correlate, and process information stored within and to indicate a lack of data. But neither an electronic nor a live computer will produce the desired result without a code and a program. A writer must tell his mind, therefore, what to search for and what to do with the information it finds.

Thinking through a Topic:
Search, Sort, Select

Search 1

For example, imagine that you have stepped outside of your mind and that you are an observer of your mental faculties. Your hand and pen serve as the readout for your computer. Using words or phrases, you list the associations your mind makes with the topic, freeing the mind from deliberate control except to keep it focused. You may think of the signal for search as saying to the mind, "Record in words or phrases as rapidly as you can all of the associations you make with _____(give the topic). My hand and pen will register as faithfully as possible the sequence of images or association you discover."

Below is a list recorded by one student on the topic *Violence*. As you read it, observe how this student's mind moved by association. In some instances the associations are easy to follow, for they are ones those who share a common culture might make. In other instances the relationships between items are less obvious because of the writer's individual perception and experience.

VIOLENCE: SEARCH 1

"Starsky & Hutch"	Anwar Sadat	firing squad
"Kojak"	President Lincoln	uprising
"Police Story"	Martin Luther King, Jr.	suicide
gun	Lee Harvey Oswald	rebellion
beatings	John Lennon	revolution
wife beatings	evening news	Alamo
child abuse	headlines	Idi Amin
loud noises	protest marches	Jim Jones
screams	civil rights	mass suicide-murder
police	P.L.O.	religious fanatics
running	Patty Hearst	Attila the Hun
jail	S.L.A.	Caesar
murder	danger	Nero
bleeding	rape	Herod
uselessness of	alarms	Pontius Pilate
insecurity	*The Godfather*	Dracula
police dogs	innocent victims	volcano
chains on doors	vandalism	Mount St. Helens
kidnapping	jury	storms
broken glass	electric chair	tornado
knives	fighting	hurricane
explosions	excitement	lightning
fire	pain	tsunami
sirens	Northern Ireland	tidal wave
disguises	drunkenness	blizzard
detectives	juvenile delinquents	Stalin
lawyers	repeat offenders	Lenin
judge	New York blackout	boxing
coroner	high-speed chase	massacre
crying	F.B.I.	earthquake

fear	emergency room	Hiroshima
Mafia	ambulance	smuggling
KKK	victims	savage
Nazis	witnesses	hate
Hitler	criminals	revenge
bank robbers	chain gang	insanity
arsonists	*Cool Hand Luke*	ransack
controversy over TV	Clint Eastwood	demolish
cowboys and Indians	bombs	torture
Sitting Bull	Kent State	Charles Manson
Custer's Last Stand	anger	duel
Waterloo	abuse	poison
Napoleon	attack	strangle
war	mangle	mutilate
Vietnam	destruction	terror
South Africa	chaos	martial law
Middle East	argument	Jack the Ripper
Aldo Morro	unrest	Son of Sam
Italy	mob	Atlanta child murders
assassinations	terrorists	death
President Kennedy	hijackers	accident
Robert Kennedy	Middle East	assailant
President Reagan	guerrillas	fugitive
Pope John Paul II	gas chamber	escape

Stop! Read no farther until you have completed Assignment 1.

Assignment 1: Search 1

Select one of the following topics (or one suggested by your instructor) and list your associations with it, filling at least three pages (one side only). You may place several columns on each page as long as you record the thoughts in sequence. The topics listed are broad ones, so everyone will have many associations with them. In fact, your mind will go on and on unless you signal it to stop. Remember that no list is "right" or "wrong"; however, occasionally a list may reveal that the writer unconsciously imposed a control on his mind beyond keeping it focused. Keep this step and all the steps that follow to turn in with your completed essay.

Suggested topics:

1. Work
2. Time
3. Power
4. Poverty
5. Handicap

The purpose of Search 1 is to demonstrate the first step in a sequence of steps employed by an essay writer: to search the mind for information on a given topic. In fact, whenever a writer has a choice of several topics, he should search each subject in this fashion to decide which one he has the greatest knowledge of. Ordinarily he would not put the survey in writing, but you are asked to do so both to emphasize the importance of this step by itself and in relationship with the procedures of inquiry that follow.

Sort 1

Now that you have assembled the information on the selected topic of Search 1, you are ready to correlate the information by grouping all of the related items. Once again your mind and pen work together. In this step your mind will need to be told, "Find relationships among the items and group the related items in columns." You may wish to devise various symbols such as ★, #, or + to place by related items as you move down the list you made in Search 1, or you may wish to draw a line through an item as you find a relationship for it. Determining the relationship involves selecting the elements that the items have in common and ignoring the elements that differ. Record the related items on clean sheets of paper (one side only), listing the items under a heading that designates the relationship. For example, the student who did her Search 1 on *Violence* arranged hers as follows (note that some items may fall under two categories and a few representing unexplored areas may not fall under any):

VIOLENCE: SORT 1

ASSAILANTS	VICTIMS	SOUNDS
Napoleon	Sitting Bull & Indians	loud noises
Lee Harvey Oswald	Custer	screams
P.L.O.	Napoleon	alarms
S.L.A.	Aldo Morro	sirens
juvenile delinquents	President Kennedy	crying
repeat offenders	Robert Kennedy	explosions
mob	President Reagan	
terrorists	Anwar Sadat	*EMOTIONAL*
hijackers	Pope John Paul II	*RESPONSE*
guerrillas	President Lincoln	excitement
Mafia	Martin Luther King, Jr.	insecurity
KKK	Lee Harvey Oswald	fear
Nazis	John Lennon	anger
Hitler	Patty Hearst	hate

Idi Amin
Jim Jones
Attila the Hun
Caesar
Nero
Herod
Pontius Pilate
Dracula
Stalin
Lenin
Charles Manson
Jack the Ripper
Son of Sam
husbands
parents
bank robbers
arsonists

VIOLENT ACTIONS

beatings
wife beatings
child abuse
murder
rape
vandalism
fighting
kidnapping
explosions
fire (arson)
assassination
protest marches
drunkenness
bomb
attack
mangle
destruction
shooting
argument
uprising
suicide
rebellion
revolution
boxing
massacre
smuggling
ransack
demolish
torture
duel
poison

Caesar
Jim Jones
wives
Atlanta children

NATURAL VIOLENCE

volcano
Mount St. Helens
storms
tornado
hurricane
lightning
tsunami
tidal wave
blizzard
earthquake

VIOLENT PLACES/ SITUATIONS

Custer's Last Stand
Waterloo
war
Vietnam
South Africa
Middle East
Italy
Northern Ireland
New York blackout
high-speed chase
Kent State
Alamo
Mount St. Helens
Hiroshima
Atlanta

revenge
terror

TV/MEDIA

"Starsky & Hutch"
"Kojak"
"Police Story"
The Godfather
controversy
 over violence
cowboys and Indians
evening news
headlines
Cool Hand Luke
Clint Eastwood

PUNISHMENT/ LAW ENFORCEMENT

police
jail
jury
electric chair
police dogs
sirens
detectives
lawyers
judge
coroner
F.B.I.
chain gang
witnesses
gas chamber
firing squad
martial law
dictatorship
death

strangle
mutilate

Stop again! Complete Assignment 2 before you continue.

Assignment 2: Sort 1

Using the associations you listed in Search 1, find relationships among the items and group all of the related items in columns under headings that indicate the relationships. Save this work to use with your next assignment and to hand in with your completed essay.

Select 1

Having completed Search 1 and Sort 1, you are ready to select a subject area for an essay. Look first at the subject headings of your Sort 1. Is there any one of these areas that interests you? If so, begin with that heading and consider each subtopic. For instance, the student who used *Violence* as her topic began with her heading of *Assailants*. Taking the first item, "Napoleon," she reflected on what she knew about him. In spite of the fact that she had taken a history course two years ago that included Napoleon, she discovered that she could recall only vague details about his actions. As for Lee Harvey Oswald, she remembered her parents talking about him and President Kennedy's assassination, she had seen reruns of the film, and she was aware that there are many newspaper accounts, magazine articles, and investigations on record; but again she thought her knowledge of Oswald too limited for an essay. Of course, if she had had the time, she could have researched the material on Oswald. However, her assignment was not to do research, and under the circumstances she preferred not to. Continuing her search, she looked at each topic under each heading until she found one that appealed to her and that she had information on.

Assignment 3: Select 1

Using your Sort 1, select a subject area that interests you and that you have information on by first considering each heading and then by reflecting on each item under the heading. Select one of the items as your subject area.

Have you completed Select 1? If not, do so before proceeding.

Search 2

As you contemplated the headings and items in Search 1, you may have noticed that once again you were directing your mind to assemble all information on a given topic—in other words, you mentally repeated the process of Search 1. Your next step is to put this process on paper by taking the item you selected and recording the associations your mind makes with it. This step, called Search 2, repeats the process of Search 1, but with a more limited subject area. For example, the student working on *Violence* decided she was interested in the subheading "juvenile delinquents" listed under the heading *Assailants*. Keeping in mind that her major topic was *Violence*, and her heading was *Assailants*, she applied the movement-by-association of Search 1 to "juvenile delinquents" and made the following list—this time searching for more details on her limited topic.

VIOLENCE, ASSAILANTS, AND JUVENILE DELINQUENTS: SEARCH 2

parental responsibility	rape
petty crime	school dropouts
television	whose fault?
newspapers	society
magazines	parents
books	outside influence (TV)
black jackets	criminal future
gangs	multiple offender
slums	family crimes
poverty	wife beating
ignorance	child beating
ethnic minorities	incest
mindless violence	children imitate
pranks	burglary
cruelty	drugs
peer pressure	car theft
leader	vandalism
followers	armed robbery
knife	rape/beatings
gun	murder
sex	

Assignment 4: Search 2

Using the item you chose in Select 1, list all of the associations your mind makes with this subject area. Keep your first subject and the heading in mind as you work with the limited subject of Select 1, for

your associations are now with the relationships you see among
the broad topic, the heading, and the narrower topic.

Halt! Do your Search 2 before you move forward.

Sort 2

After completing Search 2, your next task will be to apply Sort 2. By
now you will have guessed that each previous step of Assignment 1—
Search, Sort, Select—is being repeated as the process of inquiry moves
from larger to smaller topics until you locate one appropriate for your essay.
Sort 2 duplicates Sort 1: after the relationships among the items are determined, the items are sorted into columns under headings that indicate the
relationships. The student working on "Violence, Assailants, and Juvenile
Delinquents" grouped her items from Search 2 as follows:

VIOLENCE, ASSAILANTS, AND JUVENILE DELINQUENTS: SORT 2

KINDS   *INFLUENCES*
OF VIOLENCE   *TOWARD VIOLENCE*

burglary   parental attitudes
car theft   parental examples
vandalism   T.V.
mindless violence   newspapers
armed robbery   magazines
rape/beatings   books
murder   peer groups
                                 leader
                                 followers
CAUSES
OF VIOLENCE—SOCIAL

drugs   *RESULTS*
slums   *OF VIOLENCE*
poverty
ignorance/school dropouts   multiple offender
sex gangs   criminal future

Full stop! Take time out to do your Sort 2.

Assignment 5: Sort 2

Sort the items listed in the Search 2 assignment by finding relationships among the items and grouping the related items under headings. The headings, like those of Sort 1, stand for the relationships shared by the items.

Select 2

Although the process may be extended or all six steps repeated, your next and perhaps final act in this Search, Sort, Select sequence is to decide upon the subject of your essay from the groupings of Sort 2. You may recall that in Select 1 you chose as your subject area one of the items—that is, a subtopic—from Sort 1. Now, if you prefer, you may select one of the headings rather than a subtopic. A broader essay will result if you choose a heading. However, you may wish to use the heading when you lack detailed information or when you are writing an essay for a survey course where broad topics are commonly used. On the other hand, you may decide to write on a subtopic. Instructors in composition will probably applaud the latter choice because they know that by writing in depth on a narrow topic, you will probably produce a more interesting essay. (Should you choose a subtopic rather than a heading, before moving to "Relating Parts to the Whole," take time to apply another Search and another Sort step to gain needed details. You will, in effect, be turning your subtopic into a heading with subtopics of its own.)

The Search, Sort, Select Process
(or How to Get There from Here)

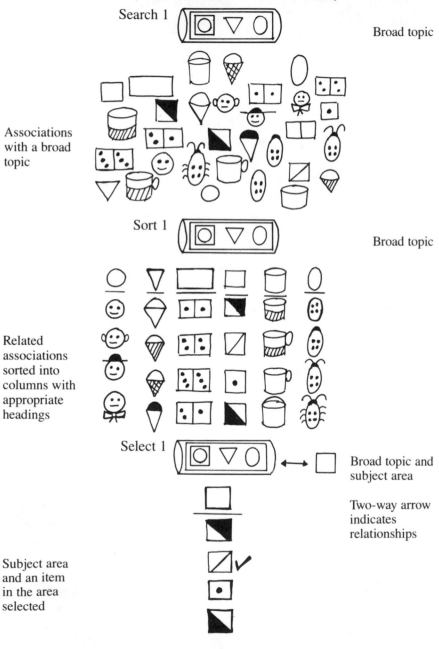

Search 2

Broad topic,
subject area,
and item

Associations
with
selected item

Two-way
arrows indicate
relationships

Sort 2

Broad topic,
subject area,
and item

Related
associations
with item, sorted
into columns with
appropriate
headings

Two-way arrows
indicate
relationships

Select 2

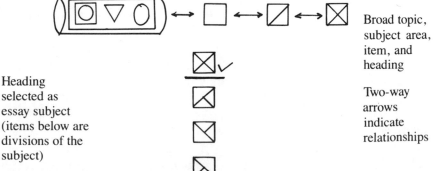

Broad topic,
subject area,
item, and
heading

Heading
selected as
essay subject
(items below are
divisions of the
subject)

Two-way
arrows
indicate
relationships

Assignment 6: Select 2

Using the groupings of Sort 2, select one heading or one subtopic
as your subject. If you select a subtopic, apply the Search and Sort
procedure to it in order to turn it into a heading with subtopics of
its own. Both a heading and its subtopics will be used in "Relating
Parts to the Whole" in this chapter.

As for the student writing on *Violence*, in spite of the fact that she did
her work rather sketchily in the last Search and Sort steps, she did reach a
decision on a subject for her essay. The topic of Sort 2 that she had the most
knowledge of and the most interest in, she decided, was the heading, "Influences Toward Violence." She planned, therefore, to write her essay on
"Influences on Juveniles Toward Violence" after having moved through a
gradually narrowing process of association, grouping, and choosing from
Violence to *Assailants* to *Juvenile Delinquents* to *Influences Toward
Violence*.

You might wish at this time to look over the six or more steps you have
taken in these assignments, following the course of thinking pursued in
reaching a subject for your essay and noting how each topic is related to the
preceding one as the area of focus grows smaller and smaller. And while
doing so, marvel a little at how fast the mind computes—in contrast with
how slowly the hand writes! Remember, too, that you directed your com-
puter-mind to assemble, correlate, and refine the information and that this
process of Search, Sort, Select furnishes a procedure that can be used to
direct your mind in investigating any subject at any time, the number of
steps depending on the size of the initial topic and the desired size of the
final subject. This procedure is one way of thinking through a subject; it is
a device that guides inquiry or investigation. With practice you can train
your mind to use this procedure easily and to extend it as necessary, and
soon you will be jotting down only the essentials you need to record.

Relating Parts to the Whole:
Outline Form

Using the Search, Sort, Select process, you have discovered what you
know, generated ideas, and derived a subject for your essay. Now you have
reached the point in preparing to write an essay where you must shape your
subject into a form that will reveal the relationships of the parts to each other

and to the whole. The outline form is an excellent one for these purposes: you will focus your ideas by identifying the details and by formulating a thesis or central idea.

In two steps you will first write an inductive outline, and then you will shift the statements of the inductive outline into the deductive outline form. Only then will you be ready to compose a deductive essay, the type of essay most teachers expect college students to write. Evolving the inductive outline first and then transforming it into the deductive outline, an approach that is another device to guide your thinking, sounds complicated—but really it is not. It is a fast, effective way to put your thoughts in order and obtain a clear focus. Later you will see how easy it is to create an essay from an outline, for the outline is the skeleton of the essay. Just keep in mind that *induction* is reasoning from particulars (details) to the general (your thesis or central idea) and that *deduction* is reasoning from the general (your thesis or central idea) to particulars (details).

Inductive Topic Outline

To begin an inductive topic outline, first phrase a question that involves a relationship and that asks what you want to say about your subject. The rule to remember is: *The question you ask determines the answer you get.* By using your subject (see Select 2) and the list that accompanied it (see Sort 2), you should have no difficulty in wording a question to fit your answers, for your headings will tell you if you are concerned with types, likenesses, differences, causes, or effects. If you chose as your subject a subtopic of Sort 2, you will need to use the subtopics you developed for it as a guide to phrasing your question (see Select 2).

For example, the student writing on *Violence* asked, "How is violence bred in the young?" Since she had decided that her topic would be "Influences on Juveniles Toward Violence," obviously she did not ask questions related to the other groups such as "What kind of violence are juveniles involved in?" or "What are the social causes of violence?" or "What are the effects of violence on the offender?" The use of Sort 2 simplified her problem.

One way to determine a question is to place across a page your broad topic, subject area (Select 1), item (Select 1), and heading (Select 2). For example:

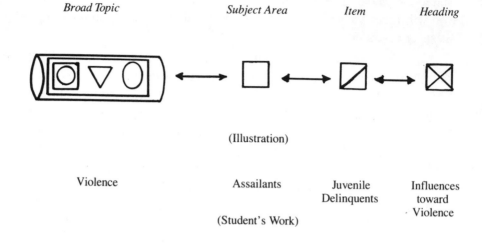

| *Broad Topic* | *Subject Area* | *Item* | *Heading* |

(Illustration)

| Violence | Assailants | Juvenile Delinquents | Influences toward Violence |

(Student's Work)

Since the two-way arrows indicate relationships, both a statement and a question can be phrased by replacing the arrows with words that reveal the relationships. Moving from left to right, you can make a statement; moving from right to left, you can raise a question.

(1) *Violence* is produced by *Assailants* who are *Juvenile Delinquents* because of certain *Influences Toward Violence*.

(2) What *Influences Toward Violence* cause *Juvenile Delinquents* to become *Assailants* thereby producing *Violence*?

To avoid awkwardness of wording, try rephrasing the question in several different ways by implying rather than stating some of the relationships. For instance:

(1) What influences juveniles to commit acts of violence?

(2) What causes violence by the young?

Now before deciding on the final form of your question, look at the items under your heading (Select 2) and their relationship to it. Observe the direction of thought taken by these divisions and the way they modify the idea of the heading. Compare, for example, the illustration and the student's work in Select 2.

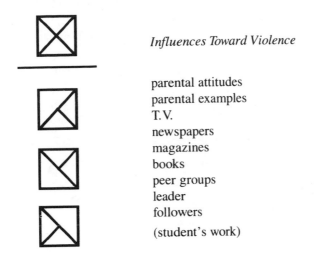

Influences Toward Violence

parental attitudes
parental examples
T.V.
newspapers
magazines
books
peer groups
leader
followers
(student's work)

The student noticed that her list consisted of factors in the immediate environment that could from childhood affect the young. Hence, she realized that she was concerned with certain influences only and with the growth period of the child—not just the child who had reached adolescence. She decided, therefore, to word her question, "How is violence bred in the young?" *To breed* is a verb that usually refers to producing offspring. But also it can mean *to propagate, to develop qualities* (desired ones, preferably), and *to inculcate by training.* She liked the implications of the verb *breed* because she felt that violence was being developed in the young by their immediate environment.

Having phrased your question, follow the trail blazed by the student asking, "How is violence bred in the young?" She jotted her question down, reflected on it, looked at her Sort 2 list with her question in mind, and observed that the subtopics in her list fell into three divisions: those related to parents, to media, and to peers. As a partial answer to her question, she listed the two subtopics related to parents as one set and then added the subtopics together to produce a summary topic. Her inductive topic outline thus far read:

Question: How is violence bred in the young?

    A. Attitudes of parents
    B. Examples set by parents
        I. Influence of parents

Next she mentally repeated the same question, produced another set of answers (media), and added them together to obtain topic II. Then she repeated the question to herself again to obtain a third set of answers (peers) and her topic III. By this time she had used all of the subtopics in her list in Sort 2—though she could have added more subtopics to her list if she had wished. Finally she added the ideas of topics I, II, and III to obtain the answer to her question. Her inductive topic outline then read as follows:

Inductive Topic Outline

Question: How is violence bred in the young?

     A. Attitudes of parents

     B. Examples set by parents

       I. Influence of parents

     A. Violence on T. V.

     B. Violence in books, newspapers, and magazines

       II. Influence of mass media

     A. Acceptance by peer group

     B. Maintaining status in peer groups

       III. Influence of peer groups

          Answer: Violence is bred in the young by the influence of parents, by the influence of mass media, and by the influence of peer groups.

Notice that she indented to show that she added the subtopics to produce I (to be able to add, she needed at least two subtopics). In wording topic I she was able to abstract the like characteristics of "attitudes" and "examples," ignoring their differences, to obtain the broader classification of "influence." Had she found it impossible to abstract for topic I, she could have written, "Attitudes of and examples set by parents." But try to abstract as she did, checking your set of answers to see what element they have in common. If they do not have a common element, chances are that they do not belong together as a set.

Assignment 7: Inductive Topic Outline

Having selected your subject, use your Sort 2 heading to help you phrase a question that involves a relationship and that asks what you want to say about your subject. *Remember that the question you ask determines the answer you get.* With the question jotted down and your heading and subtopics from Sort 2 before you (or the extension you did on a subtopic in Search 2), study the subtopics to see what divisions of idea occur among them. Then as a partial answer to your question, formulate a set of answers that includes at least two subtopics; label them A, B, and so on; and add them together to get I. In wording topic I (and the other major topics), try to abstract the like characteristics of A, B, and C.

Mentally repeat the question for a second set of answers and add them to produce topic II. Then mentally repeat the question again for a third set of answers and a topic III. (Whether you will have more than the necessary two sets of answers and the two major topics depends on the complexity of your subject and the proposed length of your essay). Finally, add topics I, II, and III together to get the answer to your question.

Inductive Sentence Outline

If you have followed directions carefully, the ideas in your inductive topic outline should bear a logical relationship with one another—that is A + B = I (or A + B + C = I); A + B = II; A + B = III; I + II + III = Answer to the question. On the other hand, the topic outline that is not preceded by careful thought may be no more than a laundry list. To be sure that the topic outline is more than a list of miscellaneous items, run another check on it by transforming it into a sentence outline that states each topic (except for the initial question) briefly but clearly in a complete sentence. As far as possible, phrase the sentences for each set of answers in parallel form without striving for sentence variety, for the aim is to reveal as clearly as possible the relationships among ideas. Be sure to use block indentation so that it can be seen at a glance how the topics relate to one another. For instance, the topic outline on violence was transformed into the following sentence outline.

Inductive Sentence Outline

Question: How is violence bred in the young?

    A. Parents transmit attitudes toward violence to their children.

    B. Parents set examples of violence for their children.

      I. Parents influence their children toward violence.

A. Television shows that appeal to children are often oriented toward violence.

B. Books, newspapers, and magazines read by children are often oriented toward violence.

      II. Mass media influence children toward violence.

A. Acceptance into a peer group is often contingent upon participation in violent acts.

B. Maintaining status in a peer group is often contingent upon continued participation in violent acts.

      III. Peer groups sometimes influence children toward violence.

      Answer: Violence is bred into the young by the influence of parents, by the influence of mass media, and by the influence of peer groups.

Assignment 8: Inductive Sentence Outline

To achieve an inductive sentence outline, transform each topic of your inductive topic outline into a complete sentence, using parallel structure for each set of answers. Strive for clear, terse statements but not for sentence variety. Use block indentation.

When your inductive sentence outline is completed, check it for the following points:

Checklist for Inductive Sentence Outline

1. Each topic and subtopic is a partial answer to the question.
   If you find errors, correct the problem either by altering the subtopics or the topics to answer the question or by altering the question to conform to the topics. If topic I gives background information, often such information, which does not belong in the outline, can be used as part of the introduction to the essay. In this case, delete the topic from the outline and renumber the remaining topics.

2. At least two subtopics precede a major topic.

   If you have an A but no B, your major topic is probably a restatement of A. Revise so that you have a set of answers—at least an A and a B— that will produce the major topics.

3. Each topic is logical in its relationship with other topics, that is, A + B = I, A + B = II, A + B = III.

   Revise the subtopic or the major topic as necessary to achieve a logical relationship of idea.

4. The major topics together equal the answer.

   If I + II + III does not = the Answer, either revise the answer to equal the major topics or the major topics to equal the answer. If a major topic is revised, the subtopics belonging to that topic may also need altering.

5. The number of topics is appropriate to the essay of medium length.

   Experience in writing from an outline will teach you to judge. Although it is difficult to generalize, sometimes when five or more topics occur, they can be rearranged in a different thought pattern to produce fewer topics.

6. The outline topics are in an appropriate sequence for the presentation of your subject.

   You will need to decide if your topics demand a different arrangement—for example, a climactic order from the least to the most important or a chronological order from the past to the present.

7. The wording of the topics maintains the sequence of idea, that is, the idea of A should precede the idea of B in the wording of the major topic unless the abstraction of the idea avoids the problem, and the ideas of I, II, III should be maintained in the same order in the answer.

8. The topics are stated clearly, briefly, in parallel form, and in complete sentences.

9. Block indentation is used to show topic relationships at a glance.

10. The question and the answer are included in the outline.

Deductive Sentence Outline

Thinking inductively has led to an answer to your question, an answer that you will discuss as the main or central idea of your deductive essay. But first your inductive sentence outline needs to be arranged in deductive form so that the skeleton of your deductive essay will take shape and you can see the relationship of the parts to the whole.

Shifting the inductive outline form to the deductive form is simple, for it requires changes only in the arrangement—not in the wording of the topics. Since the conventions of the deductive outline call for the statement of the thesis or central idea at the top of the outline and the topics arranged so that the thought moves from the general to particulars, the order of the inductive outline needs to be reversed. The *Question* is dropped (the *Answer* implies the question), the *Answer* becomes the *Central Idea* (thesis) of the deductive outline, and the major topics (I, II, III) precede the subtopics (A, B, C), the subtopics being indented beneath the major topics. Note the following example:

Deductive Sentence Outline

Central Idea: Violence is bred into the young by the influence of parents, by the influence of mass media, and by the influence of peer groups.

    I. Parents influence their children toward violence.

        A. Parents transmit attitudes toward violence to their children.

        B. Parents set examples of violence for their children.

    II. Mass media influence children toward violence.

        A. Television shows that appeal to children are often oriented toward violence.

        B. Books, newspapers, and magazines read by children are often oriented toward violence.

    III. Peer groups sometimes influence children toward violence.

        A. Acceptance into a peer group is often contingent upon participation in violent acts.

        B. Maintaining status in a peer group is often contingent upon continued participation in violent acts.

Assignment 9: Deductive Sentence Outline

Rearrange your inductive sentence outline into the deductive form by taking the following steps:

1. Omit the word *Question* and the question itself and substitute *Central Idea* (or *Thesis*, if your instructor prefers) and the answer to the question, deleting the word *Answer*.

2. Using block indentation, reverse the order of the topics by placing I first with the A and B (and C, if you have one) indented beneath the I.

3. Follow this same pattern with topics II and III and their subtopics.

If you have no questions about this outline form, you may wish to skip this section. But some of you may be wondering why this particular outline form is used rather than the one that consists of I. Introduction; II. Body; and III. Conclusion. The three-part outline, often used by speech teachers to emphasize the preparation a speaker needs to make, is sometimes longer than the outline you wrote and tends to give less clear emphasis to the logic of the thought. Your outline form is designed to give the writer the necessities only: the central idea is the basic part of the introduction in the deductive essay and the remainder of the outline is the skeletal structure of the paper. Since it is understood that the central idea is reemphasized in the conclusion of the paper, there is no need for the writer's deductive outline to state a separate conclusion. Another advantage of this outline form is its adjustability. Like an accordion it can stretch or contract to the length of any given essay.

You may also be concerned that your outline omitted subtopics 1, 2, 3, and so forth, under each A and B. Many writers feel that the omission gives more flexibility and a greater sense of creativity in the composing process; they like to think of illustrations and examples as they develop the ideas of A and B. On the other hand, the inexperienced writer may like the security provided by listing the subtopics 1, 2, 3 under the A and B. Actually, in writing the inductive essay the subtopics are helpful even to the experienced writer.

If at this time you wish to add subtopics 1, 2, 3 to your deductive outline, return to Assignment 5: Sort 2 and the heading chosen in Select 2. Take each item under the heading and apply the Search, Sort method to it. (If you chose a subtopic rather than a heading in Select 2 and extended it to arrive at a new heading with subtopics of its own, use these last subtopics.) This method will furnish the 1, 2, 3 subtopics for both the inductive and the deductive outline. The formats for the inductive and deductive outlines that include the subtopics 1, 2, 3 (at least two are necessary) are as follows:

Inductive Outline	**Deductive Outline**
Question:	Central Idea:
1.	I.
2.	A.
3.	1.
A.	2.
1.	3.
2.	B.
3.	1.
B.	2.
I.	3.
1.	II.
2.	A.
3.	1.
A.	2.
1.	3.
2.	B.
3.	1.
B.	2.
II.	3.
1.	III.
2.	A.
3.	1.
A.	2.
1.	3.
2.	B.
3.	1.
B.	2.
III.	3.
Answer:	

Are you jotting down your thoughts or observations in your pocket-size notebook?

CHAPTER III

Shaping the Deductive Essay

Audience and Voice

Although the deductive sentence outline represents the structure of thought for the deductive essay, thought cannot be shaped without considering the intended reader. Whether the particular purpose of writing is to inform, to persuade, or to convey emotions, attitudes, and beliefs, the act of writing must be motivated by a desire to share with someone.

Writing is basically an unselfish act: the writer must choose each word, phrase, sentence, and arrangement with his reader—not himself—in mind. He must be motivated by a sincere desire to communicate with fellow human beings no matter how much effort is involved in stating and explaining clearly what he wishes to share. If the writer's manner toward his reader and toward his subject implies, "I like you, I am interested in you, and I believe in what I am saying," the writer's sincerity and integrity will make contact with the reader and establish a bond of trust. The bond is strengthened if the writer looks upon the reader as someone neither inferior nor superior to himself, but as another intelligent, inquisitive human being worthy of time and interest.

Identifying the Audience

In writing essays for class assignments it will be tempting to write for the instructor, who obviously is your immediate reader, and to say what you think will interest him. There are two dangers in assuming that an instructor is your reader: first, you may allow the fact that he is your instructor to inhibit your flow of ideas; second, you may assume that he is omniscient and knows what you intend to say without clear explanation on your part. Both dangers can be avoided by recognizing that your instructor is the middleman, not the consumer; he is your editor, not your intended reader. As your editor he will review your work sympathetically and comment on your paper with the intent of showing you how to reach your audience effectively. But in doing so he will first play the role of any reader that you assign to him if you let him know what audience you intend to reach.

If your instructor is not your intended reader, then who is? Your reader is the audience you select, an audience you think your subject will appeal to. Eliminate right away the uneducated or the immature, for they seldom read essays. Avoid your classmates in a particular course (you may falsely assume that they know the subject equally as well as you and fail to give them essential information and explanations), and exclude professional audiences (even those with masters and doctorates find it a challenge to write for the experts). By omitting the uneducated, the immature, your own classmates in a particular course, and the professionals, you have limited the possibilities very little. The majority of Americans are left.

Unfortunately, *most Americans* cannot be your reading audience. You need to be more specific, focusing on certain people you can see in your mind and write to. As an aid in projecting your audience, ask yourself two questions:

1. *Who needs or wants to know about the subject I have chosen?* In answering this question, consider the sex, age group, educational level, attitudes, and values of the audience.

2. *How do I differ from and what do I have in common with this audience?* The way you differ may give a unique perspective on

the subject; what you share will give contact points with the audience.

For example, the author of the essay on "Violence and the Young" concluded that primarily her readers would be young adults, with children, probably middle class, with a high school education or beyond—though a broad audience would certainly find the topic interesting. While these young adults would share her concern for the increasing and uncontrolled violence in society, they may not have looked in their own homes and neighborhoods for incipient forces at work on their children.

Assignment 1: Describing Your Audience

First list the answers to the following questions: (1) *Who needs or wants to know about the topic I have chosen?* (Consider the sex, age group, educational level, attitudes, and values.); (2) *How do I differ from and what do I have in common with this audience?* Then write a brief description of your reading audience. Your instructor may desire you to place this description on the deductive outline page along with a statement of the purpose in writing about your subject to the audience you selected. Note: avoid describing your audience as "Someone interested in my topic," for such a statement suggests that you have not imagined your audience clearly.

In addition to eliminating certain groups and to asking questions to identify possible readers, you may also develop sensitivity to the reader by imagining that you are writing for a particular magazine. A good writer obviously selects the magazine that holds most appeal for the targeted readers. Is the magazine read by conservatives, liberals, or both? A political analyst would need to know. Can it be assumed that the readers are familiar with the literary work being discussed? A literary critic would need to know. Are the readers participants or spectators, active or armchair joggers? A sports writer would need to know.

If you are not a magazine reader except to pass the time at the hair stylist's or the doctor's office, you should spend an afternoon in the library familiarizing yourself with magazines. Your task would be to infer characteristics of the audience to which the magazine is directed. The following assignment will help.

Assignment 2: Discovering Magazine Audiences

To determine the characteristics of various magazine audiences, look at the following magazines (or others, as your instructor directs): *Atlantic, Ebony, House and Garden, The New Yorker, Playboy, Popular Mechanics, Reader's Digest, Sports Illustrated.* Consider such indicators as these: types of subject matter in essays and articles, kinds of columns, types of products advertised, people shown in illustrations, cartoons (level of humor; for example, earthy, sophisticated), level of vocabulary, reliability or factuality of material used. You may need to verify your initial impressions by looking at several back issues of the magazines. Once you have analyzed the audience of at least five different magazines, write a description of the audience of each.

Both intuition and experience are involved in the imaginative act of projecting an audience, and you must practice to increase your insight. Being genuinely concerned with sharing your subject and meeting the needs of your audience is the starting point. Describing them clearly and specifically will sharpen your perception. At the same time it is useful to recognize that a good writer can to some extent control his audience by letting his readers know what role they are expected to play.

Whether the writer informs the reader of the role directly or indirectly depends on the purpose of the essay and the voice to be used by the writer. For example, the direct approach works well when the purpose of the essay is persuasive or the conversational voice is used. Once common ground is established in the introduction, the reader will willingly suspend disbelief and participate if you make it clear right from the start what his role is. For these examples a simple phrase will do.

(1) Most teenagers agree that certain restrictions are desirable.
(2) As parents of elementary school students, we are all concerned about the safety of children on our highways.

When you write in the objective voice, however, the reader cannot be told directly what his role is because that would break the objective relationship. Instead, the reader's role is implied when you state in the introduction what is important about the topic. For example, one student began an introduction with these lines:

Scuba diving is a fascinating sport, for it opens the eyes to a whole new

> world. Under the sea there is life that no man can imagine and homes that
> no man has ever seen before. (Lisa M. Stewart)

In this essay the reader becomes a scuba diver discovering things rich and
strange. On the other hand, the reader's role is less obvious when no identifying name is suggested and he must infer his role only by the values and
attitudes the writer assumes he shares. For instance, another student expects
the reader, like herself, to be securely positioned in the mainstream of society and to view individuals sympathetically but cult membership as
abnormal:

> Still fresh in the minds of many is the horror of the Jim Jones mass sui-
> cide-murder that took place as the result of a cult movement. Although
> cults such as those of Rev. Jones and the Rev. Moon have been examined
> by the press, the appeal of cult membership is still difficult to compre-
> hend. Innocent, unsuspecting people go blindly into oblivion, some
> never to return. Yet a close look at those who join a cult shows that they
> are the less fortunate, the impoverished, the ones incapable of leading
> their own lives, or the ones who have not found a purpose in living.
> (Connie Porter)

If this view is not antithetical to the reader, he will cooperate by assuming
the part assigned to him by the writer.

Creating the Voice

Having delineated your audience, you are ready to choose the voice in
which you will convey your subject. The voice is the means by which the
writer speaks about a subject to the reader. The choice of voice reflects the
writer's own relationship with, and attitude toward, his subject and reader,
and, in turn, this relationship and attitude affect the way the reader appre-
hends the subject and perceives the writer. Thus the function of voice is a
primary one: it forms intangible links among writer, subject, and reader.

The relationships of writer to subject and reader involve subtleties that
are difficult to analyze—in fact, a writer himself may be only dimly aware
of some of them. But a writer can be fully aware of how these relationships
influence a reader's apprehension of the subject and view of the writer. A
good starting point toward understanding voice, then, is to see how the
choice of voice affects a reader. The personal, the conversational, and the
objective voices—the ones presented in this text—offer strong contrasts

with regard to a reader's awareness of the writer's presence and the directness with which a reader receives the subject.

In the personal voice (often called *first person*), a reader perceives the subject through the mind of the writer. He is aware of the writer's presence and personality and receives the idea indirectly, his interest being attracted more to the writer than to the subject. For instance, if you are writing about a personal experience unique to you, the writer, you would use "I" to focus attention on yourself. Thomas De Quincey's opening paragraph in his essay "On the Knocking at the Gate in *Macbeth*" demonstrates this personal voice. As you read the paragraph, notice that your interest is centered on De Quincey and not *Macbeth*:

> From my boyish days I have always felt a great perplexity on one point in *Macbeth*. It was this: the knocking at the gate which succeeds to the murder of Duncan produced to my feelings an effect for which I never could account. The effect was that it reflected back upon the murderer a peculiar awfulness and a depth of solemnity; yet, however obstinately I endeavoured with my understanding to comprehend this, for many years I could never see *why* it should produce such an effect.

In the case of conversational voice, a reader is much less aware of the separate identity of the writer. Instead, the reader is joined with the writer in looking at the subject. Because this voice uses "we" to represent "you and I" (reader and writer), it gives a sense of participating together in an experience.[1] When De Quincey's paragraph is revised in the conversational voice, the reader and writer focus on the subject together and share the problem.

> Why do we feel an unaccountable effect on the knocking at the gate in *Macbeth*, the action that occurs in the play immediately after the murder of Duncan? Why should this knocking seem to us to reflect back upon the murderer a peculiar awfulness and a depth of solemnity?

In the case of objective voice (often called *third person*), a reader's attention is focused directly on the subject. The presence of the writer is almost eliminated since the writer uses no pronouns to refer to himself. With this reduction of the writer's presence in De Quincey's quotation, notice that you now concentrate on the subject.

---

[1]The conversational "we" that equals "you and I" differs from the editorial "we" that represents the opinion of newspaper and magazine editors.

Why is an unaccountable effect produced on the knocking at the gate in *Macbeth*, the action that occurs in the play immediately after the murder of Duncan? Why should this knocking reflect back upon the murderer a peculiar awfulness and a depth of solemnity?

All three of these particular voices help the reader trust what the writer says. Since first person recounts the writer's own experience, the reader tends to accept the experience as valid. Because the conversational voice joins the reader with the writer and allows him to participate in the process, a feeling of togetherness develops. And the objective voice, provided the writer is careful not to use emotionally laden words and to call attention to the way he is arranging the thought, inspires trust by its appearance of impartiality, of impersonal approach to the subject. The impartiality is similar to that created by a dramatist who allows his characters to present themselves in action on stage while he remains behind the scene.

The following chart gives the personal pronouns that can be used in each of these three voices and summarizes the effect of each voice on the reader:[2]

The Personal, Conversational, and Objective Voices:
Pronoun Choices and Reader Effects

Personal: I (*me, my, mine, myself*) Tends to focus the reader's attention on the writer. The reader receives the subject indirectly as it is filtered through the writer's mind.

Conversational: We (*us, our, ours, ourselves*) Unites the reader with the writer in focusing on the subject.

Objective: No pronoun for the writer. Uses the following pronouns in referring to others: *he, him, his, himself; she, her, hers, herself; it, it, its, itself; one, one's, one, oneself; they, them, their, theirs, themselves*. Focuses the reader's attention on the subject. The reader is almost unaware of the writer's presence.

After studying the chart, try writing the following brief exercise and observing the changes that occur in relationships with the reader.

---

[2]Notice that none of these three voices includes the use of the pronoun *you*, which is direct address. However, employing *you* in speaking to the reader directly can be added to a major voice.

Assignment 3: The Voice and the Reader

The following lines are in the personal voice. Revise them first in the conversational voice and next in the objective voice.

> Of all the poems on death written by Emily Dickinson the one that to me has the most intriguing first-line title is "As by the Dead We Love to Sit." Why, I wonder, would anyone love to sit by the dead? I can think of situations in which it might be necessary for me to sit by the dead, but to love doing so seems somewhat morbid. (Kevin W. Murphy)

Even though the key to establishing the voice is the choice of personal pronouns, the writer's creation of a speaking voice involves more than the use of the right pronouns. Instead, the voice and its effect on the reader are initiated by the writer's own relationship with, and attitude toward, his subject and his audience. In spite of the fact that there are many subtleties in a writer's relationships, subtleties that even the most experienced writers and readers may not have examined consciously, there are some more obvious aspects that you need to be aware of.

The most obvious aspect of all is that you cannot evolve a voice without knowing what your subject is, what your purpose in writing is, and who your audience is. The voice is not an entity in itself; it cannot exist alone; it is not self-sufficient. The voice becomes apparent only in the writer's relationships with subject and audience. A glance at the list of pronouns on the preceding page will show you that they are merely lifeless words until they are used in context and establish meaningful relationships.

Another aspect that needs to be recognized is that the voice you write in is a voice you permit to reflect only selected qualities of your mind, experience, personality, and other attributes that make you a distinct human being. Just as a reader assumes a role when he reads, you assume a role when you write, and you do so naturally. Every time you shift subject, purpose, and audience, you alter your voice to conform to your writing role, deleting those attributes of yourself that are not appropriate to the new relationships.

Take this situation, for example. Your basketball team won a strongly contested game because you made a goal during the last minute of play. Compare the difference in the voice you would use if (1) following the game you wrote a report for the sports page of the local newspaper; (2) the next day you wrote a letter to a close friend telling about the game; (3) at the request of the coach you wrote an explanation to the team analyzing why the play was successful. Notice that although here the subject remains the same, you adjust your voice and role (as well as the details of your subject) according to your writing purpose and your relationship with the reader.

A third noteworthy aspect of writer relationships in establishing the voice is the distance you stand from your subject, a distance that affects your relationships with it and, in turn, with your audience. When you write in the personal voice, you are very close to the subject—but not so close that you become entangled in it emotionally and fail to see the experience clearly. When you write in the conversational voice, you and your reader together are at a neutral distance—yet farther from the subject than with the personal voice. When you write in the objective voice, you are at an even greater distance from your subject. Generally, the farther you are from the subject, the greater the objectivity; the closer you are to the subject, the greater the subjectivity. Since the distance is projected imaginatively, you may need to practice to obtain this sense of positioning yourself.

Assignment 4: The Voice and the Writer

Using the topic sentences below, write a paragraph on each describing an ant trying to carry a large piece of bread. Use personal voice for the first, conversational voice for the second, and objective voice for the third.

1. Ants, I think, are fascinating to watch.
2. Let's look at the actions of the ant that is trying to carry the large piece of bread.
3. Ants are fascinating to watch.

Once you have learned to use the personal, the conversational, and the objective voices—the three presented in this text—and have seen the relationship that each establishes with a reader, you will be able to experiment with voices to achieve any effect you desire. Both practice and intuition will help you choose a voice appropriate to your purpose, your subject, and your audience. Meanwhile, in writing these first few essays you are asked to use the objective voice, the voice that you will need most often in writing essays in college—just as you are asked to use the deductive form in the essay, the one generally most applicable to the discussion of ideas. Later in the text

Voice: A Few Writer-Subject-Reader Relationships

Personal Voice

Reader   Writer

Reader perceives the subject
through the mind of the writer.

Writer stands close to the subject—
but not too close.

Conversational Voice

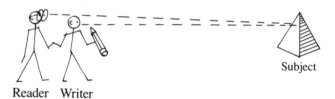

Reader   Writer

Reader and writer view
the subject together.

Writer stands at a neutral
distance from the subject.

Objective Voice

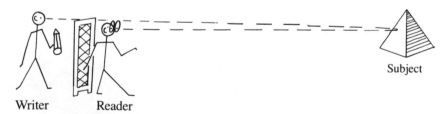

Writer   Reader

Reader unaware of writer's presence.

Writer stands at a greater distance
from the subject.

when you write in other essay forms, you will use the personal and conversational voices.

Already you have taken steps that will help you assume the right stance and the right distance in writing in the objective voice. You have selected your subject with the purpose of discussing an idea, you have determined via the deductive outline the form your essay will take, and you have analyzed your audience and its role. Now if you will think of your readers both in terms of who they are and in terms of their reading your essay (after it is published) some months from now in a faraway place, and if you will back away from your subject so that in an impersonal way you can see all of the implications of the topic, you will have the ingredients of the objective voice.

Outline to Essay

With the deductive outline prepared, the audience visualized, and the objective voice in mind, you are ready to begin building your essay on the outline. For this first essay write at least 500 words—more, if possible. Later when you have learned ways of meeting the needs of your reader, an assigned length will be unnecessary: the subject and the reader will become your determining factors. As you write, project before your eyes the usual shape of the essay with its three connected parts, the introduction, the body, and the conclusion. The body of the essay occupies the greatest portion of the space. In a 500- to 1000-word essay one substantial paragraph normally suffices for the introduction and a shorter paragraph for the conclusion.

Now think for a moment about your outline and the direction in which deductive thought moves. In a deductive outline the central idea (thesis) is first because it is the main idea, the major topics (I, II, III) follow it and divide this main idea, and the subtopics (A, B, C) divide the major topics. Thus, in a deductive arrangement the thought moves from the whole to the parts, from the general to particulars.

When an essay is based on a deductive outline, the thought too moves from the whole to the parts. You are in fact telling your readers what the essay is all about when you present the central idea (thesis); they do not expect surprises, but rather a fuller explanation and discussion. Such an arrangement achieves the purpose of the deductive essay—to present and offer proof of the main idea.

To see the general shape of the essay when the thought is arranged deductively, study the illustration that follows, observing where the topics are placed to form the skeleton of the essay.

Before beginning the actual writing of the essay keep in mind two more points. First, the outline remains flexible until the essay is completed to your satisfaction. For example, should a different idea occur to you for one of the topics or subtopics, you are free to make alterations as long as you maintain a logical relationship of the idea throughout the outline. Second, approximately equal space in the body of the essay is devoted to each of the major topics (I, II, III). If you discover, for instance, that you have little to say about one topic and much to say about the others, consider dropping the short one from the outline and, if feasible, incorporating its thought into the introduction.

The Introduction

The function of the introduction is to arouse the interest of the reader, show the importance of the topic, and state the central idea. Since it can be assumed that you are writing to a mature, intelligent audience, you do not need a gimmick to arouse interest. For example, in discussing the reasons for automobile accidents within the city limits, you need not startle your reader by beginning with, "Screech, crash, smash! The black Buick plowed into the Volkswagen that appeared out of nowhere!" Instead it may be assumed that if you give new insight to the reader by showing him why the topic is both generally important and personally significant to him, he will automatically respond with interest.

To determine why the topic is important to the reader, remember your projected readers and ask, "What do I have in common with my audience?" The values and attitudes that are alike will aid you in determining the significance of the topic both to yourself as writer and to your reader. So in presenting reasons for automobile accidents within the city limits, recognize that most of your readers drive a car, or ride in a car, in city traffic. Because their lives are at stake, knowledge of what hazards to avoid is imperative. What could be more important than self-preservation? Tell your reader, therefore, that more accidents occur within the city limits than on the highway. And make him aware of the danger he may be facing every day.

DEDUCTIVE PATTERN FOR ESSAY OF MEDIUM LENGTH

C.I. xxxxxxxxxxxxxxxxxxxxxxxxxxxxxxxxxxxxxxxxxxxx . X xxxxxxxxxxxxxxxxxxxxxxxxxxxxxxxxxxxx

I. + X xxxxxxxxxxxxxxxxxxxxxxxxxxxxxxxxxxxxxxxx . X xxxxxxxxxxxxxx

I.A. xxxxxxxxxxxxxxxxxxxxxxxxxxxxxxxxxxxxxxxxxxxxxx .

I.B. + X xxxxxxxxxxxxxxxxxxxxxxxxxxxxxxxxxxxxxxxxxxxxxxxxxxxxxxxxxxxxxx
xxxxxxxx .

II. + X xxxxxxxxxxxxxxxxxxxxxxxxxxxxxxxxxxxxxxxxxxxxxxxxxxx . X xxxxx

II.A. xxxxxxxxxxxxxxxxxxxxxxxxxxxxxxxxxxxxxxxxxxxxxxxxxxxxxxxxx .

II.B. + X xxxxxxxxxxxxxxxxxxxxxxxxxxxxxxxxxxxxxxxxxxxxxxxx .

```
III.       + Xxxxxxxxxxxxxxxxxxxxxxxxxxxxxxxxxxxxxxxxxx . X xxxxxxxxxxxxxx
III.A.   xxxxxxxxxxxxxxxxxxxxxxxxxxxxxxxxxxxxxxxxxxxxxxxxxxxxxx_____



III.B.     + Xxxxxxxxxxxxxxxxxxxxxxxxxxxxxxxxxxxxxxxxxx . _____








                                                                    Xxxxxxxxx
C.I.     xxxxxxxxxxxxxxxxxxxxxxxxxxxxxxxxxxxxxxxxxxxxxxxxxxxx    _____
```

Note: The + marks indicate transitions.

Once you have shown the reader why the topic is important, then move to the central idea. Lift it from your outline and place it at the end of the introduction. It may be necessary to add a word or two to make the thought move smoothly from the preceding sentence to the central idea or the central idea may need to be rephrased in a slightly different way to connect the thought. But unless you discover that your essay is developing in a different direction than was planned and that you must adjust the outline accordingly, hold to the thought and the sequence of thought in your present central idea.

If you are tempted to introduce your central idea with the phrase, "In this paper I shall discuss," immediately cross out the phrase and state the idea directly. The phrase breaks the objective voice and attracts the reader's attention to the writer instead of to the idea. Besides, the reader does not need to be told that you plan to discuss the thought of the central idea. He is an intelligent reader who is aware that he is reading an essay in which the main idea is stated at the end of the introduction and developed in the body of the paper—hence you may insult his intelligence by using the phrase. The objectively stated central idea automatically tells the reader both what the writer will discuss and, by omission, what he will not.

Even though you do not have to put the central idea in any one position, there are two very good reasons for placing it at the end of the introduction. First, in the deductive essay the reader expects to find it there. Second, this position for the central idea enhances communication. Imagine, for instance, that your reader is waiting in the doctor's office—and waiting and waiting. He has viewed all of the pictures on the wall and read all of the diplomas and certificates. He has observed all of the other people in the office, tried to guess their problems, and sympathized with the eight-year-old boy who has sprained or broken his finger in catching a baseball. Finally, he picks up a magazine and idly thumbs through it, looking at the pictures and the titles of the articles while occasionally glancing at his watch and wondering what the doctor's diagnosis will be. Then a subject vaguely catches his attention and he begins to read the introduction, but his mind is still occupied with other thoughts, particularly with the waste of his time and all that he still needs to accomplish this afternoon. The writer is skillful, however, and as he explains the importance of the topic, the reader begins to concentrate on what the writer is saying. By the time the reader has reached the central idea, he has blanked the doctor's office from his mind and is ready to focus on the main point of the essay. The writer has drawn him into the essay gradually and withheld the main idea until he is sure he has the reader's full attention.

In leading the reader easily to the main thought, avoid beginning the introduction too far from the central idea. For example, if in writing about the reasons for automobile accidents within the city limits you begin with the development of the automobile as a form of transportation, you have introduced an idea that is far from your central idea. You compel the reader to leap from thought to thought in reaching your central idea and, at the same time, you focus his attention on the history of the automobile rather than on the reasons for automobile accidents. When a reader's mind has to play leapfrog or is directed into channels that do not flow immediately into the main stream of thought, he becomes confused and loses interest. Be careful, therefore, to let each thought lead easily to the next and all thoughts lead to the central idea.

Although you are urged to use the described form of the introduction in writing your first deductive essays, other arrangements are possible but more difficult to compose. Instead of beginning with the importance of the topic and ending with the central idea, one form begins with the central idea, moves to the importance of the topic, and then repeats the central idea. In both cases the central idea is stated at the end of the introduction. Either of these forms functions well when the paper is a short one and the introduction is one paragraph in length. Longer papers that have several paragraphs in the introduction may begin with general statements about the significance of the topic, give historical, critical or literary background needed by the reader to understand the significance, and then move to the particular concept on which the paper will focus.

Assignment 5: Rough Draft of the Introduction

Write an introduction that (1) arouses the interest of the reader by demonstrating the importance of the topic and (2) leads to the central idea. Underline the central idea and write *C.I.* opposite it in the margin. Check to see that each thought leads easily to the next and that all thoughts lead to the central idea.

Points to remember:

1. You are motivated by a sincere desire to communicate with the readers you have selected.

2. You are writing in objective voice, using no pronoun to represent yourself and avoiding phrases that call attention to yourself.

3. If it is necessary for you to alter the thought or the sequence of thought in the central idea, then revise the outline to accommodate the change.

4. After writing and rewriting, if you are not satisfied with your introduction, put it aside and return to it after you have completed the rough draft of the essay. Be comforted—the introduction is the hardest part of the essay to write!

The Body

After all the preparation you have done so far, writing the body of the essay should be easy as long as you use your outline. Your task now is to use your outline as the skeleton of the essay and put flesh on it.

In the body you will be working with parts of the idea—not the idea as a whole. Each part becomes a paragraph or series of paragraphs so that the ideas are put together section by section. Look again at the illustration to see how parts from the outline are built into paragraph units. When the body is completed, the main idea will have been expanded or proved, thereby fulfilling the function of the deductive essay.

Start by using topic I from your outline as the lead-in to the paragraph following the introduction. Topic I signals the first major section of the essay. Now write in the more limited IA which serves as the topic sentence for the paragraph.[3] Fill the paragraph with sentences relating to IA—examples, details, illustrations, or data.

Next, indent for a new paragraph, lift IB from your outline, and write it down as the topic sentence for the paragraph. The indentation will suggest to the reader that you are taking up another aspect of I. Provide some transition to connect IB and IA (sometimes a single word such as *also* or a repetition of the previous idea will serve to relate the paragraphs). Then, as in the preceding paragraph, add sentences that flesh out the idea of IB.

Continue to use this process until section I has been completed. Then introduce the second major section from your outline. As you did with topic I, take II, use it as a lead-in for this section, and follow it with IIA as the topic sentence for the paragraph. Connect the idea of II to I by repeating the idea of I or by using a transitional word or phrase. For each of your remaining topics repeat the pattern described for topic I and its subtopics.

In connecting one paragraph to the next, notice that in deductive writing, the transitional word, phrase, or sentence is usually placed at the begining of the paragraph rather than at the end of the preceding paragraph. Observe also that the topics are linked according to their position in the

[3]The division of paragraphs depends, of course, on the size and complexity of the subject. In a very short 300-word essay, I, IA, and IB can be discussed in a single paragraph with I serving as the topic sentence. In a long essay (3,000 words or more), topic I may be introduced in an entire paragraph that serves as a transition, and IA and IB used in separate paragraphs. In even longer essays, several additional paragraph units may be needed—perhaps for IA and IA1, IB and IB1, and so on.

movement of the thought from the whole to the parts: I is linked to the central idea, IA is linked to I, IB is linked to IA, IC is linked to IB; then II is linked to I and thus the chain continues.

The linkage is sometimes provided by the natural division of the idea when the topics are placed close to one another in the essay—for instance, I is placed close to the central idea; IA immediately follows I. But a whole paragraph separates B from A and several paragraphs separate II from I. In such cases you have to provide transitions by repeating the idea of the earlier topic or by using a transitional word or phrase. These connections enable the reader to follow the development of the main idea without confusion.

When you have finished the last paragraph of the body, underline the sentences in which each topic occurs and write the outline symbols in the left margin next to these sentences. This underlining provides a visual check on how well you are following the outline and whether you are developing paragraphs in the deductive order. Compare the positioning of the skeleton of your outline with that of the illustration on pages 41-42.

Assignment 6: Rough Draft of the Body

Write the first draft of the body of the essay by incorporating your outline into the essay according to the process described for an essay of medium length. Be sure to keep your reader in mind, maintain the objective voice, connect the main points, and underline the topics of your outline as they occur in the essay, placing the outline symbols in the margin opposite the topics.

The Conclusion

The conclusion to the paper, a new paragraph that follows the one based on the last topic of the outline, serves to reemphasize the central idea and brings the essay to an end. In giving this added emphasis, the central idea per se need not be placed in a particular position in the conclusion or stated in the exact words of the outline.

The conclusion takes a number of forms such as a summary, a restatement of the importance of the idea, an anecdote or illustration that implies its significance, or a prediction for the future. The summary should not be used for a paper that is only a few typewritten pages in length, for the intelligent reader will either be bored or insulted to have the few points he has just read reiterated. He will react the same way to a conclusion that begins with the phrase, *In conclusion*, for he can see at a glance that he has reached the end of the essay. Instead, in an essay of medium length a restatement of the importance of the idea, preferably in fresh wording, an anecdote or illustration that makes the idea vivid, or a prediction for the future that is not spoiled by a didactic tone, generally functions more effectively than a summary.

The conclusion need not be a long paragraph: three to five sentences that round off the idea and bring the rhythm to a sense of completion may be sufficient. Some very short essays even omit a conclusion when the thought is completed in the discussion of the last topic and any addition would be redundant.

Assignment 7: Rough Draft of the Conclusion

Write a short paragraph that reemphasizes the central idea and brings the essay to an end. For example, use a restatement of the importance of the main idea, an anecdote or illustration that implies its significance, or a prediction for the future (in language that is not didactic). But do not be tempted to summarize the points made in your essay.

Polishing the Rough Draft

Did you think that by writing a rough draft of the introduction, body, and conclusion you had finished your essay? Unfortunately, as all writers learn, the rough draft is exactly that—it is *rough* and it is a *draft*. It has to be polished before it is ready for typing in its final form.

Before beginning to polish, set the rough draft aside until you can return to it with fresh insight. Then, ignoring as much as possible the fact that you are the author, read it through, at least twice, as if you were a member of your audience. On the second reading, mark any problems you discover that interfere with communication. For instance, you may notice an idea that is not phrased clearly or needs additional explanation, a sentence that should—but does not—develop the topic sentence, ideas that are not connected within or between paragraphs, words that are repeated unnecessarily, faulty punctuation, or misspelling. Now, as author, make the changes you noted, and then read the essay again to see if you can discover other ways to improve it.

Avoiding static paragraph beginnings and unnecessary repetition may be a particular problem when you first try to build on an outline. In the rough draft your task was to place the topics in the proper positions in the paragraphs and to provide links with certain other outline topics. In polishing the rough draft you may need to return to these paragraph beginnings and see if the thought movement can be improved. For example, topic I needs to be placed at the beginning of the first paragraph of the body, but the idea of the topic does not have to be expressed in the very first words or even the first sentence. To avoid a static opening, a phrase or a brief statement that comments on or explains topic I may separate it from the central idea in the preceding paragraph and still leave the position of the idea close enough to provide a link.

And the exact words of the outline do not have to be repeated in the essay. In the outline the repetition was deliberate to show at a glance the relationships of topics; in an essay unnecessary repetition is monotonous. So the wording of a topic may be altered as long as the meaning does not change. If you change the idea unintentionally and without adjusting the outline, you will throw the outline and the essay out of focus.

Separation of IA from I by a phrase or short sentence and a restatement of idea is also permissible and sometimes desirable. The same is true of other topics as long as their deductive position at or near the beginning of paragraphs and the connection of idea within and between paragraphs is maintained.

At this time your instructor may wish to look over your essay or ask you to exchange essays with a classmate so that each of you can offer suggestions to the other. Whether you are working by yourself or with a classmate, the following checklist should help you decide how your essay can be improved further:

Checklist for the Rough Draft

1. Is the rough draft complete with an introduction, body, and conclusion?
2. Does the introduction interest the reader by showing the importance of the topic and does it lead directly to the central idea?
3. Does the body follow the outline and are the topics placed according to the pattern described for the essay of medium length?

4. Is the focus of the essay the same as that of the outline—that is, is the essay focused on the central idea?
5. Does the conclusion provide a brief but powerful or interesting ending to the essay (without summarizing the points or being didactic)?
6. Do the transitional words, phrases, or sentences between paragraphs connect the proper topics and do so without being static?
7. In incorporating the topics from the outline into the essay, has unnecessary repetition of words been avoided without changing the meaning of the topic?
8. In developing the topic sentence does each paragraph fulfill the reader's expectation?
9. Is objective voice used throughout the essay?
10. Do the ideas flow smoothly throughout the essay?
11. Is there enough flesh on the skeleton so that the bones do not protrude?
12. Would the essay appeal to the selected reading audience?

Assignment 8: Polishing the Rough Draft

After putting your rough draft aside until you can read it more objectively, return to it and try to read it as if you were a member of your audience. On the second reading, mark places where changes are needed—for instance, to clarify ideas, to achieve a better arrangement of thought, to improve wording, or to correct errors in mechanics. Use the checklist to help you as you read, make changes, reread, and make others.

Student Essay

The following essay, written by the student who was assigned *Violence* as her topic, is included as an illustration of the format for the typed essay and of the assignments in this chapter. You may wish to study it before you put the final touches on your own essay.

Carole Bishop
English 100
Deductive Essay

Violence and the Young

Violence and the Young

Audience: Young parents with children, probably middle class, with at least a high school education, and other concerned citizens.

Purpose: To make parents and others aware of influences toward violence that exist in a child's environment.

A Deductive Outline

Central Idea: Violence is bred into the young by the influence of parents, by the influence of mass media, and by the influence of peer groups.

  I. Parents influence their children toward violence.
   A. Parents transmit attitudes toward violence to their children.
   B. Parents set examples of violence for their children.
 II. Mass media influence children toward violence.
   A. Television shows that appeal to children are often oriented toward violence.
   B. Books, newspapers, and magazines read by children are often oriented toward violence.
III. Peer groups sometimes influence children toward violence.
   A. Acceptance into a peer group is often contingent upon participation in violent acts.
   B. Maintaining status in a peer group is often contingent upon continued participation in violent acts.

Violence and the Young

Headlines scream violence, news broadcasts feature it, movies, books, and television programs dramatize it. Everywhere people turn they see or hear of robberies, shootings, rapes, kidnapping, arson, bombings, or murder. All of these individual or group acts of violence are disturbing in themselves, but even more frightening is the fact that many of these acts are committed not just by the so-called criminal elements of the adult population but by the kids who live just around the block or right down the road. Thoughtful observers of this trend toward violence by the young are taking a careful look at the environment in which they grow up to ascertain possible indirect causes. Assuming that children's beliefs and actions are shaped by the models they most frequently encounter, such observations lead to the opinion that *violence is bred into the young by the influ-*
C.I. *ence of parents, by the influence of mass media, and by the influence of peer groups.*

Though *parents* may not deliberately teach their child to at-
I. tack or rob, unconsciously they *may condition the child so that violence comes easy to him.* They do this in two ways. First, *par-*
IA. *ents transmit attitudes to their children.* Favorable responses to violence made indirectly by parents are not ignored by a child. If a father yells enthusiastically at violent encounters in hockey or boxing, even though the father is enjoying the sport vicariously, the child may infer his father's approval of violent actions. A mother who laughs as she tells of the black eye produced by their neighbor's latest family fight similarly suggests to a child the approval of violence. Even more serious consequences may result from the negative attitudes of suspicion, discrimination, or hatred expressed by parents, for these may form the seedbed of violence. Thus if parents reveal their attitude toward policemen by calling them "pigs" or "the fuzz," the child, born without prejudice or value judgments, accepts this attitude without question. Later in life this lack of respect for those who enforce the law may lead to confrontations. Or when parents blame society for all of their problems instead of assuming responsibilities and taking the initiative to improve their situation, the children will reflect this

self-pity too. This attitude may encourage a young person to take by force those things he thinks society has denied him—the watch, the bicycle, the T.V. set.

    If parental attitudes toward violence can lay the foundation for possible acts of violence by the young, *the long-range effect*
IB. *on children of direct acts of violence by parents is even more predictable.* The man who is a bully at work, brags to his family and friends about his fights on the job, and dominates his family and friends with physical force sets a pattern of action for his children, particularly for his sons, to copy. If the physical force is not possible for the son, a brick, a knife, or a gun can replace the fist. A husband who beats his wife—and a wife who submits to the beatings without seeking help—teach children to believe that such violence is a normal part of family existence. Later in their own homes the children will likely play the same roles, the violent, domineering husband and the weak, submissive wife, and the beatings will go on. When physical abuse is directed toward a child by either or both parents, the child, victimized emotionally as well as physically, will also repeat the cycle by abusing his own children.

II.   In addition to parents, *mass media influence children toward violence.* Today television is the primary form of entertainment for children. Unfortunately, however, *television shows that*
IIA. *appeal to children are often oriented toward violence.* Saturday morning cartoon shows and other shows such as "Spider Man" and "The Incredible Hulk" are filled with violence: Popeye knocks the head off Bluto; the Road Runner leads the Coyote into the path of an oncoming locomotive or steamroller; the man on the run responds to violence by instantly and incredibly becoming a giant. Even though the Hulk is a good guy and always wins, the plot is sometimes brutal. And the violence both in cartoons and in other shows is made to look like fun. During prime time hours children often join their parents in watching movies or adult shows where violence is a major and exciting ingredient. In "Dallas," J. R. gets shot by his mistress, who is also his sister-in-law; in "Kojak," muggings, drug traffic, rape, murder, and every other form of violence a policeman deals with are dramatized. The incidents on "Kojak" were claimed by one Florida teenager as the inspiration for the murder he committed. And some West Coast youngsters raped a girl with a bottle in imitation of another tele-

vision program they had seen. To imitate television violence is lots of fun!

IIB.   Like television, *books, newspapers, and magazines also present a world of violence to the child.* To protect the apes, the natives, or Jane, Tarzan is engaged in a constant battle with evil men. The Hardy boys find their jungle in the civilized world rather than the depths of Africa. Brutal beatings, murders, war-casualty counts, a bank holdup, or the Saturday night brawl at the local bar are all headlined by newspapers and often illustrated with vivid pictures—to increase circulation of the newspapers or perhaps of the reader's blood. Young children see pictures and headlines; older ones read the stories. Magazines, too, present violent stories and many contain even more details and pictures than newspaper articles. The Patty Hearst story paid the salary of many a magazine writer. All these forms of media are available to children and may have a detrimental cumulative effect, particularly if they come to see the world as a place where the moral is "Do violence unto others before they do it unto you."

III.   A third area of *influence towards violence in the child's environment is his peer group.* When a child nears adolescence, nothing is quite as important as having the approval of his friends

IIIA. and being part of the group. But *acceptance in a peer group is often contingent upon participation in violent acts.* The point emphasized in the act is the thrill and skill involved in encountering a dangerous situation and in not getting caught. Whereas in the past lifting hubcaps or battering roadside mailboxes was adequate proof of commitment to a group, now much more serious life-endangering deeds are required: steal a purse from a pedestrian on a crowded street; break into a liquor store and grab a few bottles before the police answer the alarm. These actions are not the pranks of a Tom Sawyer or Huck Finn. Belonging to certain peer groups requires much more than filching a ham, corncobs, and tobacco.

      Once a member of a peer group, the youngster frequently

IIIB. finds that *maintaining status in the peer group is often contingent upon continued participation in violent acts.* It is not enough to steal a purse or break into a liquor store. Now he discovers that he is expected to continue the role of the amateur criminal. Stealing a purse gives way to robbing a cash register; breaking into a store at night is followed by entering one in the daytime armed with a gun. Soon the amateur criminal may find himself seeking money, thrills, and peer status by even more feats such as auto theft or drug peddling. As one act of violence leads to another, the odds of someone being seriously injured or killed increase and so do the chances for years of imprisonment.

Fortunately, most children have parents who teach them to use moderation and self-control and to respect the property and lives of others. Fortunately, most teenagers have fun with friends by jogging, ringing basketball goals, or eating hamburgers and french fries. Fortunately, most children have experiences that show them the world as a place where good dwells as well as evil. *But if a child's direct experience of the world through his family and his peers and his indirect experience of the world through the media teach him only to spell V-I-O-L-E-N-C-E, it is no wonder that at some point in his young life he lays aside his toys and begins to play for real.*

C.I.

The Typed Essay

Typing the final draft of the essay is not requested just for the sake of readability. It helps you see your own writing in perspective and develop objectivity about your work. It also gives the essay a good appearance and implies that you are approaching your assignment seriously.

When you type the essay, you are expected to follow a standard format. If someone else types the essay for you, you are expected to specify the format to be used. Except for the variations that some instructors may desire, the preceding essay illustrates an acceptable format. A few points of caution may help you:

1. The title should be brief and should inform the reader of the focus of the essay.
2. The major words of the title are capitalized but not underlined. Quotation marks and italics are used only when someone else's title is included as part of your own.
3. Except for the title page, a margin of one and one-half inches on the left and one inch at the top, bottom, and right side is maintained throughout the essay.
4. The title is repeated on the page in which the essay itself begins. It is centered, placed several spaces below the one-inch margin, and separated from the first line of the essay by several spaces.
5. The first page of the actual essay is numbered at the bottom of the page. The numbers for the remaining pages are placed in the upper right-hand corner.

Assignment 9: Typing the Revised Essay

Make a good final impression by typing your essay in the illustrated format. To see the structure of the essay clearly, underline the topics from the outline as they appear in the essay and place the topic symbols in the left margin opposite the ideas. (Note: the underlining is an added feature for essays written in this course.) Before you turn in your essay to your instructor, proofread it carefully and make neat corrections with a ball-point pen that matches the color of your typewriter ribbon. Along with this essay turn in a typed copy of your inductive sentence outline and any of the other previous assignments requested by your instructor.

Paragraph to Sentence

In learning to write a deductive essay, initially it is not possible to concentrate on every element that goes into effective essay writing. Your assignments thus far have moved you by slow stages in preparing and writing the first essay. As preparation, you thought through a large topic to generate ideas and to arrive at a subject of suitable size, wrote inductive and deductive outlines, and projected your audience. In writing the essay you used objective voice, followed the outline to produce a deductive arrangement, and connected the ideas. If you achieved each of these stages and produced an organized, deductive essay in objective voice, you have begun well.

However, unless you brought a good background in writing to this course, chances are that your first essay lacked paragraph development— that is, the idea of the topic sentence was not filled out sufficiently to meet your reader's needs. If so, do not despair. Paragraph development was mentioned in basing the essay on the outline but not presented in depth. The next essay assignment is designed to shift the focus to paragraphs.

Deductive Paragraphs

In deductive essays each paragraph represents a division of the central idea and the paragraph is, in itself, a unit of thought built on that division.[4] You might think of a deductive outline as being, in some ways, like a family tree showing relationships among several generations descended from a common ancestor. Each family, represented by topics A, B, and C, is a unit with its own personality, style of living, or physical and mental attributes. These family units are related to each other and also to the particular branch from which they descended, topics I, II, or III. And topics I, II, and III are, in turn, related to the common ancestor, the central idea.

Analyzing the topic sentence. Just as the central idea tells the reader the idea to be developed in the essay, so the topic sentence tells the reader the idea to be developed in the paragraph. Not only does it tell the reader what to expect, but also it tells the writer what to do. It clues both to what the statement alone says, what the statement promises to say, what information the reader would need and want to know, and how the information

---

[4]For variations in deductive paragraphing, see n. 3 above.

should be arranged. Because it sets up a contract between writer and reader, the writer must know the terms of his agreement and fulfill these terms.

To decide what the terms of the topic sentence are, ask the following questions:

1. *What information does the topic sentence by itself give the reader—either directly or indirectly?*
2. *What information does the topic sentence promise to give the reader?*
3. *In fulfilling the promise, what information does the writer have that the reader would need and want to know?*
4. *In what sequence would the reader expect the information to be given?*

Using the following topic sentences as examples, see if your answers to the questions accord with the commentary. (Be sure to answer each question before you refer to the commentary.)

Topic sentence: Varieties of fish can be observed at Silver Springs, Florida, from the glass-bottomed boat.

Commentary on question 1: The topic sentence tells the reader that Silver Springs has different kinds of fish, that these fish can be seen (tourists presumably are the viewers and the water must be clear since the fish can be seen), and that the fish are seen though the glass bottom of a boat. Thus the sentence tells the reader what, where, and how.

Commentary on question 2: The topic sentence promises to tell the reader what kinds of fish can be seen in a particular place from a particular viewpoint.

Commentary on question 3: The writer of this sentence must know the kinds of fish that can be seen at Silver Springs in order to tell the reader what he wants to know. But the writer must be able to do more than name some of the 34 different kinds of fish. The reader would want to know some of the features of each type—their size, shape, color, or other distinctive qualities—and any additional points of special interest—for instance, a favorite environment. In other words, the writer must be able to make the reader become a viewer of the fish from the perspective of the glass-bottomed boat.

Commentary on question 4: This topic sentence calls for an arrangement of details explaining and describing some of the kinds of fish viewed in their natural habitat.

Topic sentence: River pollution has poisoned many fish.

Commentary on question 1: The topic sentence tells the reader that the writer is concerned with pollution as a cause of poison and with the effect of poison on fish. In this sentence pollution is limited to rivers.

Commentary on question 2: The topic sentence promises the reader that the writer will present proof of river pollution and proof of its effect on fish.

Commentary on question 3: The writer must know what chemicals pollute a river, what chemicals have been found by scientists in certain rivers, which of these chemicals affect fish negatively, and whether fish in the identified rivers have died, become inedible, or become incapable of reproduction.

Commentary on question 4: The reader would expect the arrangement to follow the sequence of idea in the statement: first the cause and then the effect.

Topic sentence: Catching trout is a greater challenge than catching perch.

Commentary on question 1: The topic sentence tells the reader that the writer is interested in comparing and contrasting fishing for trout with fishing for perch. More specifically, the first key word, *catching*, meaning here *to seize after a struggle*, informs the reader that the discussion is limited to hooking and landing a fish. The second key word, *challenge*, suggests to the reader a test of a fisherman's skill in tempting a fish with bait and, once it is hooked, in overcoming the fighting ability of the fish.

Commentary on question 2: The writer promises the reader that he will explain why catching trout is more challenging than catching perch.

Commentary on question 3: The writer must know that trout are generally larger than perch and therefore put up a greater fight. He must know that trout are more particular about the kind of bait they will accept and about the time of day they will bite. And he must know that light, strong equipment is used in trout fishing, enabling the sportsman to feel the play of the fish, while perch can be caught with heavier, less-sophisticated equipment—even a pole with a hook and line.

Commentary on question 4: The comparison-contrast may be arranged by discussing first the hooking and the struggle to land a trout and then the hooking and the ease of landing a perch. Or the two actions may be divided so that the first comparison-contrast is directed to the hooking of both a trout and a perch and the next comparison-contrast to the struggle and landing of each fish.

You may have noticed that each of the topic sentences above could serve as the central idea of an essay. Whether one writes a paragraph or an essay on a limited subject depends on the contract with the reader. The reader knows that a paragraph, which is only a miniature essay, will not explore an idea as thoroughly as an essay does. Nevertheless, the reader expects the writer to fulfill the promise of the topic sentence and deliver, briefly but clearly, the information that he needs and has a right to expect. Writing either a paragraph or an essay involves selecting appropriate material: in both cases, a writer always has more information than he actually uses.

Assignment 10: Analyzing Paragraphs 1

Using the four questions, try your skill at analyzing the following topic sentences. Write the four questions at the top of your page

and then each topic sentence followed by your answers. Identify
each answer with the phrase "Commentary on question #____ ."

1. Fishing as a test of man's skill and endurance has been the subject
   of many a famous story.
2. Throughout history no basic change has occurred in the tools of the
   fisherman—the spear, the net, and the hook and line.
3. The meaning of the word *fishing* varies with its context and the writer's intent. (Your dictionary will help you with this one.)

Analysis of the topic sentences above should have demonstrated the
importance of making a topic sentence state exactly what you have in mind.
If your outline topic does not express your idea, then change it and make
any other adjustments in the outline necessitated by the change. Only when
you are sure that the idea is clearly stated are you ready to concentrate on
building the paragraph.

If you apply the questions to your own topic sentences, the answers
will give you the basis of good paragraph development. The question that
may give you the most trouble is question 3 in which you must decide what
you know and what your reader needs and would like to know. This question
first calls for you to reflect on your own ideas and experience with the topic.
Then it asks you to imaginatively transform yourself into the reader, see
what knowledge he lacks, and recognize that what is in your own mind
needs to be put in his. Of course, you will have far more information in your
own mind than you can convey to a reader in one paragraph, so information
will have to be selected that is pertinent to the contract you have made.

A paragraph such as the following may result if you do not fulfill your
contract—especially if you not not apply question 3:

Good warm-up exercises serve to prevent severe injuries to the body.
During a warm-up the dancer's body is stretched to its capacity. This
massive stretching works like a rubber band and is a preventive measure
against cramping when the stretching is done correctly.

Here the writer, in her essay about ballet, assumes that the reader knows
what warm-up exercises for ballet are and, therefore, does not describe
them. She does not show the reader how they are done correctly and does
not explain in detail why the muscles need stretching or what injuries may
be prevented by this preliminary warm-up.

By neglecting to apply all of the questions to her topic sentence, the writer of the above paragraph may have fallen into another paragraph trap—judging a paragraph's completeness by the amount of space it takes up on a handwritten page. Everyone has had the experience of seeing what appears to be a healthy paragraph shrink to a few lean, undernourished sentences when the paragraph is typed. Other traps also await the unwary writer. A writer may end a paragraph when his hand becomes tired or when his sense of rhythm tells him that he has completed a rhythmic movement. All of these subconscious factors, once recognized, can be negated by forcing yourself to judge a paragraph by its content.

Building the paragraph. Although you can write a good paragraph without knowing that paragraphs can be classified by their structure, identifying the structure aids in discussing paragraphs. The major types are enumeration or arrangement of details, cause and effect, comparison-contrast, example (one or more); definition; or a combination of these types. The topic sentences discussed above or placed in the assignment illustrate these types:

In the discussion of topic sentences—

Topic sentence 1	(*Varieties of fish*)	arrangement of details
Topic sentence 2	(*River pollution*)	cause and effect
Topic sentence 3	(*Catching trout*)	comparison-contrast

In Assignment 10: Analyzing Paragraphs 1—

Topic sentence 1	(*Fishing— famous stories*)	example (here several)
Topic sentence 2	(*Throughout history—tools*)	arrangement of details (here chronological)
Topic sentence 3	(*meaning of "fishing"*)	definition plus illustrations

Because topic sentences are always phrased on an abstract level, it is necessary to explain the ideas to the reader. And that explanation is what paragraphs are all about. In explaining the topic sentence, regardless of the structural pattern of the paragraph, it is necessary to use details. These details move from the abstract statement of the topic sentence to more concrete statements in the sentences that follow. Normally, the movement occurs in three or four stages, each stage less general and more specific than the first.

For instance, if you move from *fruit*, to *apples*, to *Golden Delicious apples*, each step is less abstract and more concrete than the former. Your task in the paragraph is to extend the idea of the topic sentence (fruit) to a second but lower level of abstraction (apple) and then to a third and even lower level of abstraction (Golden Delicious apples). This third level is the concrete level that lets your reader see or understand on a very specific basis the idea you are discussing in the paragraph. And that last level is what instructors mean when they say, "Be specific."

For a little practice in dealing with different levels of abstraction, see if you can fill in the blanks below:

1. medicine	2. _____	3. Phillips' Milk of Magnesia	
1. star	2. star of a T.V. series	3. _____	
1. _____	2. Cairn terrier	3. brindle female	4. Holly
1. plant	2. _____	3. African violet	4. Ontario clear white
1. doctor	2. heart specialist	3. _____	4. Dr. Michael DeBakey

Perhaps you will recall that when you were in grammar school, your teacher tried to show you how to write definitions. In doing so, she asked you to define a word such as *punishment*. And you may have replied, "Punishment is when you are not allowed to watch T.V. for a week." Your definition was in terms of your own concrete experience. But what your teacher wanted was an abstract phrase such as "penalty for wrongdoing." Possibly she merely confused you by commenting: "You can't define by using 'is when.' *Is* is a linking verb and should be followed by a predicate noun." Instead, she might have explained (and illustrated in terms you could understand at that time) that to define a word it is necessary to do as the dictionary does: list many different instances of its use, sort out the characteristics these instances have in common, ignore the differences, and produce a word or phrase that represents the common characteristics. Hence, *punishment* is "a penalty for wrongdoing." Now, as an adult, you tend to write on abstract levels. What you need to do in paragraphs is to return momentarily to your childhood and move the idea down until it reaches the "is when" level. The "is when" level is needed to clarify the thought of your topic sentence for your reader.

For example, note how the paragraph below, structured by an arrangement of details, proceeds from the abstract to the concrete. The topic sentence is abstract; the second sentence, which identifies the meaning of "important things" (part of the major idea of the topic sentence), is less abstract; and the details that follow illustrate the important things on a concrete level. Then another sentence introduces the less important things (a second part of the major idea of the topic sentence), identifying them by contrast as insignificant compared with life and death. This sentence is also less abstract than the mother topic sentence. In turn, it is followed by a series of illustrations of unimportant things phrased on a concrete level:

> Another function of reading is that of informing—informing people of important things and of things not so important. It tells them some things which are vital to their health and perhaps even to their survival. When a pedestrian reads the "Don't Walk" sign on the traffic light, he knows to stay on the sidewalk lest a driver knock him down. The "Poison" label on strychnine warns that it is not to be used for mouth wash. The caution on a pack of cigarettes lets people know they may be endangering their health by smoking. Reading a book on communist techniques may enable an FBI agent to recognize infiltrators. Daily reading of newspapers keeps people informed of what is happening today, what might happen tomorrow, and how they can prepare for it. In contrast to this important information is reading that informs about less important things. A couple reads movie advertisements in the afternoon newspaper before deciding how to spend the evening. Television fans read *TV Guide* to know which programs will interest them most. Diners order their dinner after reading a menu. When students read a bulletin board, they know where to be at what time. Careful reading of the tags on two pairs of pants tells the buyer which pair will last longer. In a matter of life and death or in the choice between two movies, reading informs.

In building a paragraph, begin by analyzing your topic sentence to see what it tells both you and the reader, what it leads the reader to expect, what you will need to tell your reader to make the ideas both interesting and clear, and the sequence in which the ideas should be presented. Then as you present these ideas in the sequence suggested by the topic sentence, move from the abstract to the concrete. Suppose, for example, your topic sentence reads: "The visual communication of animals is understandable even to humans." You then add a second sentence explaining the first one in language that is less abstract. Your second sentence might be: "Because animals and humans have the same basic survival needs and the same basic feelings, they are able to communicate through body movements." Now you will have explained "visual communication" and given the reason why humans can interpret certain body movements of animals—the shared expression of survival needs and basic feelings. Through this less abstract statement you have made the ideas of your topic sentence clearer and also led the reader to anticipate more specific explanation of the terms. You then fulfill the reader's anticipation by moving to the "is when" level, that is, to concrete examples of how basic needs and feelings are expressed through body movements. Finally your paragraph might read:

> The visual communication of animals is understandable even to humans. Because animals and humans have the same basic survival needs and the same basic feelings, they are able to communicate through body movements. For example, just as a cat indicates antagonism or anger by snarling and baring her teeth, a human also reveals these reactions by contorting his face or gritting his teeth. Metaphorically, he may also, like a cat, get his back up when he is defensive. One way a horse shows his fear is to open his eyes so wide that the white part is revealed. Likewise, if a human is shocked or frightened, one of his first reactions is to widen his eyes. In winter a pair of rabbits will cuddle together for warmth and affection and so will a teenage couple. A dog will stand on his hind feet for a dog biscuit; a child will tug at his mother's skirt for a cookie. (Becky Cates)

Not all paragraphs, however, follow the simple arrangement of: topic sentence, followed by a second sentence clarifying the ideas of the first on a more specific level and anticipating fuller explanations, followed by additional sentences that illustrate on a concrete level. You may need to use several sentences to explain the topic idea before you move to a single, extended example or to short, specific illustrations. A comparison-contrast sequence may be presented in different ways (see, for example, the commentary on question 4 under the topic sentence "Catching trout is a greater challenge than catching perch") and still incorporate abstract to concrete movement. Or if you are working in a cause-effect structure, you will need to clarify the cause and discuss it and then clarify the effect and discuss it.

By understanding the purpose of a paragraph and the principles of developing it and by being genuinely concerned with communicating with your reader, you can produce good paragraphs, each one uniquely structured according to the demands of its topic sentence. Variations of paragraph structure prevent monotony in an essay and help hold the reader's attention. Study the following paragraph to see how one student solved her problem of arrangement. Note that she used an analogy to clarify the idea:

> Keeping a journal also fosters direction in life by providing order. The day's events are a jumble and days on end may seem the same. Order must be put in life—rather, sometimes the task is to find the order which is there, but hidden. This sorting does not of itself give direction but it helps set the stage. To straighten a room one walks around and simply begins by picking up a newspaper, folding the lap rug, emptying the ash tray, putting pillows in place, taking dishes to the kitchen, and suddenly the room is sorted out and usable. Then one can see what to do with it— how to decorate it, how to put it to a different use, or how to enjoy it as it is. This ordering did nothing to aid one in making a decision about the room; it merely allowed the room to be seen. Writing a few lines or a few pages about a cluttered day helps make sense of that day, clarify it, put it in perspective, own it. Events then are not as likely to be loose cannon on the decks of one's life but a part of the structure of that life. (Jane Turner)

Assignment 11: Analyzing Paragraphs 2

Select one of your own topic sentences from your first essay. Copy it down by itself on a clean sheet of paper, ignoring the paragraph that you wrote earlier. Using the four questions, analyze your topic sentence and list the answers to your questions as you did in Assignment 10. Then with the answers before you, write a rough draft of the paragraph, arranging the ideas to follow the structure identified in question 4 and to move the thought from abstract to concrete.

Checking the paragraph. When you have completed the rough draft of a paragraph, you need to use your eyes and ears to check it for unity, coherence, and completeness. If the paragraph has unity, that is, oneness of thought, each sentence will be an extension of the ideas of the topic sentence. Building your paragraph on the answers to your questions should have produced unity. But if you did not maintain a consistent relationship with your subject and reader through voice, you may have broken the unity. Check for oneness of thought by using your eyes to determine if you have inadvertently added an opinion, thrown in a remark, shifted your attitude, or even changed the subject. If there is any break in the unity, yank out the evidence and fill in the hole.

Now use your ears to determine if the ideas flow smoothly and clearly from sentence to sentence. The arrangement of your paragraph according to the sequence suggested by the topic sentence and to the abstract-concrete movement within the structure should have produced a coherent paragraph. Yet there may be places where you did not connect the ideas, and the loose relationship may confuse the reader. So read the paragraph aloud very slowly and listen to it as if you were hearing it for the first time. As you listen, check for any thought that is not connected to the next either by placement in a natural order, by a transition that relates the idea to a pre-ceding one, by words that repeat the thought, by pronouns that reflect the nouns they represent, or by verbs or other words that signal time or place. If you find a loose connection, repair it. Then read the paragraph aloud again to be sure that the reader's way through the paragraph is clearly illuminated.

Finally, use both your eyes and ears to check for completeness. First see if you have fulfilled your contract with the reader. Have you given him the information you promised in the topic sentence? Have you told him what he needs and wants to know? Make alterations if your answer is no. Next you will need to hear if the paragraph has been completed rhythmically. Read it aloud slowly again and listen now for the rhythm of your prose. Lo-cate any place where the phrasing is rough or a sentence seems exceedingly short or long and make necessary adjustments. In listening to the rhythm, pay particular attention to whether or not the last sentence gives a sense of completeness. When it does not, change the sentence or add another one. Prose rhythm, of course, does not have the beat of traditional poetry, but like free verse it does have asymmetrical balance. Instinctively you should feel the movement and sense where it is satisfying and where it is not.

To be satisfying to the reader the last sentence should fully carry out both the thought and the rhythm. When the thought of the topic sentence has been divided and presented in sections within the paragraph, then a final sentence to unite the idea once more may be indicated. Such is the case in the paragraph above on "Reading informs." The student presents the idea in two parts, the first part explaining that reading informs about important things and the second that it informs about less important things. She brings the idea together again with a final sentence that also completes the rhythm: "In a matter of life and death or in a choice between two movies, reading informs." In contrast, because the paragraph on "The visual communication of animals" has one simple movement from the concrete to the abstract, the idea of the topic sentence does not need to be reiterated. Instead, the last sentence gives a final detail as it terminates the rhythm, "A dog will stand on his hind feet for a dog biscuit; a child will tug at his mother's skirt for a cookie." In the paragraph on "Keeping a journal," the more complex arrangement is ended by the sentence, "Events then are not as likely to be loose cannon on the decks of one's life but a part of the structure of that life." This sentence gives the final detail of the thought, echoes the idea of the topic sentence, and completes the rhythm, thereby scoring in three ways. (A word of caution: in writing a deductive essay, a paragraph ending to avoid is a sentence citing the next idea to be discussed. Remember that the transitional word, phrase, clause, or sentence connecting the idea of one paragraph to the next belongs at the beginning of a new paragraph and not at the end of the preceding one.)

Assignment 12: Checking the Paragraph

Check the rough draft of the paragraph you wrote for unity, coherence, and completeness. Make any alterations that are necessary and then type it. Check the paragraph again after you have typed it because seeing your work in typed form often enables you to spot problems that you overlooked in a handwritten copy.

Return now to the paragraph you wrote in your first essay and compare it with your new paragraph. You should see a great improvement if your first one was not adequately developed. Your instructor may wish to have members of the class critique each other's work or may request that you turn in this entire assignment.

Checklist for Paragraph Development

1. Have you analyzed the topic sentence by asking the following questions:
   a. What information does the topic sentence by itself give the reader—either directly or indirectly?
   b. What information does the topic sentence promise to give the reader?

    c. In fulfilling the promise, what information does the writer have that the reader would need and want to know?

    d. In what sequence would the reader expect the information to be given?

2. When your topic sentence does not say what you want it to say, have you altered it, and, if necessary, altered the outline?

3. Have you structured the paragraph according to the sequence suggested by the topic sentence?

4. Within the structure have you moved from the abstract to the concrete?

5. Does your paragraph have unity?

6. Does your paragraph have coherence?

7. Is your paragraph complete—both in terms of the contract your topic sentence made with the reader and in terms of being rhythmically satisfying?

    For the subject of the following essay assignment, select one that interests you and that you know something about. Choosing an idea that is being discussed in one of your other courses would be practical. To write about an idea, you have to understand it and be able to explain it—thus, as you write, you are studying for the other course. And you might be lucky enough to choose an idea that turns up as an exam question! Another bonus: it might be possible with the permission of both instructors to write one essay that will be accepted for credit in two different classes. However, if you cannot find a suitable topic, your instructor will have other suggestions.

Assignment 13: Deductive Essay #2

Use the Search, Sort, Select method to think through your subject, generate ideas, and arrive at a suitable subject area. Write the steps if it helps to do so, but learning to do them mentally saves time.

Next write an inductive sentence outline and turn it into a deductive sentence outline. (Do not skip the inductive outline step). Then following the directions given for Essay 1, write a deductive essay based on your outline—but this time develop your paragraphs fully.

Use the "Checklist for the Rough Draft" and the "Checklist for Paragraph Development" to help you polish the rough draft. Then type the essay, underlining the topics from the outline and placing

the outline symbols in the left margin. Hand the inductive sentence
outline to your instructor along with the completed essay.

Sentence Variety and Emphasis

When you have achieved a satisfying level of paragraph development,
you need to turn your attention to another important element of communication—the sentence. An even smaller composition unit than the paragraph, the sentence is the basis of meaning. It signals meaning in two ways:
through its external form or structure and through its internal arrangement
of words.

External form. What the form or structure of a sentence communicates
is an idea's relative importance—that is, it helps the reader decide which
ideas the writer considers of greater importance and which ideas he considers of lesser importance. Even when a reader does not consciously identify
a simple, compound, or complex sentence, from these three major forms he
receives subconscious signals about the importance of one idea in relationship with another. The simple sentence, consisting of one subject and one
verb (either or both of which may be compound), says to the reader, "This
idea is important enough to stand alone." The compound sentence, composed of two or more main clauses joined by a coordinating conjunction or
a semicolon, announces, "Each of my ideas is equally important." Being a
little more sophisticated, the complex sentence, formed of one or more subordinate clauses and a main clause, exclaims: "It should be obvious that the
idea in my subordinate clause is less important than that in my main clause
because the *sub* of *subordinate* means *inferior* or *secondary.*"

For example, compare the relative importance of ideas signaled by the
following sentences:

Simple: Sociologists can list characteristics common to all large cities.
Most sociologists agree that a large city is difficult to define.
(*Ideas are important enough to stand alone.*)

Compound: Sociologists can list characteristics common to all large cities,
but most agree that a large city is difficult to define. (*Ideas are
of equal importance.*)

Complex: Although sociologists can list characteristics common to all
large cities, most agree that a large city is difficult to define.
(*One idea is more important than the other.*)

As long as the sentence functions to give the idea proper weight, no one sentence form is superior to another. The simple, compound, and complex structures are all significant and necessary.

In writing paragraphs, however, you are concerned with more than the individual sentence, for you are dealing with sentences within a larger structure. First you concentrate on developing the idea of the topic sentence in an arrangement that moves the idea from the abstract to the concrete. Then you focus on paragraph unity, coherence, and rhythm, all of which have to be reviewed with every change in the paragraph. In the process of revising, you look at the structure of sentences to see if you have indicated the relative importance of the idea. Then you check for unnecessary repetition of the same sentence form. Although sentence structure can convey meaning, unnecessary repetition of like forms can detract from meaning.

Lazy or immature writers tend to use too many simple and compound sentences because these forms do not force them to weigh the value of ideas. Even though a close friend receiving a hastily written letter may forgive such a grammar-school style, most readers will not. A mature writer will always review his rough draft to see if he has lapsed into a multiplicity of simple and compound sentences. At the same time, he may allow himself to repeat like forms as many as three times for emphatic effect.

In inspecting the rough draft, you should look at sentence length as well as form. Sometimes monotony is not caused by the repetition of sentence form alone but by sentence length. Too many short sentences or too many long ones can be tedious. But place a short sentence after several long ones and you gain attention. Thus to rhythmically underscore the movement of an idea and to accentuate its significance, sentence form and length should work together.

One warning: do not confuse sentence length with sentence form. Many assume that a simple sentence is short; a compound one, longer; a complex one, even longer; and a combination of the latter two, a compound-complex sentence, the longest of all. Instead, as a study of prose will show, length is often determined by the number and type of modifiers. After all, ideas can be subordinated in many ways other than by subordinate clauses. And simple sentences, dressed in modifiers and carrying a compound subject or predicate, can assume many guises. For instance, the following paragraph, developed through a series of illustrations, is composed entirely of simple sentences. (Read the paragraph through once and then return to it to see how the writer subordinated his ideas and varied his sentences with participial phrases, infinitive phrases, and appositives instead of clauses. Notice also the compound predicate in the last sentence.)

> Laurence Olivier spares no pains in preparing for his roles. His body, a precisely tuned acting machine, is ready to respond to the most exacting dramatic situations. Nothing is left to chance. Preparing for the role of Coriolanus, Olivier embarked on a weight-lifting program designed to develop a warrior's musculature. To obtain the voice resonance demanded by the role of Othello, he trained for weeks with a special singing coach. The resulting voice, described by one critic as "dark, deep, sinister," astonished his audiences. He will gain or lose weight, grow his hair long or shave it off, speak in a whinny or a roar, in convincing dialect or in standard diction, all according to his conception of his role. (Douglas Davidson)

The writer above, using only the simple sentence but avoiding the appearance of too many like forms in sequence, proved what is really important in relating ideas. He placed main thoughts in main clauses and subordinated less important ideas. In doing so and in simultaneously varying the length of sentences according to rhythmic demands, he achieved variety.

The writer above also avoided another pitfall—a series of subject-first sentences. These can produce a static rhythm and dull reader interest. Because English, having lost most of its inflectional endings, is a word-order language, the natural sequence of words is subject-verb-object. Nevertheless, it is possible to place a word or words before the subject to circumvent the repetitive clunk of "The _____, The _____, The _____." A transitional expression, a conjunction, an adverb, a subordinate clause, a participial phrase, or a prepositional phrase preceding a subject lends grace and prevents a truncated rhythm without deflecting interest from the subject. For example, note the ways in which the following subject-first sentence is varied:

> The frightened cat crouched on the edge of the roof and cried piteously for help. (*subject first*)
> Meanwhile the frightened cat crouched on the edge of the roof and cried piteously for help. (*transitional expression*)
> But the frightened cat crouched on the edge of the roof and cried piteously for help. (*conjunction*)
> Piteously the frightened cat cried for help as she crouched on the edge of the roof. (*adverb*)

As she crouched on the edge of the roof, the frightened cat cried
    piteously for help. (*subordinate clause*)
Crouching on the edge of the roof, the frightened cat cried pite-
    ously for help. (*participial phrase*)
On the edge of the roof crouched the frightened cat, crying pit-
    eously for help. (*prepositional phrase*)

Revising to gain emphasis and to maintain a smooth flow of thought
can revive a paragraph whose ideas are submerged in repetitious sentence
patterns. Read the first paragraph below (an introduction to a deductive essay) and then compare it with the revision that follows:

Original

Becoming familiar with the life of a large city is probably an impossible undertaking. Sociologists have never even agreed on a working
definition for what makes a large city. Most sociologists can list some
characteristics common to all large cities, but cities seem to have a life
of their own and refuse to stand still to be labeled. Robert Park, an early
sociologist in Chicago, recognized that the city as a whole was too complex a structure to study. He noticed that there seemed to be natural partitions in the city that could be isolated. He called these "natural areas."
To understand a city one must start with its parts. The face, future, and
problems of a city can be defined by studying its natural areas. The city
has a handle if not a label once one recognizes the natural areas.

Revised

Although sociologists can list characteristics common to all large
cities, most agree that a large city is difficult to define. The problem lies
in the complex structure of the city. Recognizing the difficulty of examining an urban composition as a whole, Robert Park, an early Chicago
sociologist, decided to begin with its parts. Once he had isolated what he
termed "natural areas," he studied these partitions. Such an analysis enabled him to define a city's face, future, and problems.

Can you see how much easier it is to read and understand the revised paragraph? By subordinating the less important ideas, varying the type and
length of sentences, and altering some of the subject-first structure, the
writer has now created a paragraph in which the relationship of ideas is
much clearer. Moreover, while maintaining the same sequence of ideas, he
has produced a paragraph that has become rhythmically more satisfying
and richer through its loss of unnecessary words.

Try your hand at revising the sentences in the following paragraph. See if you can relate the ideas better, vary the type and length of sentences, alter some of the subject-first beginnings, and rhythmically underscore the thought movement.

> Many people find their honesty tested in accepting welfare. Some feel that they have been victimized by society and do not deserve their present situation. They see no reason why they should suffer while others enjoy comfort, so they resort to cheating the welfare program. Some feel that it is their right to grab all they can get. They think the government has deprived them, so they fight back by bucking the system. On the other hand, some honest citizens lose their integrity as they succumb to basic need. The welfare checks are just not enough to live on. They cheat to survive. Cheating to survive may increase as the government begins to cut the welfare program. But whatever the reason for the fraud, the welfare program tests the honesty of those it tries to help.

Internal arrangement of words. In building a sentence around its core parts, the subject and verb, a writer has many ways of stating his meaning with exactness and adding variety to his expression. He may use adjectives, adverbs, appositives, phrases, and clauses and is bound only by the necessity of placing these modifiers so that the connection with the subject or verb is clear. Yet the astute stylist does more than conduct random experiments with combining words. With a sure touch derived from knowledge of how a reader responds, he places words where they will have the greatest force and effect.

How can you obtain this knowledge of how a reader responds? From reading and observing how other writers get effects; from observing your own response to the written word; and from constant practice in writing and revising. At the same time, knowing a few basic principles of word placement can increase your perception of subtle ways to emphasize ideas and can aid you in revising. Here are a few principles: (1) place the most important thought at the end; (2) make equal ideas parallel; (3) occasionally place a word out of natural order; (4) within limits, repeat single words and variations of those words.

Place the most important thought at the end. Because the end position in a sentence is stronger than the beginning, place the idea you wish to emphasize at the end. Note how the second sentence of the two sets below gives more prominence to the main thought:

Unemphasized: Husbands often resort to violence to vent anger
and frustration, according to battered wives.

Emphasized: According to battered wives, husbands often resort to violence to vent anger and frustration.

Unemphasized: He missed his flight to Atlanta because the plane
was late in arriving at Minneapolis.

Emphasized: Because the plane was late in arriving at Minneapolis, he missed his flight to Atlanta.

Since the end position is strong, occasionally use a periodic sentence
instead of a loose sentence. The periodic sentence withholds the complete
meaning of the sentence until it reaches the period. The loose sentence arranges words in natural order with the main idea first (*loose* applied to sentences does not mean ill-formed). Often longer and more complex in
structure than the loose sentence, the periodic sentence may seem contrived
and should be used sparingly. But when it is used, it keeps the reader in sus-
pense until the end of the sentence. Compare the following:

It never entered his mind that she was insincere, that she was enjoying her power, and that she was an accomplished flirt.
(*loose*)

That she was insincere, that she was enjoying her power, and that
she was an accomplished flirt, never entered his mind.
(*periodic*)

The principle of holding the important idea until the end applies also
to arranging information in order of climax. Moving from the least to the
most significant idea builds reader anticipation:

She lost a contact lens, caught her heel in the escalator, and
rammed her car into a taxi cab—all on the same day.

For a surprising shift in treatment, use anticlimax. Reader expectation
of climax is so entrenched that by moving unexpectedly from the serious to
the light, you hit your target:

Not only have you ruined my entire life, you have spoiled my entire day.

Alexander Pope offers a famous poetic illustration of anticlimax:

> Then flashed the living lightning from her eyes,
> And screams of horror rend the affrighted skies.
> Not louder shrieks to pitying heaven are cast,
> When husbands or when lapdogs breathe their last.

Make equal ideas parallel. The equality of two or more ideas is indicated by phrasing in two or more similar grammatical structures—whether the structures are single words, phrases, or clauses. The rhythm produced by the repetition of the structure gives additional emphasis. For example:

> The abandoned lighthouse stood like a sentinel—tall, lonely, forbidding. (*adjectives*)
>
> Over the river and through the woods to grandmother's house we go. (*prepositional phrases*)
>
> He knew that he had to study, that he had to arm himself with knowledge, and that he had to prepare himself for job competition after graduation. (*clauses*)

Contrasting thought can also be set off by using like structures. Everyone remembers Pope's example:

> To err is human; to forgive, divine. (*infinitives*)

Occasionally place a word out of natural order. Although the unexpected position emphasizes the word, be careful not to muddle the idea with awkward phrasing. The following sentences are arranged to emphasize the words *never, tall,* and *green.*

> Never will I purchase a product advertised by telephone. (*adverb*)
>
> The pines, tall and green, poured their fragrance over me. (*adjectives*)

Within limits, repeat single words and variations of those words. The old superstition that bad luck comes in threes does not apply to writing. Repetition—up to a point—is good, for humans learn by repetition. Paralleling equal ideas produces a structural repetition automatically; a deliberate repetition of words or variations of them can be added to this technique or used alone to emphasize ideas. Generally, however, repeating parallel structures or single words more than three times (whether in sequence or not) becomes monotonous and loses the effect desired. But apply judicious repetition and rhythm to good thoughts and the result, as in the quotations below, can be memorable:

> Reading maketh a full man, conference a ready man, and writing an exact man.—*Francis Bacon.*

> Some men are born great, some achieve greatness, and some have greatness thrust upon them.—*William Shakespeare*

> I know not what course others may take; but as for me, give me liberty, or give me death!—*Patrick Henry*

On a sheet of paper list the above four principles, applicable to internal arrangement of words, along with their variations. Then see how many of these principles the student writer used to gain emphasis and variety in the paragraph below. Place the number of the sentence by the principle you think he illustrates:

> (1) A series of films is judged not on the quality of the first movie alone but on the quality of the following movies. (2) In the history of film sequels, the reputation of many quality first movies was affected by their sloppily made sequels. (3) The movie *Shaft* won an Oscar from the movie industry, but its sequel *Shaft in Africa* won only a thumbs down. (4) *Jaws* was a classic, but *Jaws 2* and *Jaws 3-D* were little more than celluloid jokes. (5) In contrast, Lucasfilm was able to continue its production of quality motion pictures through the second and third installments of the *Star Wars* saga. (6) *The Empire Strikes Back* was as good as *Star Wars*, if not better. (7) It was well written, well directed, well produced, and well promoted. (8) Just as good was the third movie, *The Return of the Jedi*. (9) By producing these two quality sequels, Lucasfilm proved to the movie industry that it was not a one-time success story but a force to be reckoned with. (Howard Simms)

Checklist for Sentence Variety and Emphasis

External Form

1. Have you structured your sentences to indicate the relative importance of ideas?

2. Have you varied the type of sentence?

3. Have you varied the length of your sentences?

4. Have you varied the beginnings of some of your subject-first sentences?

5. Do your sentences function together to rhythmically underscore the thought movement?

Internal arrangement of words

6. Have you gained emphasis by placing the most important thought at the end? Occasionally using a periodic sentence? Arranging information in order of climax? Using anticlimax, if appropriate?

7. Have you made equal ideas parallel? Set off contrasting thought by using like structures?

8. Have you occasionally placed a word out of natural order?

9. Within limits, have you repeated single words and variations of those words?

Assignment 14: Deductive Essay #3

Choose a subject, mentally use the Search, Sort, Select method to think through your topic, and arrive at an appropriate limitation. Next write an inductive sentence outline followed by a deductive sentence outline. Describe your audience and state your purpose.

After you have based your essay on the deductive outline and developed your paragraphs, use the "Checklist for Sentence Variety and Emphasis" to see if you have (1) arranged the ideas in sentences to gain the desired emphasis, (2) arranged the sentences themselves so that the thought flows easily from one sentence to the next, and (3) varied your sentences in form and length.

Then type the essay, underlining the topics from the outline as before and placing the outline symbols in the margin opposite the topic. Hand the inductive sentence outline to your instructor along with the completed essay. (The description of audience and purpose and the deductive outline are part of the completed essay.)

Word to Punctuation

Word Choice

In conveying degrees of meaning, writers must be especially sensitive to word choice. Unlike a speaker, who employs gesture, facial expression, and voice tone to aid in reaching an audience, a writer can use only words.

In spite of this limitation, the power of words alone gives the writer the opportunity of making a reader understand every nuance of his thought. Some writers demonstrate this power by selecting words with the eye of an artist, the ear of a musician, and the touch of a poet, but not everyone has such talent. Yet even an ordinary person can learn to savor the quality and uniqueness of words—and bless the English language for providing him with words of all hues. An ordinary person can also meet the challenge of writing if, as he selects words, he matches them with the exact thought he wishes to express and tunes them to the reader's needs.

As every dedicated writer discovers, finding words to convey thoughts precisely, however rewarding, is not always easy. You may wish to write your first draft rapidly and then, while revising, seek more exact words. In revising, if the right word is not at hand, run a search, sort, select process through your mind to see if you can find it. (Even then, a word may be elusive, refusing to emerge from the mind one day only to arise from the subconscious the next.) Turn freely to a dictionary and a thesaurus when you need aid. Be prepared to rewrite today what you revised yesterday. Above all, be patient: take the time to select words that will transfer your exact thought to the mind of a reader.

Which words to select no one can tell you—you must use your own mind, imagination, and sense of communication. But you can bring your talents into play by following Peter Elbow's advice, ". . . if you want your reader to *experience* your thinking and not just manage to understand it—if you want him to feel your thoughts alive inside him or hear the music of your ideas—then *you* must experience your thoughts fully as you write."[5] Experiencing your thoughts as you write (or again as you rewrite) will help you express your thoughts graphically. Suppose, without experiencing it, you allowed yourself to phrase this thought in abstract terms: "The man avoided the problem." Immediately your reader would question, "Which man, what was the problem, and how did he avoid it?" But, on revising, if you recreated the experience in your mind's eye, you might alter your words to read, "The instructor avoided classroom cheating by giving new essay topics." Or you might write, "His face masked, his body encased in coveralls and his hands in gloves, the hold-up man avoided recognition." Whatever the experience, seeing it yourself will lead to word choice that enables your reader to see it also. Then you will not leave your reader with

---

[5]Peter Elbow, *Writing with Power* (New York: Oxford University Press, 1981) 339-40.

who, what, where, when, why questions. Instead you will choose words that either specify or describe the experience.

Another approach, based on certain principles of selecting words, is more analytical, but it can give you ways of measuring the effectiveness of word choice—your own and that of others. These principles are not rules a teacher devised. They were discovered by those who took time to evaluate why some writing communicates vividly to a reader and some does not. Try to keep these principles in mind as you reflect on your word choice:

1. Sentences are built on nouns and verbs. Make these building blocks strong and specific. Do not rely on adjectives, adverbs, and prepositional phrases to prop up weak basic structures. In the following examples, compare the revised second sentence with the first:

   Original: The leaves of autumn hung like a flash of red from the tree.

   Revised: The sugar maple flashed its autumn leaves.

   Original: His eyes twinkling, the speaker from the south voiced his reply slowly.

   Revised: His eyes twinkling, the southern senator drawled his reply.

   Original: The original intense color of the brick building had become mellow under the weathering of time.

   Revised: Time had mellowed the yellow brick building.

2. Gain strength in writing by using active elements.

   a. Gain energy in a sentence by using active voice rather than passive—unless passive is necessary to the thought. For example:

      active: The farmer grew wheat in Kansas. (The subject, *farmer*, is the agent of the action.)

      passive: Wheat was grown in Kansas by the farmer. (The subject, *wheat*, receives the action.)

   b. Gain energy by using specific verbs (*saunter, stride, stroll* instead of *walk*) and verbals (*Running* down the hill, Jack fell, and Jill came *tumbling* after).

3. Eliminate unnecessary words. Thought can disappear from view in a morass of words. Note the wordy sentences below and the steps taken to reduce wordiness:

> There were three hundred students attending the rally. Owing to the fact that the students dressed in green and red colors, the school football rally looked like a Christmas celebration. One reason why the students dressed in green and red colors is because of the fact that green and red are the school colors.

Pull out the major thoughts:

> Three hundred students attended the rally.
> Because the students dressed in green and red, the football rally looked like a Christmas celebration.
> Students dressed in green and red to represent their school colors.

Then combine these major thoughts, using only necessary words:

> Dressed in green and red to represent their school colors, the three hundred students made the football rally look like a Christmas celebration.

4. Use words that have the right social connotation for the context of the sentence. Connotation is the aura of association one brings to a word, both personal and social. Everyone can agree on the denotation of *dog*, that is, the abstract dictionary definition, but the word *dog* may bring varying images to individuals. To one person, *dog* may suggest a fawn-colored Chihuahua named Mitzi; to another, a Sheltie named Beau; to a third, a tail-wagging, mixed breed named Elvis. Beyond these personal associations are associations that much of society shares whether or not they are dog owners or dog lovers. Dogs are noted for their attributes of faithfulness, loyalty, love—they are man's best friend. These established social connotations are what you need to be aware of in choosing the right word for the context of a sentence. Test your sense of social connotation by trying the following exercise. Select from the words in parentheses the one that fills the blank with the appropriate connotation:

   (1) The presidential _____ in Washington, D. C., is a gracefully designed structure. (retreat, mansion, cabin)

   (2) After recess was over, the children _____ back to their kindergarten class. (scampered, jogged, hastened)

   (3) Socrates, a famous Greek thinker and teacher, _____ a dialogue with his students. (ran, presided over, conducted)

    (4) The judge entered the silent courtroom and _____ tapped his
        gavel. (frantically, quietly, enthusiastically)
    (5) The perfume was advertised as subtle and _____. (alluring,
        fetching, beckoning)

5. Occasionally use a figure of speech (simile, metaphor, personification)
to picture an abstract idea, but do not shift your basis of comparison. In
the first of the following sentences the metaphor is mixed and the picture
gets muddied. In the second, the sustained comparison produces visual
clarity.

Original: Sometimes a writer will make a home run the first time he
bats, but more often than not he will wind up in a sand trap or
lake before he lands his words on the green.

Revised: Sometimes a writer will make a home run the first time he
bats, but more often than not he will have a number of strikes
against him before he connects with the right words.

6. Be consistent in your level of English usage. Whatever you write,
whether it is a personal letter, a business letter, a report, or an essay, you
automatically adjust the level of language to your purpose and to your
reader. You know, for example, that a letter applying for a position with
a company would be more formal than a letter to a personal friend, and
an essay discussing the structure of the contemporary novel for *Saturday
Review* would be more formal than an essay on jogging for *Sports Illustrated*. And you know that as a college student it would be unacceptable
for you to write as if you were illiterate—unless you were creating a
character who speaks on that level. In other words, the measure of the
level of English usage is whether or not it is appropriate to the writer
(speaker), the situation, and the reader (audience).

      Read the following gradations of usage and note the characteris-
tics of each level:

Standard English

Formal: I think that I shall dine at the hotel this evening. (*Word
choice is dignified; relative pronoun is stated.*)

Upper informal: I think that I shall have dinner at the hotel tonight. (*Word
choice is less formal.*)

I think I shall have dinner at the hotel tonight. (*Relative
pronoun is omitted.*)

Lower informal: I think I'll eat dinner at the hotel tonight. (*Contraction used; word choice is more relaxed.*)
I think I'll grab a bite at the hotel tonight. (*Slang is used*)

Nonstandard English
(generally spoken—not written)
I'm gonna git ma vittles at thet ther hoe-tell ternite.

Although many college teachers prefer that you write essays on the upper informal level unless there are reasons for using the lower informal, once you determine the level appropriate to your writing purpose and audience, be consistent. For instance, if you write, "I think I shall have dinner at the hotel tonight," do not shift to contractions and slang in sentences that follow.

Checklist for Word Choice

1. Does your word choice reveal that you experienced your thoughts as you wrote? Have you answered the who, what, where, when, why questions your reader might ask?
2. Have you made your nouns and verbs strong and specific? Have you avoided reliance on adjectives, adverbs, and prepositional phrases to prop up weak structures?
3. Have you gained energy by using active voice rather than passive voice—unless passive was necessary to the thought? By using specific verbs? By using verbals?
4. Have you eliminated unnecessary words?
5. Have you used words that have the right social connotation for the context of the sentence?
6. Have you occasionally used a figure of speech to picture an abstract idea?
7. Have you been consistent in your level of usage?

Assignment 15: Revising the Word Choice

Look over your second deductive essay (or the third one if it has been returned to you) and select a paragraph whose word choice you think you can improve. Revise the word choice, using your "Checklist for Word Choice" as a guide. Turn in a typed copy of your original paragraph followed by your revised one. Designate them *Original* and *Revised*.

Punctuation

Some people sprinkle punctuation like salt and pepper, hoping to give a little flavor to bland fare. Others throw it in whenever they take a breath or whenever the rhythm seems to demand something. Still others leave it out as often as they put it in. Such writers look upon punctuation as meaningless squiggles that excite only English teachers. What they have never experienced is the pleasure derived from recognizing punctuation as an art and using it to enhance communication.

To know the science of punctuation, you need only to study a handbook. Here are listed all the rules and the explanations of the grammatical structure on which these rules are based. To know the art of punctuation, you must go beyond those codes to delve into the symbolic value of punctuation. Punctuation is the smallest element of communication; it is sign language; it signals directions to the reader. Without these directions the reader would always be snarled in sentence traffic and might never get to his destination. For example, try reading the following sentences:

> Samuel Becketts Waiting for Godot is a modern morality play but there is no progress for these pilgrims no Celestial City There is only waiting waiting for someone or something that will infuse life with meaning Unlike Bunyans allegory there are no tests and temptations to overcome only boredom futility and endurance The play cannot be approached objectively To ask such objective questions as Who is Godot and Why are they waiting for him would be as absurd as responding to Prufrocks anguished cry that he has measured out his life with coffee spoons with the question Was it Folgers or Maxwell House (Maria Garcia)

Even with the help provided by the capital letters (and capital letters themselves are really a form of punctuation), would you agree that without other punctuation the above passage is difficult to read?

To recognize that the reader needs the signals provided by punctuation is the first step toward understanding the art of punctuation. The next step is developing a sensitivity to the signal conveyed by each mark. To develop this sensitivity, play with the image each punctuation mark suggests to you and relate the image to its function. For instance, you might write:

> Period: The period, like a red traffic signal, warns the reader to come to a full stop. One thought has been completed.

Comma: The comma, a period with a tail, tells the reader to pause briefly but to hang in there, for something else is coming.

Semicolon: The semicolon, half period and half comma, is stronger than a comma but weaker than a period; it clues the reader to pause a moment without coming to a complete stop. That it is a half-and-half mark also reminds the reader that it separates thoughts of equal importance.

Colon: The colon, a gate formed by two periods, halts the reader but does not stop him fully: it is a gateway to the thought that follows.

Dash: The dash, a single long horizontal mark when printed and two small marks in succession when typed, both separates and acts as an arrow—it directs attention to what follows. It is less formal than a colon.

Parentheses: Parentheses (a pair of bow-legged lines) make the explanatory or qualifying material they enclose less important.

From these examples, can you sense what is implied by the art of punctuation? Once you do, and once you combine the art with the science of punctuation, you can add power to your writing. For example, you can set off an appositive in three ways—your choice affects the amount of stress placed on the idea. Compare the difference in emphasis created by the parentheses, the comma, and the dash:

Parentheses: The coming of spring (a sign of regeneration) made Chaucer's folk yearn to go on pilgrimages. (*Idea in the appositive is de-emphasized. It could be omitted.*)

Comma: The coming of spring, a sign of regeneration, made Chaucer's folk yearn to go on pilgrimages. (*Idea in the appositive is subordinated but not de-emphasized.*)

Dash: The coming of spring—a sign of regeneration—made Chaucer's folk yearn to go on pilgrimages. (*Idea in the appositive is emphasized.*)

But to see the creative power of punctuation at work in context, turn to the speech made by Winston Churchill when, following Dunkirk, the very survival of England was threatened. In the long sentence below, a psychological masterpiece, he uses the comma and the semicolon to enhance the impact of his words. Of the many ways the punctuation in this sentence functions, you should notice particularly that, as the fight continues, the comma pause serves to shift the fight to another battle front. And the longer pause of the semicolon both underscores the words *we shall never surrender* and brings the Empire and the New World in as partners to help carry on the fight. (Can you explain these two functions and point out others?):

> We shall go on to the end, we shall fight in France, we shall fight on the seas and oceans, we shall fight with growing confidence and growing strength in the air, we shall defend our island, whatever the cost may be, we shall fight on the beaches, we shall fight on the landing grounds, we shall fight in the fields and in the streets, we shall fight in the hills; we shall never surrender, and even if, which I do not for a moment believe, this island or a large part of it were subjugated and starving, then our Empire beyond the seas, armed and guarded by the British fleet, would carry on the struggle, until, in God's good time, the New World, with all its power and might, steps forth to the rescue and the liberation of the old.[6]

Churchill was able to use punctuation creatively because he understood language as well as the signals called by punctuation. If you study the science of punctuation and then evaluate what each mark of punctuation signals to a reader, you, too, can learn to employ this smallest element of communication with artistic appreciation and subtle power.

Assignment 16: Deductive Essay #4

Choose a subject and use the Search, Sort, Select process to find a topic and generate ideas. Compose your inductive and deductive outlines, describe your audience, and state your purpose. Base your essay on the deductive outline, build your paragraphs, vary your sentence structure and arrange ideas to achieve emphasis, choose exact words on the appropriate level of English, and use punctuation that signals your meaning to the reader. Much of the polishing will need to be done after you have written your first draft.

After you have revised your first draft (perhaps again and again), type the essay, underlining the topics from the outline and placing

---

[6]Winston Churchill, "Dunkirk, June 4, 1940," in *Into Battle: Speeches by the Right Hon. Winston S. Churchill, C.H., M.P.,* comp. Randolph S. Churchill, M.P., 8th ed. (Toronto: Cassell and Company Ltd., 1941) 223.

the symbols in the left margin. Hand in the inductive outline to your instructor along with the completed essay.

> Are you keeping your pocket-size notebook
> with you and recording your observations?

CHAPTER IV

Shaping the Inductive Essay

Once you have gained skill in developing a deductive essay,[1] you are ready for the challenge of an inductive essay. And it really is a challenge compared with the deductive, for it demands a constant and more immediate awareness of the thought sequence, a greater control in arranging sentences and placing transitions, and a closer, more subtle relationship with the reader. Yet some of you may discover that the inductive arrangement itself seems very natural—in fact, if you have had difficulty in arranging ideas deductively, it may be that you have been accustomed to using the inductive order.

Establishing Perspective

Characteristics

An inductive essay is more than a deductive essay written backwards. In the deductive essay you were concerned with presenting a main idea and

---

[1]If you are beginning a second writing course with this chapter, review chapters 1, 2, and 3 first.

offering proof of this idea. Since you knew that the reader did not expect surprises, you told him the general idea in the introduction and fulfilled your contract by giving a fuller explanation and discussion in the body. In contrast, the inductive essay builds anticipation because the introduction poses a question or problem, and the essay progresses through stages of thought to an answer or solution. Of course, the writer knows the answer or the solution before he begins to write, having used the outline to record, order, and check his thoughts, but to hold the reader's interest he does not reveal this knowledge.

In addition to the difference in reader expectation involved in reverse thought arrangements, another major difference between deductive and inductive essays is their focus. It might be said that a deductive essay is product while an inductive is process. The deductive essay begins where the inductive ends: it emphasizes the results and implications of a thought, achieving a favorable response primarily with the details offered to explain and justify the thought. On the other hand, the inductive recreates the thought process itself by demonstrating how the conclusion is evolved from the details. And in moving from details to a conclusion, the writer purposely tries to involve the reader in every stage of reasoning in order to convince him of the validity of the question's answer or the problem's solution.

The writer's knowledge of the answer or the solution before he begins to write obviously distinguishes the pure inductive form, the type you will write, from the pseudo-inductive essay. In the latter, the writer states the question or problem and then, uncertain of the answer or solution, lets his pen meander through the composition as he tries to reach a decision. Almost everyone has written at some time the pseudo-inductive essay—perhaps as an aid to thinking or under the desperation of a test situation. But it lacks the strength of the pure inductive form that is derived from a writer's control of the movement of thought as he shares the thinking process with a reader.

Creating the Reader

Before writing the deductive essay you projected your reading audience by asking questions to identify the readers and ascertain their likenesses and differences from yourself. You thought of them as a group, and because you knew that they would not read the essay until it was published, you conceived of them as removed from you in time and space. In addition, the objective voice placed you at a distance not only from your readers but also from your subject. Maintaining a distance from your subject fostered impartiality, thereby gaining the reader's trust in the fairness of your judgment. Keeping yourself at a distance from your readers helped focus each reader's mind on the idea without intrusion from your presence.

In contrast, in an inductive essay you are asked to imaginatively create one reader close to you in time and space. The reader you create should be a person with the intellectual curiosity necessary for participating in the idea and the judgment needed to evaluate and appreciate the idea. Moreover, he should be a person that you like and desire to communicate with. Once his interest is aroused, he will be willing to play the particular role you assign him—provided you approach him with sincerity and treat him as a person of intelligence. Thus, as the writing theorist Walter Ong observes, you create a reader to play a particular role and the actual reader assumes the assigned role.[2]

Achieving Closeness

Two aids to achieving closeness with a reader are the imaginative location of the reader himself and the use of the conversational voice in writing. As you write, try to imagine that your reader is present and seated close enough to you for a conversation. If you are interpreting a short poem, perhaps a copy is on the table before the two of you. If you are explaining how you solved a problem, perhaps he is sitting in an easy chair near yours. Of course, you need to remember that your audience will actually read your essay after it is published, so you will have to record everything your reader needs to know. Nevertheless, it is helpful as you write the inductive essay to imagine that your reader is present and that you are speaking to him. The reader does not reply, but the writer should anticipate or even formulate questions he might ask.

The use of the conversational voice is another way to achieve closeness with a reader. The pronoun *we* is employed in this voice to mean *you and I*—not "in the opinion of the editor" as in the editorial *we*. With both writer and reader positioned at a neutral distance from the subject, the conversa-

---

[2]Walter J. Ong, S.J., "The Writer's Audience Is Always a Fiction," *PMLA* 90 (January 1975): 12.

tional use of *we* joins the reader with the writer in looking at the problem and ascertaining the answer to the question (see chapter 3). Other pronouns that may be used are *us, our,* and *ourselves.*

One caution: the writer needs to be careful not to allow himself to substitute "I" or "you" for "we," for using either "I" or "you" automatically breaks the sense of sharing and the unity of focus by giving a separate identity to the writer and to the reader. Because you are deliberately trying to involve the reader in the reasoning process as you move from question to answer or from problem to solution, such a break will negate your purpose.

Choosing a Subject

Certain subjects lend themselves easily to inductively shaped essays, but the range of suitable topics is not as wide as for the deductive form. The inductive essay demands a subject in which the thought process used to answer the question or solve the problem is in itself significant. Thus the lawyer can use the inductive form in preparing a brief to argue a case; a scientist can use it in demonstrating how via experiment he has made a discovery or verified an assumption; a philosopher can use it in presenting the mode of thought that led to his conclusion; a student of literature can use it in offering a fresh interpretation of a literary work; a minister, rabbi, or priest can use it in presenting a problem of ethics; a detective can use it in detailing clues that led to the murderer; a doctor can use it in describing symptoms and tests suggesting his diagnosis. In addition, certain aspects of the form are often used orally by lawyers in addressing juries and by teachers in stimulating their students to reason through problems.

In choosing a topic for your inductive essay, select one in which the thought process is important. Consider the courses you are currently taking or have recently completed. Is there some idea you arrived at by reasoning through a number of steps? Do you recall beginning with several possibilities, sometimes taking a direction that proved false, and eventually eliminating all steps except those that led logically to the idea? Perhaps you analyzed a short poem in literature, solved a problem in math or physics, did an experiment in chemistry, interpreted a legal case in political science, or demonstrated the causes of a marketing problem. It is not necessary, of course, to choose a topic that you have already thought through—your Search, Sort, Select steps and your outline can guide your thinking. But in seeking an appropriate subject keep the process of the inductive essay in mind.

Since the inductive essay that is written with deliberation (and not by chance) will be a new writing experience for many of you, read the following student essays to identify the type. Try to read each one in the spirit in which it was written, playing the role the author has assigned his reader. Though the essays vary in quality, all are successful inductive essays.

Willie D. Simpkins
English 100
Inductive Essay

What is Objectivity?

———————

What is Objectivity?

Audience: A young friend who has difficulty in understanding objectivity.

Purpose: To get her to consider the physiological and psychological processes involved in objectivity.

Inductive Sentence Outline

Question: What is objectivity?

    1. Let's define the relationship between our brain and the external world.

    2. Let's refer to the world as an object and to the brain as a movie screen.

    3. We can understand from this analogy that the image of each object is transmitted to our brain through our five senses.

       A. Our nervous system functions as a link between the object and our brain.

    1. We know that the images have a source.

    2. We know that the movie screen cannot be the source.

    3. We can infer that the object that is not perceived cannot project an image on our screen.

       B. The characteristics of an object are contained in and projected by the object.

    1. We realize that no two objects are exactly alike.

    2. Let's consider the example of identical twins.

    3. We can say that no two pencils, or cars, or animals are exactly alike.

       C. Our brain can distinguish one object from another by contrasting the characteristics that it receives from each object.

I. The distinct and independent characteristics flow from the object through the nervous system to the screen in our brain where the brain distinguishes one object from another by contrasting the characteristics.

1. Let's recognize another characteristic of our brain that the movie screen lacks.
2. It would be very inconvenient if we had to list all of the characteristics of an object each time we wanted to talk about it.
3. Our brain gives each set of distinct characteristics a name.

    A. Our brain receives and interprets the images.

1. Our brain may expand its interpretation beyond mere identification.
2. The beauty we see is not a distinct characteristic of a rose.

    B. Our brain adds a characteristic to the object.

        II. When our brain perceives an object, it identifies and expands the characteristics of the object.

1. Our movie has an audience and some are wearing tinted glasses.
2. The tints of the lenses represent a different view of the images perceived by our audience.
3. Each member of our audience has a different perspective of the world.

    A. The tints represent the preconceptions, the personal prejudices, and the emotions of the wearer who views our movie.

1. Let's not forget the fourth member of the audience whose glasses are not tinted.
2. We see the images are not changed as they pass through his clear lenses.
3. We also see that his judgment is made after the facts are clearly perceived.

    4. The judgments of the tinted-lens members come before the facts, for the tints distort the facts.

    B. The person who withholds judgment until all the facts are clearly perceived, we believe, will obtain a clearer picture of reality.

    III. We can infer that accurate judgments about the material depend upon the perspective of the observer.

    Answer: Objectivity is the realization that the external world is independent of our perceiving it plus the realization that when we do perceive it, we must withhold judgment until all the facts are clearly observed.

What is Objectivity?

Almost every day we hear people emphasize the importance of objectivity. We hear politicians proclaiming that their ability to be objective is one of their best assets for political office. We hear of scientists performing objective observations and of judges objectively considering the evidence while our friends are telling other friends to be more objective. We even say it ourselves, "Well, I tried to be as objective as possible in considering such and such a matter." Even though we all use the idea and the terms in our daily conversations and thoughts, only a few of us ever take time to ask what we are talking about. Let's pause right now and ask ourselves, What is objectivity?

Question
1A I.   First, let's define the relationship between our brain and the external world. To expedite our discussion let's refer to people,

2A I. events, and things as objects and compare a part of our brain to a movie screen. That is to say, our brains are receivers of images in a similar way that a movie screen receives the images that are

3A I. projected onto it by a projector. The image of each object is transmitted to our brain through our five senses. In other words,

A I. our nervous system functions as a link between the object and our brain.

1B I.   What is the source of the images that pass through our nervous system to the movie screen in our brain? Since the movie

2B I. screen is the receiver of images, it cannot at the same time be the source of the images. For example, if we are viewing a movie and the projector is turned off, the screen will become blank, and immediately we realize that without a projector there can be no

3B I. movie. On the other hand, if an object is removed out of our sight, touch, and hearing range, the object cannot project an image onto the movie screen in our brain. It follows then, that the object is the source of the images, and they exist independently of our

B I. perceiving them. The characteristics that we perceive from an object are contained in and projected by the object itself.

1C I.   Can we also say that no two objects have exactly the same characteristics? But if this statement is true, what about identical twins? Wouldn't they be exactly the same? No, because their

2C I. mother can distinguish between a set of twins. Her ability to tell one twin from the other must be based on the differences she perceives in the similar characteristics that are projected by each object, while we only see the similarities. From this obser-

3C I. vation we can also say that no two pencils, or cars, or animals,

C I. or even people are exactly alike. Our brains can distinguish one object from another by contrasting the characteristics it receives from each object. Thus when we look at an object, the object projects distinct and independent characteristics which are con-

I. ducted by our nervous systems to the screen in our brain, and there the brain distinguishes the object from other similar objects by contrasting the characteristics.

1A II.   With these observations in mind, let's recognize the characteristic of our brain that a movie screen lacks. We have said that both movie screen and brain receive images of objects that

2 A II. are projected onto them. It would be very inconvenient if we could describe these objects only by listing all of their characteristics. We would have to say that we saw and heard a green rectangular object with four round objects on the bottom of it; but for purposes of efficient communication, we say that we saw an automobile. In other words, the distinct characteristics that are

3A II. projected upon the movie screen in our brain are given a name based on our past experiences with similar sets of characteristics. The object is not just a rectangular with letters on it: it is a book. Or the object is called Jane, or Dan, or an airplane. Our

A II. brain receives and interprets the images that are projected onto its screen.

1B II.   But, in addition, does our brain expand its interpretation of the image beyond mere identification? When we perceive an image and call it a rose, we may also call it beautiful. Of course, we

2B II. know that the beauty is not a distinct characteristic projected by the object because another person may say that the same rose is ugly. Or, for example, we have seen people disagree about the taste of a coke or a cup of coffee. To be sure, we know that everybody does not think that any one particular style of clothes is the most beautiful, for if this attitude were true, would not all of us dress just alike? From these observations, then, we can say that the beauty is a quality that is projected back into the object by

B. II. our brain itself. Our brain differs from the movie screen because it adds characteristics to the objects that it perceives. So when

II. our brain receives an image, it identifies and expands the characteristics of the object.

Let's take our analogy a step further. Can we agree that a movie is always viewed by an audience? Now, let's suppose that

1A III. there are only four people in the audience and that all are wearing glasses with three of the four having tinted lenses in their

2A III. glasses. Also, let's suppose that each tint represents a different

3A III. perspective of the images perceived by the wearer. We can now say that a rosy tint will give the wearer a rosy view of the images, and no matter what is projected on the screen, he will see the good and not the bad. A pair of dark-tinted lens worn by a second member of the audience would cause him to see evil in all of the images presented on the screen. Let's say that purple-tinted lenses represent an emotional perspective of the images.

A III. In our example, the tint of the lens represents the preconceptions, the personal prejudices, and the emotions of the person who is wearing the glasses.

1B III. Oh yes, let's not forget the fourth member of our audience: his lenses are not tinted by any preconceived perspectives

2B III. about the images on our screen. The images are not changed as they pass through his clear glasses. They are perceived as they actually are projected by the object. If, after the movie is over, each member of the audience is asked to interpret its meaning, which member's judgment should we rely on as being the most accurate? Obviously, we would pick the member wearing the

3B III. clear glasses because his judgment comes after all of the facts have been clearly perceived. The judgments of the tinted-lens

4B III. members come before the facts, for the tints distort the facts before they can be received by the brain. From this analogy we can

B III. conclude that the person who withholds judgment until all the facts are clearly perceived will obtain a clearer picture of reality

III. than one who puts his judgment first. And we can infer that accurate judgments about the material depend upon the perspectives of the observer.

Now, let's collect our thoughts and see if we have answered the question of objectivity. We have said that objects exist independently of our perceiving them and that each object projects its own distinct characteristics. We have seen that our brain can both receive the characteristics and interpret them on the basis of our past experiences with similar sets of characteristics. And we have recognized that the brain contains some preconceptions that may interfere with a clear interpretation. With these

Answer points in mind, we can now say that objectivity is the realization that the external world is independent of our perceiving it plus the realization that when we do perceive it, we must withhold judgment until all the facts are clearly viewed. If we are to be truly objective, then, we need to know ourselves well enough to recognize the tints in our own glasses and their influence on our interpretations.

Newton Galloway
English 100
Inductive Essay

Beware: Chicken Crossing

———————

Beware: Chicken Crossing

Audience: A psychologist with a sense of humor.

Purpose: To apply scientific testing and observation in an attempt to answer a question that has plagued society.

Inductive Outline

Question: Is there any way to determine why or why not a chicken crosses the road?

1. If the chicken crosses the road to a pizza place, we can assume that his purpose is to obtain a pizza.
2. If the chicken crosses the road to a library, we can assume that he wishes to enhance his knowledge by checking out a book.
3. If the chicken crosses the road to a bank, we can assume that he may wish to deposit, withdraw, or open a new account.

    A. We may postulate from this raw data that the reasoning behind the move across the road is dependent on the location where the chicken is placed.

1. If the chicken crosses the road to a pizza place, he may be attracted by the smell of pizza as opposed to the smell of exhaust fumes from cars.
2. If the chicken moves from the side that contains a red-brick post office to the side that contains a white library, he may prefer the color of the latter.
3. If the chicken crosses to the bank, it may be that he feels at home around money if his father was an egg magnate.
4. If the chicken crosses to the bank, it may be that he has spotted a hen standing under the bank's sign.

    B. We can infer that a chicken's psychological preferences may influence his motivation in crossing the road.

        I. Both the location where the chicken is placed and the chicken's psychological preferences may be influential in his crossing the road.

1. If a chicken exercises his option and does not cross the road, it may be that he does not know how to walk.

2. If he does not cross the road, he may be suffering from heart and lung disease and fear the strain of the noise and the hazards of crossing.

3. If he does not cross the road, he may be high on alcohol or drugs and fear that he will be arrested for Crossing Under the Influence.

    A. Such cases give us evidence supporting the assumption that a chicken, due to his physical condition, may not cross the road.

1. The chicken may be too frightened of cars and buses to cross the road.

2. He may be content with our company on the original side and would have to be strongly motivated to move to the other side.

3. Our chicken may just not want to do anything but stay where he is without being bothered.

4. Our chicken may be stubborn; he may not want to be forced across the road.

    B. These points add up to show us that the chicken's psychological factors may cause him not to cross the road.

        II. The physical condition of our chicken and psychological factors may influence him to remain on our side of the road.

Answer: The evidence shows that we can pre-
         dict why or why not a chicken will
         cross the road, but the predictive
         power of our reasoning is small be-
         cause we cannot determine any set
         probability on external surroundings,
         physical conditions, and psychologi-
         cal preferences.

Beware: Chicken Crossing

"Why does a chicken cross the road?" has been one of society's most puzzling questions for generations. Because it has puzzled both scientists and philosophers, major corporations have now invested money and advertising in determining this age-old question's solution. A case to cite is the most recent advertising by the Citizens and Southern Bank (C&S). This advertising maintains that the chicken crosses the road in order to complete its banking operations. While this hypothesis may or may not be correct, it will undoubtedly be disputed and contested by the future advertising of other corporations whose proposals maintain that the act of crossing the road is caused by the pleasure the chicken derives from their services. Alas, is there no end in sight? Will future generations continue to be plagued by more chicken jokes? We can save our posterity from this burdensome task by simply evaluating the evidence that is
Question available pertaining to this problem. We must ask, "Is there any way to determine why or why not a chicken crosses the road?"

Let us assume that we take an experimental male chicken as a test animal. We place the chicken across from Shakey's Pizza on Riverside Drive; we watch him then cross the road to
IA I. Shakey's. From this act, we deduct that he is crossing the road for a pizza. In a similar case, suppose we place him at the corner of the United States Post Office facing Washington Street Library.
2A I. Obviously, his reason for crossing will be in order to enhance his knowledge by checking out a book. Next, we decide to test the accuracy of the C&S Bank advertising. We take the chicken to the other side of the street across from the bank. The chicken
3A I. then walks across the road and to the bank. Once there, he may deposit, withdraw, or open a new account. What do these inci-
A I. dents tell us? We may postulate from this raw data that the reasoning behind the move across the road is dependent on the location where the chicken is placed.

Our same three cases may illustrate another reason for crossing the road. If our chicken is again placed across from
1B I. Shakey's Pizza, he may simply cross the road because the smell of pizza (and steak since Shane's is next door) appeals to him

more than does the car exhaust emanating from vehicles on both
2B I. Riverside and Interstate 75. We can interpret a move from the
post office to the library as an individual chicken's preference of
white (the color of the library) as opposed to red brick (the color
of the post office). In the chicken's crossing over to the bank, we
3B I. may have overlooked the fact that because our chicken's father
4B I. was an egg magnate, he feels at home around money. We also
 B. I. may not have noticed the hen standing directly under the C&S
    I. sign. Thus, a chicken's psychological preferences, along with
the location at which he is placed, may influence why the chicken
crosses the road.

     If we take our experimental chicken out and place him on the
sidewalk, he may not cross the street. If he chooses, he may exercise his other option and stand there. We may find that the reasons for his not moving are not quite as readily apparent as those
1A II. influencing his movement. If the chicken is placed beside the
road, he may not move because he does not know how to walk.
Naturally, if he does not know how to walk, regardless of what is
2A II. on the other side of the road, he cannot move. Our chicken may
also be among the twenty million American chickens suffering
from heart and lung diseases. If this is the case, the noise and
speed of the cars would put too much of a strain on him. Depending on his age (generally this condition is prevalent among
teenage chickens), he may not be able to cross because he is
3A II. high from alcohol and drugs. If he is an intelligent chicken, he will
remain on the sidewalk out of fear of being arrested for CUI
(Crossing Under the Influence). Such cases give us evidence
 A II. supporting the assumption that a chicken, due to his physical
condition, may not cross the road.
1B II.   However, it may be that our chicken is frightened of cars and
buses. In such a case, the chicken would never cross the road
by himself; he would be too scared. The street would have to be
well guarded by a police chicken in order to attempt to cross the
2B II. road. Or the chicken may find himself completely content in our
company on the original side of the road. A great reward would
be necessary for him to give up what is on this side of the road
3B II. for what is on that. Our chicken might also possibly just not want
to do anything but stay exactly where he is without being both-
4B II. ered. He may be stubborn; he may not want to be forced across
 B. II. a road. All these points add up to show us that just as the chick-
en's psychological factors cause him to cross the road, they may

II. also cause him not to move. The psychological factors and the question of the chicken's ability may cause him to stand still on our side of the road without a step taken.

Answer

The evidence shows that we can predict why or why not a chicken will cross the road. Both the chicken's external and internal conditions and psychological preferences may influence his decision to cross or not to cross. However, the predictive power of our reasoning is small because we cannot determine any set probability on external surroundings, physical conditions, and psychological preferences. Each chicken's individual surrounding differs from that of another, and a chicken's health and preference varies from individual chicken to individual chicken. Thus we assume that society will continue to be plagued with chicken jokes for as long as roads and chickens exist.

Mary Cantwell
English 100
Inductive Essay

A Childhood of Pegasus

———————

Caballitos
by Antonio Machado

Tournez, tournez, chevaux de bois
Verlaine

1. Pegasos, lindos pegasos,
2. caballitos de madera.
. . . .
3. Yo conocí, siendo niño
4. la alegría de dar vueltas
5. sobre un corcel colorado,
6. en una noche de fiesta.

7. En el aire polvoriento
8. chispeaban las candelas,
9. y la noche azul ardía
10. toda sembrada de estrellas.

11. Alegrías infantiles
12. que cuestan una moneda
13. de cobre, lindos pegasos,
14. caballitos de madera.[1]

Translation

1. Pegasuses, beautiful Pegasuses,
2. merry-go-round made of wood.
. . . .
3. I knew as a child
4. the joy of turning round and
5. round up on a red-colored charger
6. on a night of festivity.

7. In the dusty air
8. the lights would sparkle brilliantly,
9. and the night would burn blue
10. all strewn with stars.

11. Childish joys

---

[1]Ernesto G. Da Cal and Margarita Ucelay, *Literatura del Siglo XX* (New York: Holt, Rinehart and Winston, Inc., 1968) 160.

12. that cost a copper coin,
13. beautiful Pegasuses,
14. merry-go-round made of wood.[2]

---

[2]The translation and the numbering of the lines in the original poem and in the translation are mine.

A Childhood of Pegasus

Audience: An adult who dismisses Machado's poem as one directed to children.

Purpose: To demonstrate that only adults have the knowledge and experience to appreciate the poem.

Inductive Outline

Question: What is the real sense of loss that "Merry-go-Round" conveys to us?

1. Each of the three stanzas contains a different verb tense.
2. In the first stanza Machado uses the past tense.
3. In the second stanza he uses the past progressive.
4. In the third stanza he uses the present tense.
5. The first provides a push to begin the movement of the poem.
6. The second sustains the movement.
7. The third brings the movement to a stop.
8. The refrain frames the poem at both ends.

   A. Machado takes us full circle just as though the poem were a turn on the merry-go-round.

1. In the first stanza, Machado begins with the child on a merry-go-round horse.
2. He then directs us to the air.
3. He next directs us to the lights.
4. Finally, he directs us to the sky.

   B. Machado constructs a spatial movement upward toward an unlimited horizon.

      I. Both movements serve to create a feeling of nostalgia for the joyous freedom the child experiences while riding the merry-go-round.

1. Something in our adult nature prevents us from experiencing the "childish joys" as the child does.
2. Children's pleasures are cheap: they "cost a copper coin."
3. Adult pleasures are expensive.
    A. We regret the loss of simplicity.

1. The child imagines his wooden horse is a charger.
2. The dusty air, the sparkling lights, and the clear, starry night all create a mysterious and magical atmosphere in which the child's imagination takes flight.

    B. This quality of imagination is peculiar to children, and we regret the loss of it.

1. In mythology Pegasus threw his rider when he tried to become immortal.
2. This myth reminds us of our mortality.
3. The child does not recognize limits.
4. The child has not yet confronted mortality.
5. As adults we know that the horse is made of wood.

    C. Unlike children, we know that immortality is beyond our grasp.

        II. Because we know we will die, recalling the simplicity of childhood and our fanciful childhood dreams is painful.

        Answer: Machado leads us to regret the loss of childhood that does not yet know limits of death.

A Childhood of Pegasus

The simple imagery and spare language of Antonio Machado's fourteen-line poem "Merry-go-round" are deceptive. Our first impression after reading the poem is that Machado has done nothing more than recall the pleasant childhood memory of riding the merry-go-round horses. Thus we can't account for the mood of melancholy that pervades the poem. Words like *joy* and images that create a carnival-like atmosphere seem inconsistent with the deep, human feeling of loss and regret that is sug-

Question gested. This inconsistency compels us to ask, "What is the real sense of loss that 'Merry-go-round' conveys?"

To answer that question, let's begin by looking closely at the
1A I. movement of the poem. First we notice that each of the three
2A I. stanzas contains a different verb tense. In the first stanza, Ma-
3A I. chado uses the past-tense verb *knew*. In the second stanza, he
4A I. uses the past progressive verbs *would sparkle* and *would burn*, and in the third, the present tense *cost*. In this way Machado seems to take us on a journey from the past, through a continu-
5A I. ous past, up to the present. The use of past tense in the first stanza seems to provide a push to begin the movement of the
6A I. poem, while the use of the past progressive seems to sustain a
7A I. spinning motion, and the appearance of present tense stops the
8A I. motion. In addition, we notice that the words, "beautiful Pega-suses, / merry-go-round made of wood," are placed at the be-
 A I. ginning and end of the poem and serve as a frame. Machado thus takes us full circle, just as though the poem itself were a turn on the merry-go-round.

Next we notice that there is a second directed movement
1B I. within the poem. In the first stanza Machado begins with the child up on a red-colored horse on the merry-go-round. Next we
2B I. see, in line seven of the second stanza, that he directs our eyes
3B I. to the dusty air. Then, in line eight, he directs our attention to the lights—perhaps Chinese lanterns or bare bulbs hanging from
4B I. wires that are strung across the fair grounds. Finally, in lines nine and ten, we see the night and the stars. The directed movement,
 B. I. then, is from eye level to the air and lights above our heads, and to the open night sky strewn with stars—a movement towards an

I. unlimited horizon. Machado, therefore, constructs a spatial movement upward as well as the circular-time movement of the merry-go-round. In both movements we are made to share nostalgically the joyous freedom experienced by the child riding the merry-go-round.

1A II. But does this nostalgic feeling fully explain the sense of loss that we feel when we read "Merry-go-round"? In approaching this question we need to read closely the clues that Machado gives us. For example, in lines eleven and twelve, he writes, "Childish joys / that cost a copper coin." Thinking about these lines, we conclude that there must be something in our adult nature that prevents us from experiencing the same joy that the child has while riding the merry-go-round. First, we notice that

2A II. children's pleasures, costing no more than a copper coin or a

3A II. penny, are inexpensive compared to those of adults, for we must buy an education for ourselves, have a beautiful home, and prepare to raise a family before we count ourselves happy. The child, on the other hand, needs only to have a penny or two to buy candy or comic books or, as here, to take a ride on a merry-go-

A II. round. "Merry-go-round," then, causes us to grieve somewhat for the simplicity that we lose when we become adults.

1B II. We notice another quality of children as well. In line five of the poem, we note with some amusement that the child imagines his wooden carousel horse to be a "charger" or stallion. While riding the wooden horse, he dreams that he is up on a wild and

2B II. airborne animal. The dusty air of the fair grounds, the lights sparkling through the dust, and the clear and starry night all create a mysterious and magical atmosphere in which the child's

B II. imagination takes flight. We sense that this quality of imagination is peculiar to children, and again we feel the loss of something precious belonging to our childhood.

However, we can only understand our feeling of melancholy fully when we examine Machado's use of the metaphor of Pegasus to describe the merry-go-round horses. Remembering the myth of Pegasus, we note that Bellerophon tried to ride the winged horse Pegasus up to Mount Olympus to take his place

1C II. with the immortals. Pegasus threw his rider to his death, an act

2C II. that serves to remind man of his mortality and his place in the limited world. When we recall that our eyes were directed upward in the second stanza and that the child imagines he is riding a winged horse, we can see the real loss we experience when we

3C II. become adults. For the child still believes in the impossible—his
4C II. merry-go-round horse is a beautiful Pegasus. He has yet to face
5C II. limitations that clearly reveal his mortality. As adults we know that
C II. the horse is made of wood: we know that immortality is beyond
II. our grasp. Aware that we are bound to the present and that we will die, we can remember, but not recreate, the fanciful dreams of our childhood, and thus we feel a deep sadness when our lost childhood nature is recalled to us in "Merry-go-round."

Although the imagery and language of "Merry-go-round" are simple, Machado leads us with great skill to remember our childhood. As we observed, he does this by using movements of time and space to create for us the joyous feeling and spirit of children riding a merry-go-round and also by giving us clues to the childlike qualities we have lost since becoming adults. By doing so, Machado makes a profound and moving statement
Answer about our common human mortality. This sense of mortality accounts for the sadness and regret we feel when we read "Merry-go-round."

Keith Salmon
English 100
Inductive Essay

The Braves' Chances in 1982

_____

1981
FINAL OVERALL STANDINGS
NATIONAL LEAGUE*

EAST DIVISION					WEST DIVISION				
CLUB	W	L	PCT.	G.B.	CLUB	W	L	PCT.	G.B.
St. Louis	59	43	.578	....	Cincinnati	66	42	.611	....
Montreal	60	48	.556	2	Los Angeles	63	47	.573	4
Philadelphia	59	48	.551	2.5	Houston	61	49	.555	6
Pittsburgh	46	56	.451	13	San Francisco	56	55	.505	11.5
New York	41	62	.398	18.5	Atlanta	50	56	.472	15
Chicago	38	65	.369	21.5	San Diego	41	69	.373	26

BRAVES' FINAL BATTING STATS*

ATLANTA	PCT.	G	AB	R	H	2B	3B	HR	RBI	GW	SB
Smith	.333	5	3	0	1	1	0	0	0	0	0
Washington	.291	85	320	37	93	22	3	5	37	3	12
Porter	.286	17	14	2	4	1	0	0	4	0	0
Sinatro	.281	12	32	4	9	1	1	0	4	2	1
Horner	.277	79	300	42	83	10	0	15	42	6	2
Chambliss	.272	107	404	44	110	25	2	8	51	9	4
Linares	.265	78	253	27	67	9	2	5	25	3	8
Benedict	.264	90	295	26	78	12	1	5	35	4	1
Harper	.260	40	73	9	19	1	0	2	8	1	5
Runge	.259	10	27	2	7	1	0	0	2	0	0
Asselstine	.256	56	86	8	22	5	0	2	10	3	1
Butler	.254	40	126	17	32	2	3	0	4	1	9
Murphy	.247	104	369	43	91	12	1	13	50	3	14
Hubbard	.235	99	361	39	85	13	5	6	33	3	4
Miller	.231	50	134	29	31	3	1	0	7	2	23
Nahorodny	.231	14	13	0	3	1	0	0	2	1	0
Ramirez	.218	95	307	30	67	16	2	2	20	1	7
Royster	.204	64	93	13	19	4	1	0	9	1	7
Gomez	.200	35	35	4	7	0	0	0	1	0	0
Jacoby	.200	11	10	0	2	0	0	0	1	0	0
Whisenton	.200	9	5	1	1	0	0	0	0	0	0
Pocoroba	.180	57	122	4	22	4	0	0	8	2	0
Hall	.000	6	2	1	0	0	0	0	0	0	0
Owen	.000	13	16	0	0	0	0	0	0	0	0

BRAVES' FINAL PITCHING STATS*

ATLANTA	W	L	ERA	G	CG	IP	H	BB	SO	ShO	SV
Alvarez	0	0	0.00	1	0	2	0	0	2	0	0
Hrabosky	1	1	1.06	24	0	34	24	9	13	0	1
Camp	9	3	1.78	48	0	76	68	12	47	0	17
Garber	4	6	2.59	35	0	59	49	20	34	0	2
Mahler	8	6	2.81	34	1	112	109	43	54	0	2
McWilliams	2	1	3.08	6	2	38	31	8	23	1	0
Niekro	7	7	3.11	22	3	139	120	56	62	3	0
Montefusco	2	3	3.51	26	0	77	75	27	34	0	1
Bradford	2	0	3.67	25	0	27	26	12	14	0	1
Perry	8	9	3.93	23	3	151	182	24	60	0	0
Boggs	3	13	4.09	25	2	143	140	54	81	0	0
Bedrosian	1	2	4.50	15	0	24	15	15	9	0	0
Walk	1	4	4.60	12	0	43	41	23	16	0	0
Hanna	2	1	6.43	20	0	35	45	23	22	0	0
Matula	0	0	6.43	5	0	7	8	2	0	0	0
Gomez	0	0	27.00	1	0	1	3	2	0	0	0

*The Sporting News 192 (24 October 1981): 16.

The Braves' Chances in 1982

Audience: A loyal Braves fan who dreams of a winner and remembers all of those bad years.

Purpose: To examine the chances of the Braves in realistic terms.

Inductive Sentence Outline

Question: What are the Atlanta Braves' chances for becoming a winning ballclub in 1982?

1. A look at the 1981 home run production of the Braves shows us an obvious deficiency compared to past seasons.
2. A look at the 1981 batting averages of the Braves shows us a failure to meet past seasons' performances.
3. The potential is there in spite of the season-long slump.

   A. We can see the potentiality of the players and the possibility of a return to the powerful hitting of the past seasons' form.

1. A look at the 1981 earned run averages for pitchers shows us a marked improvement over last season.
2. A look at the excellent 1981 seasons of Rick Camp, Rick Mahler, and Phil Niekro shows us three consistent performers for next year's pitching staff.

   B. We can see the steady improvement of the pitchers and be confident in their pitching strength for future years.

      I. We can conclude that offensive potential and pitching improvements are favorable factors for a winning season in 1982.

1. A look at the firing of manager Bobby Cox shows us a need to hire a new manager with winning, major league experience.
2. A look at possible managerial candidates shows us that Dick Williams is available and meets our experience requirements.
   A. We can see the importance of hiring a new manager with winning major league experience such as Dick Williams.
1. A look at some of the actions of owner Ted Turner shows us that he lacks the ability to operate a major league baseball club.
2. A look at the similar situation the Atlanta Falcons faced several years ago shows us that the Falcons' hiring of a knowledgeable front-office executive to operate the club helped create a winning team.
   B. These observations lead us to believe that Turner should turn over the operations of the Braves to a knowledgeable baseball executive.
      II. We can infer that the hiring of Dick Williams as manager and a knowledgeable baseball executive to run the club could solve the Braves' problems.
         Answer: Although the strong possibility of a return to powerful hitting, the development of pitching strength, and the hiring of an experienced manager are favorable factors for success, until Turner makes the decision to hire a knowledgeable baseball executive to run the ballclub, the Atlanta Braves will never be a winning team.

The Braves' Chances in 1982

Each year in October we sit at home in front of our television sets and watch the hoopla of the World Series. But we as Atlanta Braves' fans have very little to cheer about. Our Braves have finished another season and finished in their usual manner—fifth or sixth place. Not since 1969 have we had a winner in Atlanta. The Braves won the pennant that year, but went on to lose to the Miracle Mets in the championship series. From that point on there has been nothing but one annual disaster after another. When will we ever get a break? We were led to believe that a break would come in 1981, but, alas, once again pre-season hopes fell far short of post-season reality. Tempted to believe "This could be the year" by promises from club officials that Atlanta's long-proclaimed potential had arrived, we let our excitement run high. Veterans Dale Murphy, Bob Horner, and Chris Chambliss were returning, and we were reminded of all the good things they could do to a baseball. Officials encouraged us to go ahead with World Series ticket purchases because there was no way the Braves could miss with the addition of free-agents Gaylord Perry, John "the Count" Montefusco, and Claudell "3.5 million dollars" Washington. Could our dream for a winner finally come true? Had owner Ted Turner finally put together a winning team? We were answered at the end of the season by the club's record—50 wins and 56 losses with a fifth place finish ahead of only the lowly San Diego Padres. So we were let down once again. But wait, with the firing of manager Bobby Cox last week, that annual prophetic optimism of club officials is beginning to surface again. Nevertheless, let's put them on hold for a while. Before we hear that promising sales pitch for next season, let's be realistic and ask

Question ourselves, "Can the Atlanta Braves be a serious contender in 1982?"

The first step we must take in the logical evaluation of the Braves' chances in 1982 is to reflect on the miserable statistics

1A I. of last year. The most astounding figure of all is the incredibly low total of home runs. If we add the home-run productions of the Braves' top three hitters (Murphy, Horner, and Chambliss), we have a grand total of thirty-six four baggers. When this record is compared with the thirty-one home runs hit by one Mike Schmidt of the Philadelphia Phillies, the deficiency is obvious. A similar

2A I. failure appears if we look at the batting averages for the team: not one starter hit in the .300's and the team average was a lethargic .243. Can a team consistently win with these offensive statistics? All spring and summer we were told that the hitting would eventually come around to the potential showed in the two previous years, but it never materialized. Yet, in spite of the poor record,

3A. I. all hope is not lost if we look at the potential. The youngsters Horner and Murphy are future superstars. Chris Chambliss has always been a consistent .290 hitter and so has Claudell Washington. It would appear that the players went into a season-long slump all together this past year. Thus as we evaluate the

A I. status of Braves' hitters, we can be confident that last year's slump will come to an end and the hitting will return to past seasons' form.

Just as we did for hitting, let's look now at statistics for Braves' pitchers. No one need remind us that pitching has always been a weak spot for the Braves. It is the single, most-quoted reason used to explain the failure of the club to produce a winner. Our Braves have always had adequate hitting, but never quality pitching. However, this past season brought a reversal of that trend with pitching in 1981 being quite adequate. In fact, we would call it magnificent considering our memories of past years.

1B I. To prove our point, let's look at the ERA (earned run averages) for Braves' pitchers. We can see that the team average last season moved to an excellent 3.45 from a ridiculous 4.00-plus figure. The most notable improvement occurred among the relief pitchers, the leader being Rick Camp. We are well aware of the accomplishments of Camp. In the games the Braves did manage to win, Camp won nine of those and saved seventeen. If we are ever

2 B I. to see a winner in Atlanta, we can predict that Camp will be a major factor. And what about the excellent season of Rick Mahler? Only a rookie, Mahler led the Braves' starting staff in a number of victories (tied with Gaylord Perry) and also in earned-run average (2.81). We can look forward to many more superb seasons for Mahler. Nor do we want to forget that always consistent mainstay of the staff, Phil Niekro, who had another good year, winning seven with an ERA of 3.11. Based on last year's performances, we can safely say that the Braves are in fairly good pitching shape. In that case, perhaps we can expect some trades over the winter

B. I.
I.

1A II.

2A II.

A II.

1B II.

in which the Braves use some of this pitching talent to acquire a quality power-hitter to take some pressure off of Horner and Murphy. Whether or not a trade occurs, we can conclude that the Braves appear set in pitching talent. So overall, then, the team is in good shape regarding both offensive potential and pitching strength.

Now let's turn our attention to manager Bobby Cox. Citing the need for a change, Ted Turner fired Cox last week. Let's look over the situation. After four seasons with the Braves, Cox failed to produce better than a fourth-place finish. The circumstances are as simple as that. Let's put ourselves in Turner's shoes. Should the whole team be blamed for bad play? Of course not—the manager must assume responsibility for this. When Cox consistently failed, there was little choice but to fire him, as Turner did. But this action poses a new question, "Who is to be hired as a replacement?" One of Cox's coaches? A minor league manager? Or should some new blood be infused in the club? Under the present conditions, we can agree that Cox's coaches should be ruled out. If it is time for a change, let's make a complete change. Still in Turner's shoes, let's look at a possible minor league candidate. Eddie Haas has been managing at the Braves' Richmond Club and doing a fine job. He has consistently produced winning teams. Yet he has no major league experience and this is not the situation for him to gain any. A manager with major league experience must be found, but more than that, he needs winning experience. Who then should be hired? It so happens Dick Williams is available at the present time. Williams has many years of managing experience and took the Oakland A's to the World Championship in 1971. Thus, even though the current managing status is uncertain, the hiring of Dick Williams could remedy the situation.

When we place ourselves in the shoes of Ted Turner, we hold a tremendous responsibility. The owner is the key to success for a ballclub. In the Braves' case, Turner is a failure. We can recall several incidents in which Turner showed his incapability as an owner. The most recent example is Turner's signing of free-agent Claudell Washington. Other baseball owners were furious at Turner for awarding Washington a huge contract (3.5 million for six years) when Washington is no more than a career .290 hitter—not a bad statistic, but no way worth that much money. These other owners blame Turner's action as a major factor in the rising salaries that must be paid to free agents. And we have other actions depicting Turner's baseball ignorance, including the trading away of Doyle Alexander, Gary Matthews, Jeff Burroughs, and Dick Ruthven. Also, he almost lost Bob Horner over what was a small salary dispute compared with the tremendous amount he dished out to Claudell Washington. It would be possible for us to list many other incidents, but the point is proved: Ted Turner, a good yachtsman and a good Cable News operator, knows nothing about running a major league baseball team. The solution? Let's look at the Atlanta Falcons. Like the Braves, the Falcons were once perennial losers; like Turner, owner Rankin

2B II. Smith was once a total flop. But having the intelligence to bring in a man capable of running the team, Smith put Eddie LeBaron in complete control of the team and from then on kept his hand out

B. II. of the operations. Will Turner ever find this wisdom? Will Turner step aside and place the daily operations of his club under the control of a qualified baseball official? If he asked our opinion, we

II. would say that the hiring of Dick Williams plus the hiring of a knowledgeable baseball executive would solve the Braves' on-the-field management problems.

Now that we have examined closely the current player and management situation in Atlanta, we are in a good position to deal with the Braves' chances in 1982. To be a serious contender a team must have big hitting or big pitching. It is often necessary to have both these requirements, but sometimes a team can be carried on by one or the other. For the Braves the latter is not the case. That the Braves now have the adequate pitching requirement is not enough to carry the team. They must return to the powerful hitting of past seasons—but, as we found, the return is a good possibility. So we can say, "Yes, the Braves will be a serious contender." No, let's not answer yet. We can assume that if the Braves do hire a qualified, experienced manager such as Dick Williams, their chances will increase. Nevertheless, the important roadblock to success still remains: the owner, Ted Turner. For the Braves to win, they can no longer afford any lame-brain

Answer decisions by Turner. Until Turner makes the decision to hire a knowledgeable baseball executive to handle the ballclub, the Atlanta Braves will never be a winning team.

Having read the four sample essays, you can now judge better how to select a topic for your own essay. If you have difficulty in thinking of an inductive topic, then try asking a question that will induce a thoughtful examination of an idea. As you noticed, the student who wrote "Beware: Chicken Crossing" sought the answer to an age-old question that he modified for his purposes. The author of the first essay asked, "What is objectivity?" and the sports fan questioned, "What are the Braves' chances for becoming a winning ballclub in 1982?"

By using your initiative, you too can find questions that will require a thought process to answer. For instance, one student turned assignment 2 in chapter 3 into an inductive essay by choosing a magazine new to the market and asking what audience it was directed to. And a student interested in the problems of communication posed the question, "What causes failures in communication between two people?" After she mentally answered the question, she wrote the following anecdote for her essay and analyzed the situation she had described.

> As was his custom when he went to a western movie, Bob was dressed in his favorite jeans and shirt, an outfit that was important to Bob on these occasions but ridiculous to Debbie. After all, he had worn the same outfit every Saturday night for the last two months—that's how often they had been to drive-in westerns. Bob noticed she didn't have much to say when she got into the car and she didn't sit as close to him as she usually did, but Bob thought she probably didn't feel well. Because the movie started at eight o'clock, he hurried so they would not miss any of it. Incensed because Bob had not asked her which movie she would prefer, Debbie scooted even further across the car until she was almost at the window. It was easy to fall asleep during the boring movie and Debbie hoped Bob would take a hint. After the movie ended, Bob took Debbie home, walked her to the door, and told her he would call tomorrow. Bob left convinced that women are strange creatures. (Pam Emert)

Another student, inspired by a physics course, discovered a thought process when he asked, "When a tennis ball and a baseball are dropped from the same height at the same time, why do they hit the ground simultaneously?" Thus you can easily unlock the door to the inductive essay if you seek the right key.

Structuring the Essay

The Inductive Outline

Once you have a topic that lends itself to recreating a thought process as you move from question to answer, then the outline is your next concern. You will need to write both an inductive outline and a deductive one, the latter for double-checking the logic of your thinking.

Because you have already written inductive outlines, you are familiar with the outline format. But look once more at the outlines with the preceding essays. Do you notice a difference between these inductive outlines and the ones you have been writing? Yes, these outlines are in greater detail, for you need the details represented by subtopics 1, 2, 3, and so forth, to determine what thoughts or specific points led you to your A, B, C topics. Another difference you can see is that these outlines employ conversational voice. So you will need to describe your reader and state your purpose at the top of the outline page before you compose your outline. The conversational voice can only be captured when you have your reader and your purpose in mind.

As you read the essays, did you also observe that two writers placed information for the reader before the outline page? The author of "A Childhood of Pegasus" included a copy of Machado's poem and her translation, making it available for the reader to see and the writer to refer to, and the author of "The Braves' Chances in 1982" used statistical information for the same purpose. This information can be helpful both to writer and reader if the topic lends itself to such material. If you have a similar topic, then have the material before you as you prepare your outline.

In composing the inductive outline, first look at the format for the detailed inductive outline given at the end of chapter 2 and at the outlines of the inductive student essays. Then follow the procedure described in chapter 2 for evolving an inductive outline. (If your paper is dealing with a problem, you will need to phrase the problem in the form of a question.) A broad outline will result from following this procedure.

Then you will need to add subtopics 1, 2, 3, 4, and so forth, before each A and each B topic (and C, if you have one) by reproducing the steps in your thinking that resulted in each A and B. For the small subtopics you may recapitulate your thoughts by two methods. One simple way is to ask yourself, "What thoughts or ideas led me to topic A?" Once you have these answers, then repeat this question for B (and C) and continue repeating it until you have supplied the subtopics for all A's, B's, and C's. Another method is to deliberately apply a third Search and Sort to the items under the heading you chose in Search 2. This method will also provide the needed elements.

In both instances you may have to force your mind to slow down and allow you to capture the fine points of your thinking, for the mind moves swiftly in reaching conclusions and you may be unaware of the bases on which you are building. To help your mind slow down, think of the television slow-mo and freeze-frame techniques used to recapture the details of a football play. Then pace your mind as if you were running a film in slow motion, stopping the film when necessary to look at each picture, frame by frame.

Once you have completed the inductive outline, check to see if it is logical (See the checklist in chapter 2 but add the small subtopics to the questions) and then turn it into a deductive outline to recheck the logic. When you are sure that your outline is logical, reread it to see if you employed the conversational voice in your wording. If not, revise. Of course, the outline remains flexible until you have composed your essay, and you may alter it if the need arises—as long as you retain a logical relationship among the ideas.

Assignment 1: Inductive Sentence Outline

After you have identified your reader and your purpose in addressing the subject to him, write an inductive sentence outline using conversational voice. Be sure to include the small subtopics 1, 2, 3, 4.

Then check your outline to see if it is logical, using the checklist in chapter 2 and extending it to include the small subtopics. Finally, turn your inductive outline into a deductive one to recheck the logic.

The Introduction

You know already that the deductive introduction arouses the interest of the reader, shows the importance of the topic, and states the central idea, a central idea that is identical with the answer derived in the inductive outline and normally placed at the end of the introduction. In the inductive introduction you still capture the interest of the reader by showing him the importance of the topic, and you lead him to the end of the introduction before you ask the main question. But alterations are necessary in the inductive introduction because you are raising a question instead of presenting an answer, and using the conversational voice instead of the objective voice (and thus you have changed your relationship with the subject and reader). Moreover, your essay has a different purpose.

To involve the reader in the thought process, you must now establish a rapport with him, provide him with enough background information to follow the reasoning of the essay, and lead him to the question without revealing the answer and without suggesting by a superior tone that you know the answer.

To see how four writers constructed inductive introductions, return to the sample essays and reread the introduction with these questions in mind:

1. How does the writer indicate the significance of the topic?
2. How does he establish rapport with his reader?
3. How does he provide background information?
4. How does he arrange his introduction so that it leads to the question?
5. How does he avoid revealing the answer?
6. How does he avoid sounding superior?

In answering the first question, did you notice that the first three writers all began with the significance of the topic and gave examples to illustrate the significance? The fourth writer, however, assuming that a Braves' fan would know that the topic is momentous, does not state the importance. Instead, he implies the significance to the sports world as he reveals the poor record of the Atlanta Braves, the ups and downs of the team and its followers, and the "annual prophetic optimism" of the club officials.

From analyzing the introductions you can also infer that before each writer began his essay, he took the basic step toward achieving rapport with his reader by creating a reader and imagining the reader present as he talks with him. Only when a writer has achieved this imaginative projection and looks at a subject with his reader and himself positioned at a neutral position from it (see illustration in chapter 3) can he successfully use the conversational "we." The "we" helps the reader relate to the writer and become involved in the thought process. You can also observe that the writer bases the importance of the topic on the common ground he shares with the reader, another way of establishing rapport.

Did you discover how each writer provides background information? See if you agree with the following observations:

1. In "What is Objectivity?" the writer gives instances of how the term is used.
2. In "Beware: Chicken Crossing" no background information is really necessary because everyone is familiar with jokes about why a chicken crosses the road. But by his mock treatment of the seriousness of the subject and by showing that the subject is of current interest (for example, its use by advertisers), the writer establishes an attitude that prepares the reader for the scientific experiments conducted in the essay.
3. In "A Childhood of Pegasus" the writer gives the reader the opportunity of familiarizing himself with the subject by placing a copy of the poem along with her translation on a page before the outline. Then, in the introduction, she points out the conflicting impressions that occur on a first reading, impressions that give additional background and establish the reason for the question.
4. The author of "The Braves' Chances in 1982" also provides separate information—in this case, the overall standing in the National League and the batting and pitching stats of the Atlanta Braves. He then reviews the recent past history of the team.

To follow the sequence in which each essay writer arranged his or her material to lead to the question should have been easy. Nevertheless, you may wish to compare your answers with these comments:

1. The author of the first essay moves from the emphasis placed on objectivity by most people to examples of the use of the term by professionals, then by friends, and finally by "ourselves." He then points out that though the term is used frequently, few of us ever ask exactly what we mean when we say the term, a statement that furnishes a natural preface to his question, "What is objectivity?" The sequence, by progressing from others, to friends, to us, helps involve the reader in asking the question.
2. The author of the second essay moves from the age-old question, to the reasons for reviving it for serious consideration, to the problem of solving the persistent question.

3. The author of the third essay moves from the statement that the imagery and language are deceptive, to the two conflicting impressions made on the reader, to the question that is concerned with the less obvious reason for one of the impressions.
4. The author of the last essay reviews in a longer introduction the past record of the Atlanta Braves, the successes and failures of the team (including the writer's and reader's response), and the constant prediction of achievement by the club officials. Then he moves to the question, which calls for a current evaluation of the Braves' chances.

How did these essay writers avoid revealing the answers to their questions as they composed introductions? Here your reply needs to reflect your ability to see relationships between writer and reader. In each instance the writer, by projecting the reader, establishing rapport, and sincerely trying to involve his intelligent reader in asking the question, has avoided the deductive essay trap of telling the reader the answer. He has led his reader rather than telling him, knowing that he must withhold the answer until he reaches the conclusion and sustain the reader's anticipation throughout the essay.

Your replies to the final question on the introductions, "How does the writer avoid sounding superior?" also involve your sensitivity to writer-reader relationships. Briefly, your answer should be, "By sincerity of intent and respect for the reader's intelligence." But deeper analysis might have revealed how essays 1 and 3 contrast with essays 2 and 4. The authors of essays 1 and 3 tend to guide the thought; the authors of essays 2 and 4 manage to suggest that they are exploring the idea with the reader. For example, the author of essay one sounds like an older person talking to a younger one: he is in control of the thought and indicates by his sure and direct building of the thought that he knows the answer. The reader becomes increasingly aware of this fact as the question is answered in the body. Even so, you will have to forgive him, for he has stated that his audience is "A young friend who has difficulty in understanding objectivity" and that his purpose is "To get her to consider the physiological and psychological processes involved in objectivity." And the author of essay three, by implication a younger person talking to an older one, indirectly reveals that prior analysis has occurred—else she could not have discussed the particular aspects of the poem. She, too, acts as a guide through territory known to her, but she has given the reader the opportunity of studying the poem. In contrast, the authors of essays two and four are more successful in maintaining the reader's feeling that writer and reader together are exploring the problem for the first time. Do you agree? You may need to reread the rest of each essay to decide.

Assignment 2: Rough Draft of Introduction

The introduction is always the most difficult part of the essay to write, so write it first to allow plenty of time for revising. As you write, keep your imagined reader close enough to you for a conversation with both of you positioned at a neutral distance from the subject. If you are referring to material that you plan to include on a separate page for your actual reader, have this material at hand.

Now try your luck at writing an inductive introduction using conversational voice. Be sure to (1) indicate the significance of the topic, (2) establish rapport with the reader, (3) provide any necessary background information, (4) arrange your introduction so that it leads to the problem or question placed at the end of the introduction, (5) avoid revealing the solution or answer, (6) avoid sounding superior to your reader, and (7) underline the problem or question and by it, in the left margin, place the word *question*.

The Body

Before you begin the body of the essay, look at the following abbreviated pattern to see the skeleton of the inductive essay of medium length. Note that after you have raised the question (or stated the problem) at the end of your introduction, you begin the body of the essay by moving from the parts to the whole, from particulars to the general, for this is the direction of inductive thought.

Your small subtopics 1, 2, 3, 4 come first in each paragraph to furnish the details or particulars, and each A, B, and C is placed at the end of its respective paragraph to become the topic sentence. Topic I, representing a partial answer to the question, follows the B in the same paragraph unless you have a C. In that case, the I follows the C.

This same pattern is repeated for the II section of your essay and, if you have one, for the III. Finally, you form the concluding paragraph of your essay with the answer. Thus the skeleton of the outline as it occurs in the inductive essay represents an arrangement that is the reverse of the deductive, for the thought pattern is also the reverse.

INDUCTIVE PATTERN FOR ESSAY OF MEDIUM LENGTH
(ABBREVIATED)

QUESTION _____ ?

+ _____
1A | _____
2A | _____
3A | _____

4A | _____

A | _____

+ _____
1B | _____
2B | _____

3B | _____
4B | _____

B | _____

| _____

Now to see the pattern as it is worked into the essay, return to the sample essays and look at the sequence of the outline symbols placed in the left margin of each essay. Because there are so many topics involved, these printed essays do not underline the outline topics. Yet it would help you visualize the pattern if you underlined the question, topics A, B, C, topics I, II, III, and the answer. At the same time, be sure to put all of the outline symbols, including those for the small subtopics, in the left margin opposite the ideas in the essay.

In building the essay on the inductive outline, an initial problem is what to say in the opening sentence of a paragraph. After all, the topic sentence that you are so accustomed to relying on for the deductive paper now comes at the end of the paragraph. And to begin with an abrupt statement of small subtopic 1 does not always indicate the direction of thought for the reader—whom you cannot ignore if he is to participate. To solve this problem, let your opening sentence of each paragraph clue the reader to the area of thought to be explored in the paragraph. Sometimes you can accomplish this purpose with a statement and sometimes with a question. For example, compare the various arrangements reflected in the opening sentences of the first essay's paragraphs with the outline's subtopics 1:

Subtopic 1: Let's define the relationship between our brain and the external world.

Opening sentence: First, let's define the relationship between our brain and the external world.

Subtopic 1: We know that the images have a source.

Opening sentence: What is the source of the images that pass through our nervous system to the movie screen in our brain?

Subtopic 1: We realize that no two objects are exactly alike.

Opening sentence: Can we also say that no two objects have exactly the same characteristics?

Subtopic 1: Let's recognize another characteristic of our brain that the movie screen lacks.

Opening sentence: With these characteristics in mind, let's recognize a characteristic of the brain that a movie screen lacks.

Subtopic 1: Our brain may expand its interpretation beyond mere identification.

Opening sentence: But, in addition, does our brain expand its interpretation of the image beyond mere identification?

Subtopic 1: Our movie has an audience and some are wearing tinted glasses.

Opening sentence: Let's take our analogy a step further.

Subtopic 1: Let's not forget the fourth member of the audience whose glasses are not tinted.

Opening sentence: Oh yes, let's not forget the fourth member of our audience: his lenses are not tinted by any preconceived perspectives about the images on our screen.

Of course, having written his outline in conversational voice, the author already had the basis for paragraph openings that maintained rapport with the reader and directed the reader's thinking. But he varied some of the statements by transforming them into questions and added transitions to others.

Once you have your opening sentence, keep your reader close and talk to him even though you do not record his response. Let your language in this voice be sincere, relaxed, and informal (contractions, for example, are permissible) as you try to capture the impressions of a real conversation. In doing so, be careful not to use "we" with every breath, for such frequency is unnatural. Instead, use the conversational pronouns only when needed to maintain your reader's sense of partnership. And do avoid the language of debate with its "therefore," "we have proved," and "in conclusion"—such language makes a reader aware of an argumentative intent and an overt effort to prove your points.

In each paragraph you will need to connect the ideas of the small subtopics as you marshal the thought toward the topic sentence. Fill in with details and illustrations and occasionally pose a question that your reader himself might ask. Any awkwardness you might feel in arranging ideas inductively will soon disappear when you begin to sense the flow of the thought and enjoy the challenge of involving your reader in thinking with you.

In moving from paragraph to paragraph, you must also be conscious of relating the building blocks of your thoughts. In the deductive essay the transitions between paragraphs used to join B's to A's, C's to B's, II to I and III to II are necessary to show the reader the connections among the divisions of your central idea. In your inductive essay, however, you are adding rather than dividing, and the process of adding ideas carries with it a natural cohesion. Thus it is not necessary in the inductive essay to follow a formal pattern in relating one paragraph to the preceding one as long as you indicate the progression of the idea or a change in direction.

Most writers of inductive essays connect the ideas between paragraphs intuitively because they are leading the reader to follow the sequence of ideas. Generally, the paragraphs between each major topic (I, II, III) indicate a continuation of related thoughts, and the paragraph following a major topic indicates a change of direction. For example, the author of "A Childhood of Pegasus" relates the ideas of the first two paragraphs, the second of the two ending in topic I, and then opens the third with a change in direction. She then relates the ideas of the fourth and fifth paragraphs to the third, the fifth ending in topic II. But the author of "What is Objectivity?" uses a different scheme—in fact, he knits the points of his more closely reasoned argument by making the opening sentence of each paragraph refer to the last topic of the preceding paragraph whether it is an A, B, C, I, or II. Thus the subject itself, the movement of the idea, and the writer's relationship to the reader all indicate to the writer how to connect one paragraph to the next.

The Conclusion

In the deductive conclusion of either a short essay or one of medium length, you were cautioned not to insult your reader's intelligence by summarizing the points he had read only seconds before. Now, in the inductive conclusion, you are allowed, even encouraged, to use the summary technique. The reason lies in the arrangement of thought and the purpose of the essay.

As you know, the deductive introduction states the main thought and the body discusses its divisions, expanding the idea and revealing its implications. Once you have accomplished this purpose, the only way to conclude the discussion is to give the importance of the main idea a final emphasis. An application, an example, or a prediction for the future will provide this emphasis, but a summary of points adds nothing but boredom. In fact, a conclusion is sometimes omitted if the writer reached a terminal point in the final paragraph of the body.

In the inductive essay the conclusion is far more important. You are not rounding off an idea already presented and explored, but rather giving the final answer or solution to the question or problem. You have built your whole essay toward the conclusion: it is your finale. Yet giving the bare answer or solution is not enough. To add a little more, to hold off your reader one moment longer, to be sure the major points that led to your answer are clear, you may summarize—and then give the answer. After that you may need another sentence to underscore the answer or bring the rhythm of the essay to a close, but do not remain on stage too long after you have taken your bow.

Assignment 3: Rough Draft of Body and Conclusion

In writing the rough draft of the remainder of the essay, remember the following points:

1. As you write, place all outline symbols in the left margin and underline topics A, B, C, I, II, III, and the answer.
2. Let the opening sentence of each paragraph clue the reader to the area of thought to be explored in the paragraph.
3. Keep your reader close and talk to him in language that is sincere, relaxed, and informal.
4. Within paragraphs, connect the ideas of the small subtopics as you move the thought toward the topic sentence. Fill in with details, illustrations, and, occasionally, with a question.
5. Relate paragraphs to each other by indicating the progression of the idea or a change in direction.
6. As you add the ideas throughout the essay, build toward the answer. Then make your conclusion the pinnacle of the essay.

Assignment 4: Revising and Typing the Essay

After you have polished your rough draft, have someone else read and respond to your essay. Often your reader can see what you may have overlooked—mechanical errors, lapses in voice, or places where the thought is not clear.

When you are satisfied that the essay represents your best effort, then type it. Finally, reread it and correct any typographical errors you find. Be sure your inductive outline is included as part of your paper along with information to be placed on a separate page for your actual reader.

Some perceptive—or lucky—writers produce a good inductive essay on the first assignment. Others may have problems—such as achieving the conversational voice along with the inductive structure—and need to try again and perhaps a third time before they capture the voice and movement of this essay type. Whether you belong to the first or second group of writers, writing another inductive essay in the conversational voice and even a third one is necessary to strengthen your skill.

Assignment 5: Inductive Essay #2

Choose another subject appropriate to an inductive essay and write another essay. Strive to sharpen your control of the thought arrangement and your use of conversational voice.

Assignment 6: Inductive Essay #3

Choose a third subject appropriate to an inductive essay and demonstrate your ease in writing in this form.

In the next chapter you will use the notations
made in your pocket-size notebook.

CHAPTER V

Shaping the Familiar Essay

If you have maintained the small notebook as suggested in chapter 1, jotting down your observations, reflections, or passing thoughts about ideas, objects, and people in everyday life, it is time to bring it forth to see if your notes contain possibilities for a familiar essay topic. However, before you can make a choice, you will need to understand the characteristics of the familiar essay.

Establishing Perspective

Characteristics

Although usually written in first person, the familiar essay sometimes employs a voice other than the personal one and is classified as familiar primarily by the style, the subject, and the treatment of the subject. Generally the familiar essay, using association as the basis of thought, employs a pattern that circles from the introductory presentation of the subject and the author's unique attitude toward it, through illustrations and an occasional anecdote, then back to the initial idea or attitude. The style in which it is written is an easy, informal style that in itself is sometimes called the familiar style, particularly if it has charm and lightness of touch. But the term *familiar* also refers to the subject, for, as its name implies, it deals with a subject that most people are familiar with—hence, the genuine familiar essay is a true essay and not an article on an ephemeral topic. The writer's purpose in this essay is to disclose his individual apprehension of and attitude toward this common subject, an apprehension and attitude colored by his own mind, personality, and experience. In brief, it is a personal essay about a familiar topic.

The term *personal essay*, an essay written in first person about the author's observations and experience, is a wide umbrella under which many types can find shelter. Yet, the familiar essay, the type of personal essay you are asked to write, has a distinctive quality—even though professional writers may not find it necessary to make that distinction. The reason lies in the difference between the professional's interpretation of *personal* and the nonprofessional's. A nonprofessional may falsely assume that because he is human, what happened to him or how he responded emotionally to a situation will interest other human beings—as it would if he were telling a member of his family or a close friend. What he does not recognize is that he cannot rely on this response from a reading audience unless he turns his experience or his reaction into an essay that illuminates human life. A professional writer, on the other hand, is always concerned with his audience, and he knows that while he may speak in a personal voice and illustrate his idea with personal experience, his aim is to give his reading audience new insight into human experience, thereby turning the personal into the universal.

Assuming a Stance

One prerequisite to achieving the familiar essay is to assume the required stance. To do so, you need to step outside of yourself mentally and concentrate on the subject and reader. Only then will you be able to achieve the personal voice of the familiar essay, for this voice represents a writer who is able to look at himself and his subject objectively—to look with a detachment that is conscious of any emotional bias. This detachment of the writer does not imply that he is coldly impersonal, but it does mean, for example, that if he is treating his subject with warranted emotion, he knows that he is doing so: he recognizes the difference between sentiment and sentimentality. The "I" that speaks in the familiar essay has been able to apply the Socratic dictum "Know thyself," and he knows himself well enough to recognize—and even at times to be amused at—the human foibles he discovers in himself.

In addition to looking objectively at yourself, you must be able to look objectively at the relationships of human beings to each other, to objects, and to situations—relationships that furnish the topics for most familiar essays. You should strive to present the relationship with a tolerance that reveals the humorous aspects or the special attributes of being human. By standing far enough away from your subject so that you can observe it (See the illustration on voice in chapter 3), you can attain what is called in drama an aesthetic distance. You may approach the subject, for example, with the comic verve of an Erma Bombeck as she comments on family living, or the gentle touch of a Charles Lamb as he reflects on the pleasure of owning old china, or the geniality of an E. B. White as he says farewell to the days of the Model T Ford. Whatever the treatment of the subject, that "I" that speaks in the familiar essays knows himself and generally views life from the perspective that belongs also to the writer of comedy, for the realm of human life is still claimed by the comic muse.

On the other hand, there are a few famous familiar essays that, by suggesting the infinite, recall the reader to the fact that human life is finite. Such essays move toward the realm of the tragic muse. For instance, in E. B. White's "Once More to the Lake" a continuing cycle of life is described as the author relives through his son his own childhood experience at a lake. As he looks at this experience, he becomes aware not only of the present and the past but also of the future, a future that he will not share directly as the cycle of life continues. The subject is not treated as a tragic one: the essay, based on personal experience, explores with warmth and understanding one facet of what it means to be human and part of the phenomenon of life. Nevertheless, the reader is left with a feeling of solemnity that is not evoked by the majority of familiar essays.

Thus whether you are approaching your subject with a comic view characteristic of most familiar essays or with a more serious view, you need to stand far enough away from yourself and your subject to obtain an aesthetic distance. This distance will allow you to be objective about yourself and your subject and to present implications and relationships clearly to the reader even while you are writing in the personal voice.

Other Elements

The thoughts in a familiar essay are intuitive and are arranged by association rather than by the logical relationships used in deductive and inductive essays. You will employ your Search, Sort, Select steps to record and sort the associations your mind makes with the topic, but you will not compose an outline. Nevertheless, it is always helpful to raise a question to bring your subject into focus. The question will also aid you in determining the universal significance of the topic. Once you have narrowed the topic to an appropriate size for an essay of medium length, then work from the list of items under your heading. You may, of course, add other associations as they occur to you, but each association must be selected carefully to help illustrate the point of your essay.

Because you are neither dividing nor adding an idea in the familiar essay but moving intuitively from one association to the next, the structure of the essay, unlike the pyramidal forms of the deductive and inductive, is circular. Such a pattern is necessary to terminate a movement by association, for associations with the topic could go on and on. To let your conclusion circle back to the idea of the introduction gives a sense of completion that a mere trailing off would not provide.

Just as a familiar essay's arrangement differs from that of the deductive and inductive essays, so does its purpose. In the latter essays your purpose was either to inform the reader by presenting an idea and expanding on it or to convince the reader of the validity of an idea by involving him in answering a question or solving a problem. In the familiar essay you are more concerned with giving the reader pleasure. The personality of the writer, the special way he or she views the topic, and the style of writing are as important as the idea reflected upon. You are trying to share yourself and your apprehension of some aspect of everyday living, regardless of the significance or insignificance of the topic.

This difference in purpose is reflected in the relationship you establish with the reader by the personal voice. The personal voice (*I, me, my, mine, myself*) tends to focus a reader's attention on the writer, the reader receiving the subject indirectly as the writer filters it through his mind (see chapter 3). You will recall that the objective voice, employed in the deductive essay, focused a reader's attention on the subject so that he was almost unaware of the writer's presence, and that the conversational voice, used in the inductive essay, united the reader with the writer in looking at the subject. Now in using the personal voice you are in the spotlight, so do not be afraid to take center stage.

Of course, while the reader's attention is directed toward you, you must not forget that you are performing for an audience. Consequently, you must project your audience before you begin the essay and keep this audience in mind as you write. To do so, return to the method used in imagining an audience for the deductive essay (see chapter 3) and conceive of a group of readers—rather than an individual—as your audience. In a familiar essay you will be more concerned with likenesses and differences between yourself and an audience than with their sex, age group, educational level, attitudes, and values. In a few familiar essays the latter may have significance in the reader's response, but, on the whole, the common experiences of life they share with you are more important. Equally important is the difference in the way you and your readers view the subject, for the uniqueness of your view will determine your success in treating a familiar topic.

The overall effect of the familiar essay on the reader to a large extent depends upon writing style. The style should be informal and should reflect your personality. Its tone is keyed to the attitude you take toward the topic— it can, for example, be charming, reflective, genial, vivacious, or amusing. Since your purpose is to delight the reader rather than to instruct him, your touch should be light. In revealing your attitude toward the subject, you open the door graciously rather than shoving the reader through.

Choosing a Subject

Because of the personal nature of the familiar essay, no one can give anyone else a subject to write on. You must arrive at your own topic and interpretation of the topic—otherwise it would lack individuality. And you must be able to draw on your own mind, personality, and experience to develop the topic.

So where do you begin? For a start you might read a few familiar essays by professional writers to see the kinds of topics they chose and the ways in which they treated their topics. (See essays at the end of chapter 6.) Erma Bombeck's syndicated column appears in newspapers throughout the United States and some of her columns have been published in her books. Collections of the essays of Charles Lamb and of Robert Louis Stevenson can be found in most libraries. You may also be able to locate James Thurber's *The Thurber Carnival* (1945), Robert Benchley's *My Ten Years in a Quandary* (1936), and the *E. B. White Reader* (1966). *Modern Essays*, edited by Russel Nye and Arra Garab (1969), contains a number of familiar essays along with a variety of other types.

Once you have read a few professional essays and glanced at the topics of others, you will see that as long as the subject deals with everyday life and the author's view toward it differs from the usual, almost any topic will serve. Now you will need to look at your notebook of jottings to see if you have recorded a thought, opinion, or observation that will lead you to a topic.

After reflecting on your notation, it may be necessary to phrase a question in order to examine your idea and determine its significance in human life. For instance, you may have observed that people you pass on campus often respond to a "hello" with a "hi" and to a "hi" with a "hello" or a "hey" but seldom repeat the exact form of the greeting. Naturally, you will wonder why the form of the reply differs from the greeting. And once you find the reason, you will discover something about human beings. The same would be true if you observed the types of customers who are attracted to a convenience store during the midnight shift. What, you might ask, do these people have in common? And, after consideration, you might decide that what many of them share is loneliness and what they really seek in the dark hours is human contact bought with a small purchase.

The possibility for familiar essay topics is as varied as human experience. A song title such as "Dream the Impossible Dream" from the musical *Man of La Mancha* might lead you to show how foolish mortals can be if they set their sights on impossible achievements. Barbra Streisand became famous for her voice, but she did not win—or try to win—a Miss America contest. The health craze for jogging could produce a humorous discussion of the hazards and pitfalls you encounter as a jogger. An idea might be engendered by an ordinary question about grammar such as "What is the difference between *that* and *which*?" Having searched a grammar book for the answer, you may discover that the answer leads you to thoughts of all the tangles a writer can produce by confusing the two. Certainly if you have read Thurber's essay on "Which" in *Ladies' and Gentlemen's Guide to Modern English Usage*, you will know to avoid "whichmires" at all times. A single word discovered in the dictionary or thesaurus by thumbing through the pages might make your imagination soar. The word *statistics* did so for Don Marquis, whom you might know as the author of *Archie and Mehitabel*. He produced an essay of pure delight by claiming that there should be an art rather than a science of statistics. To him statistics represented sound, color, and motion: to tie them down to facts was a gross irreverence!

However, if none of these suggestions produces a topic, if you are in a genuine funk and bereft of any sense of originality, try listing some aphorisms such as "A rolling stone gathers no moss" or "Early to bed, early to rise, makes a man healthy, wealthy, and wise." Choose one, disagree with it, reinterpret it, or use it as a starting point for an idea. (The latter saying, for instance, was obviously composed by a day person. But night people need to speak up against the injustices caused by the day people who seem to have society under their control. For example, with the excuse of saving energy, they have imposed daylight saving time on society. They may have saved electrical energy and their own energy, but they have squandered the energy of night people, giving them jet lag for six months of the year! And have you ever noticed how intolerant day people are? A night person is perfectly willing for a day person to go to bed at dusk and get up at dawn-thirty—so long as the day person is equally as tolerant. But the day person has no understanding of the night person and insists that the only way to live is "Early to bed and early to rise." Many a marriage has ended in divorce and many roommates have split up because of such inflexibility. . . .) But if forcing mileage from a maxim is not appealing, then all you have to do is look at the peculiar habits or attitudes of human beings—yourself included.

While your own ideas about a familiar essay topic are simmering, read the following essays written by students. As you will see, the essays are as individual as the personalities of the authors. The first, entitled "Procrastination," disagrees with the point of view of the aphorism, "Never put off until tomorrow what should be done today." The second, "The 1960s," presents an extended but controlled anecdote that makes its point with the deliberate naiveté of the ironist. The third author laughs at herself as she relates how strongly she is influenced by reading. And the fourth comments with zest and humor on the family's selection and decoration of a Christmas tree. Relax and enjoy them—they were written to give pleasure.

Lib Williams
English 100
Familiar Essay

Procrastination

———————

Procrastination

Audience: All who, at one time or another, have felt guilty about procrastination.

Purpose: To show the values of "putting off until tomorrow what should have been done today."

Procrastination

Ever since I can remember, I've been a procrastinator. When I look back, I see that I came by the quality very naturally, for both my mother and father were and still are procrastinators. My sister used to be a procrastinator until she married a man who was an overachiever. (They eventually found a balance between the two extremes.) Even my dog used to wait until the fire engines had passed before he would decide to get up and bark. Today I deliberately carry on the family tradition in spite of criticism and mockery because I realize that many of my assets were born of my dedication to procrastination.

As a novice procrastinator, I discovered that although most things could be put off easily, there came a point where certain things had to be done. Homework had to be finished before going to bed and one was obligated to dress before going to school. So I learned to do things quickly and at a standard of acceptability to those figures of authority surrounding me. I could wash up, choose an outfit for school, dress, and comb my hair in the space of five minutes and still get a pretty-little-girl comment from my mother.

As I gained my amateur status in procrastination, I became adept at doing things well in a short amount of time. Could anyone but a procrastinator have read *The Odyssey* in two nights and written an "A" paper on it? Could anyone but a procrastinator have practiced the "Rhapsody in Blue" concerto by George Gershwin for only a month and brought it to a performable level?

As it is natural to select friends whom we see as reflections of ourselves, most of my friends were procrastinators and ne'er-do-wells. In school we avoided those smug early birds who were always waving around their mandatory and extra-credit assignments like flags. While these doers were becoming skillful in one area or another, my friends and I were busy planning many things that never quite materialized. But through our unfulfilled dreams we became the philosophers of the day. We could discuss any subject of great or little importance and see it from angles and perspectives never considered by achievers. Because we were not doers, we became thinkers. We procrastinators searched for reasons not to do things, and in doing so gained a wide-angle-lens view of life. I always knew where I stood in relation to the world, and I also saw where my fellow humans stood and was quick to verbalize my thoughts (many times to take my teacher's mind off what I had not done). Though I was never a teacher's pride, I was constantly a teacher's stimulant.

Being a teacher's stimulant, or anyone else's for that matter, does not help much when I make the mistake of waiting just a little too long. Missing a bus, being late for work or on an assignment, or getting to the bank just a minute after it closes on Friday is always frustrating. To counteract, or at least lessen, the consequences I would have to suffer, I developed techniques of persuasion which could be applied to different personalities and situations. In learning to open bank doors and to be excused from being late when I had no good reason for being late, I also learned to talk my way into much-needed jobs for which I have no skill and to gain access to things and places which are generally off limits. (For a journalist this is a necessary ability.)

Before the skill of persuasion was mine, I, as a procrastinator, suffered abuse at home, in school, and during outside activities. What being a procrastinator has forced me to learn is how to take knocks. I know that I can withstand the anger of people and emerge all in one piece. I am strong and spiritually self-supporting. When someone comes to me now—for any reason—with that painfully disappointed comment or look, I can say to that person, "Either you trust me or you don't" because I've learned to trust and depend on myself.

Of all the things procrastination has done for me, the most important has been the development of my own ideas. I never had time to belabor someone else's idea or incorporate it into my own work consciously because I waited until the last minute to work on a project. I could only do what I thought was the best, and whether or not that coincided with anyone else's idea was purely by chance. My instinct for survival and my sense of pride always told me I had to do well; but my procrastination forced me to count on my own concepts, to think them through, and to express them in an understandable manner. Had I taken the time to do exactly what I was told, I might never have realized my ability to analyze things on my own or the many original and exciting ideas I could come up with.

If I hadn't delayed in marrying an earlier fiancé, I might never have known the joy of being with my husband. If I hadn't delayed in making a career choice, I might never have known the joy of performing on stage. If I hadn't delayed in getting my bachelor's degree, I might never have known the joy of the learning experience.

Lately I've leaned toward modified procrastination rather than pure procrastination. Certain things have become too important to me to put off. Why were things never so important before? Who knows what I could have done if I had never procrastinated! Yet, in spite of my modified attitude, I do know what I gained from procrastination is far greater than what I might have lost.

Sylvia Henry
English 100
Familiar Essay

The 1960s

———————

The 1960s

Audience: Those Americans who remember the 1960s and those who were too young at that time to be aware of how those years revealed negative human attitudes.

Purpose: To dramatize prejudice toward minorities.

The 1960s

When most Americans think of the 1960s, they remember a restless and violent period—of protest marches against Vietnam, sit-ins for integration, and college students joining nature communes or throwing themselves into social action. But at that time I was too young to participate in such upheaval or even to be aware of it. Instead, my most vivid memory is of my family's move to another house and of a strange neighbor.

The summer I was twelve, my family, a black family, moved from a neighborhood that was entirely black in population to a neighborhood that, until my family made a home there, was entirely white. Since we had always enjoyed moving about the city or state, we looked forward to a new location. This one was very convenient—a nearby school for the kids, an accessible church, and an easy drive to work.

Though the location was ideal for us, it may not have been ideal for many of the people who were already residing there: most of them immediately began selling their houses. Even though the majority of the people in the neighborhood had lived in their houses for several years, perhaps their place of employment, their church, or something of that nature had suddenly changed, thus making their present residence inconvenient.

In the new neighborhood Mr. Jones lived to the right of my house. A fence separated our yards. I can remember sitting in the driveway of my new home wondering why Mr. Jones could possibly be selling his beautiful home. He had lived in his house about twenty years and had markedly increased its value by adding such accessories as burglar bars and a large, built-in swimming pool.

Each day at ten o'clock Mr. Jones came out of his house and onto his patio where he had a late breakfast. His wife always set a beautiful table for him, but all that he ever consumed was one cup of black coffee and a slice of buttered bread. I can remember standing on tiptoe, peering at him over the fence and through the shrubbery. He always placed the morning paper to the right of his plate as he wiped his glasses in preparation for reading it. After reading the paper, he tossed it into the same patio chair. Before eating, he would take the cup of coffee in his right hand while harshly pushing away the cream pitcher with his left—as though expressing a definite refusal to mix the strong black coffee with the cream. After sipping his coffee, he immediately picked up the slice of bread and hurriedly tore the brown edges from the bread, leaving only the white portion to butter and eat. Then, having finished his breakfast, he went back into the house and I retired from the fence, just as an audience departs after the performer is finished. In the months shortly following, I had no more performances to view, for Mr. Jones and his family had moved away.

I had new neighbors now, and as time passed I rarely thought of Mr. Jones. A few years later, however, mail for Mr. Jones arrived at the home of my new neighbors (the site of Mr. Jones's old place of residence). Suddenly filled with curiosity about Mr. Jones's whereabouts, I volunteered to take Mr. Jones his mail. I grabbed the telephone directory, located his name, and drove to the new address. But when I arrived, I was told by the occupants at that address that Mr. Jones no longer lived there. They suggested that I go next door and talk with their neighbor, Mrs. Rodriguez, who had lived there longer than they had and could possibly know more about where Mr. Jones presently lived. I accepted their suggestion and walked to the next house where Mrs. Rodriguez informed me that Mr. Jones had moved some time ago. As a matter of fact, she remembered the exact month and year in which he moved because it was very close to the time she became his neighbor. She then told me that the last report she had heard was that Mr. Jones had moved into a housing area called Delamar Estates. Thanking Mrs. Rodriguez for her help, I jumped back into the car and headed for Delamar Estates.

As I drove around Delamar Estates, I spotted a large black Doberman pinscher and immediately recognized the animal. Why, it was Poopsie, Mr. Jones's dog! I inferred that Mr. Jones lived in the house where the dog lay resting in the front yard. Filled with a sense of conquest, I ran to the door and excitedly rang the door bell. To my surprise, the person that answered the bell was not Mr. Jones nor any member of his family. Instead, it was a Mr. Jack Ryan who immediately expressed his regrets to me. Speaking oddly with an Irish accent, he told me that Mr. Jones had lived next door to him at one time, but had left very abruptly after he (Ryan) moved in, leaving Poopsie behind without care. Mr. Ryan then gave me another address at which he thought Mr. Jones lived.

Again I got into the car and drove to the new address. While driving into the new neighborhood, I noticed a group of small children who were playing Cowboys and Indians along the side of the road. The amusing thing about the children's play was that the Indians were *real* Indians. It was at this particular time that I decided to give up my search for Mr. Jones. Somehow I had no faith that he would be found at this new address either. Puzzled and defeated, I returned the letter to the post office. Perhaps the post office would have more luck at finding Mr. Jones than I had.

Lori Crump
English 100
Familiar Essay

On the Persuasiveness of Print
or
Why I Appear Schizophrenic

On the Persuasiveness of Print
or
Why I Appear Schizophrenic

Audience: Those who think of art as an imitation of life or who live a
book as they read it.
Purpose: To demonstrate what happens when life imitates art or
when one lives a book after reading it.

On the Persuasiveness of Print
or
Why I Appear Schizophrenic

I am convinced that the old adage "Don't believe everything you read" was coined especially for me. Though I admit it shamefully, I have yet to read a book that has not, in some way, joggled my precariously perched perspectives on life. I realize that such vulnerability warrants disgust in this age of skepticism, but I just can't help it. No matter how hard I try, I cannot seem to protect myself from the insidious persuasiveness of the printed word. Consequently, some people may think me a wishy-washy, vacillating person. This, I hasten to point out, is a most erroneous judgment of character. I happen to be a very fair, judicious, open-minded individual who is unfortunately susceptible to the magic of eloquent rhetoric. This open-mindedness could be considered a praiseworthy attribute, but I have come to dread picking up a new book because of the inevitable re-assimilation of ideas that results. I often feel that my mind is a hodgepodge of personalities patched together with Scotch tape. Each new book that I read shatters the neatly constructed picture as fresh ideas are taped into the collage.

Before I entered high school, I was nearly perfect—I mean *life* was nearly perfect. I knew who I was and where I was going and I sanctimoniously pitied anyone whose ideas didn't agree with my own. Suddenly, my structured, stable philosophy of life shuddered convulsively and crashed into rubble at my feet. I read *The Fountainhead* by Ayn Rand and saw the light of truth. No longer would I be an innocent, misled, sacrificial lamb believing that good would always triumph in the end. Now I realized the folly of emotionalism and the decadence of having fun. I was impressed by the Nietzschean hero of *The Fountainhead*, by his cool, level-headed objectivity and his stoic practicality. I started wearing dark glasses and crossing my arms a lot. I abhorred sentimentality and practiced scowling in the mirror for hours, varying my cynical expressions with a slightly arched eyebrow or a contemptuously curled mouth, depending on the degree of disgust warranted by the imaginary situation. I bought a black jacket to signify the somberness of life.

"I will never live for the sake of another man, nor ask another man to live for mine" was my new motto. No more listening to people with personal problems; no more loaning money to destitute friends; and definitely no more dancing and laughing and mingling with the herd. My friends and family, who were obviously incapable of recognizing a potential Nietzschean hero, found my behavior quite disturbing. My best friend suggested that I see the school counselor, and for her concern received my most contemptuous scowl, complete with raised eyebrow, flared nostrils, and twisted lips. My family received scowls too, especially my mother, who constantly hid my sunglasses and refused to wash my black jacket. I would not touch the comic strips or *Mad* magazine, so my brother and sister refused to associate with me in public, saying that I was a disgrace to our freewheeling generation. But their behavior did not perturb me. Aspiring heroes like being left to themselves and appreciate every opportunity they have to frown.

I would have made an impressive Nietzschean hero, but my propensity for reading and my impressionable mind caused my perspectives to collapse once again. I read Eric Fromm's *The Art of Loving* and went from extreme stoical pragmatism to extreme irrational sentimentalism. How could I have been so inhumanly detached? I wondered how I could have ignored the most important thing in the world, the essence of existence, the force that makes the world go around. But no longer was I blind to the secret of life, now that Mr. Fromm, an obvious expert on the human condition, had introduced me to the stupendous powers of love. Out went the sunglasses and the black jacket and in came yellow blouses and Oil of Olay (to smooth out the frown wrinkles). I fairly dripped with love for my fellow man, and no one was safe because I sympathized with and offered my assistance to everyone, whether he wanted it or not.

I practiced smiling in front of the mirror—sad smiles, inspiring smiles, sympathetic smiles, good morning/afternoon/evening smiles. I began to develop a second set of wrinkles, distinctly happier than the first. My face looked like a synthesis of those two masks that symbolize the happy and sad sides of the theatre. I was altruistic and concerned. I wanted to save the whales and the seals, and I wanted to feed the poor and clothe the needy. I even began reading the comic strips and *Mad* magazine again now that it was not against my philosophy to be happy. I swooned over the poetry of Wordsworth and Keats and wailed for the world's wrongs. I never crossed my arms in public.

Luckily, I emerged from my love-saturated state before I went off to college. I say "luckily" because I would have been spiritually crushed had my noble and chaste ideal of love been denigrated by the base interpretation of love commonly found on college campuses. However, I am not sure that reading Sartre enabled me to better withstand the college experience. Whereas Rand had made me pragmatic, and Fromm had made me sentimental, Sartre served to make me nihilistic. This time I didn't buy clothes or practice faces in the mirror in concurrence with my new philosophy. "What's the use?" I reasoned, "I'm going to die anyway." Sometimes I stayed in bed for days, speculating on the futility of action and reasoning that twenty years from now, no one would care that I had skipped English 60 three days in a row. I procrastinated a lot on the rationale that "the sun also rises." Now, I have no earthly idea what this phrase means, but it bears an existential tone and seemed to fit my philosophical ennui. It had the same glossing effect as "We're all gonna die anyway," and I used both lines at every opportunity, much to the chagrin of my roommate, who wanted me to vacuum the carpet regardless of the fact that I planned on dying someday.

Sometimes the ennui was replaced by reckless energy and I would run down the halls encouraging my fellow students to discard their laborious pursuits and grab a little of life's gusto. "Study?" I would say, "What is study? We're all gonna die anyway and the liquor stores close at ten." I concluded that most alcoholics were probably existentialists.

My existentialist phase eventually passed, much to the improvement of my grades and health. But, since then, exposure to Shakespeare and Milton and Socrates and Plato has kept my psyche in a perpetual state of confusion, and I have yet to encounter myriad influential authors. Sheer mental exhaustion and personality strain may force me to give up reading, or at least force me to prepare for the inevitable cracking of my philosophical collage by buying Scotch tape by the crates. Yes, I admit it—I believe and try to put into practice most everything I read. However, I have had the foresight to stash Masters and Johnson away until I am at the prime of my, uh—life. Maybe by then I will have become immune to the persuasiveness of print, but if I haven't, I certainly plan on putting my vice to the best possible use.

Scott Brooks
English 100
Familiar Essay

"O Christmas Tree, O Christmas Tree!"

"O Christmas Tree,
O Christmas Tree!"

Audience: All families who share the tradition of decorating a Christmas tree.
Purpose: To reflect the impact of conflicting standards of tree decorating on one American family.

"O Christmas Tree,
O Christmas Tree!"

"I think that I shall never see,
A poem as lovely as a tree."
I think that I shall never see,
A Christmas tree as lovely as it ought to be!

I have no idea who wrote the first two lines of that poetic masterpiece; but so as not to risk being unjustly accused of plagiarism, I will gladly admit that it wasn't I. I did, however, write the poem's final, considerably less polished, couplet which is, I think, equally as astute as the poet's original observation, and much more timely. For Christmas is upon us once again!

'Tis once again the time for holiday shopping and wrapping and caroling and baking and sledding—if we had snow in Georgia that is—and baking and caroling and wrapping and shopping and, most important of all, selecting the family Christmas tree. Selecting the tree is always the highlight of the holiday season for me and my family. We take our time and we choose with great care, for the tree must be just right, absolutely perfect in every detail. It must be neither too tall nor too short, nor too broad nor too narrow, nor too full nor too sparse; and it must possess all of the many and various qualities that each individual in my family demands.

My father will claim again this year, as he does every year, that he doesn't care what the tree looks like just as long as he doesn't have to bother with it. This is, of course, pure, unadulterated humbug—a seasonal euphemism for bullshit. Dear old dad only claims disinterest in the tree in order to avoid being responsible for its appearance. For he knows, as we all know, that to bring home an unattractive, imperfect tree is to feel the wrath of that most awesome of all Christmas spirits—my mother.

My mother is what might be called a Christmas tree purist. The tree itself must be flawless, certainly, and never too large; yet the main brunt of my mother's attention falls not on the actual tree, but on its decoration. There must be balls, and there must be lights, and they must, I repeat *they must*, be of the same color, preferably red since we own—or, perhaps, I should say stockpile—only red decorations. There most certainly may be no tinsel or icicles—the tacky things. Occasionally in the past, ornaments of a different color—if you'll pardon the expression—have been found on our tree, but only as the result of long and fearsome arguments, after which mother submitted with an air of hurt that hinted at a sacrifice tenfold greater than that of Isaac. She still loved the trees on those off-color years, but she made it quite obvious to all that her Christmas spirit had been broken.

I am always the villain in these decoration debates, for I am the only one with enough temerity, and stupidity, to challenge the honorable lady of the red tree. I like red as much as anyone, except for my mother, of course; but I like other colors as well, and I am willing to fight for my tree in an attempt to bring a little color and excitement into its short, seasonal existence. After all, the poor plant gives up its very life so that our Christmas might be made a little merrier, and I feel that it is the least I can do to try and spare it the embarrassment of spending its last few days spruced up like the guiding light of a cathouse.

My sister shares my love for colorful Christmas trees, but our yearly battles over the right to lights have always made her extremely tense, so she is little help to the cause. Two years ago the strain of pre-tree squabbling became more than she could stand, and on the first day of Christmas, she wed. She then spent a glorious honeymoon decorating her own little tree with ornaments, lights, and tinsel of every size, shape, and color, and even included that tackiest of all adornments among her decorations—icicles.

Of my family's five immediate members, only my grandmother never enters into our Christmas tree clamor. She, being concerned solely with the giving and receiving aspects of the holiday, tells us to do whatever we like to the Christmas tree, but not to worry her about the "damn little thing."

This year, as every year, I will select our tree, for mother and I do, at least, have the same stringent requirements for Christmas trees in their naked state. I will take the tree into our home, and the annual battle will begin. I will, as always, lose the battle, and our tree will once again be a shining scarlet tribute to my mother and her iron will.

I will once again go downtown on Christmas Eve, as I have for so many years. I will stare, in utter defeat, at the huge, brightly colored tree high atop the Atlanta Rich's building, and I will think to myself, "By God, red lady or no red lady, next year I am going to have icicles on my tree!" I will feel better for having thought such a thought, but in my heart I will know that I have lied. There will be a tree next year, and that tree will be wearing red. It has always been, and so it will always be.

Structuring the Essay

In reading the sample essays, probably you were first impressed by the differences among them. And they are different—in topic and in treatment of topic and in the personality and style of the author. Yet they are all familiar essays, and what they share classifies them as such. By analyzing what they have in common, you can verify the preliminary steps taken by each writer, the components of the introduction, the body, and the conclusion, and the total effect on the reader.

The Preliminary Steps

Obviously, the topic selected by each writer was a familiar one. In "Procrastination," the subject is a known foible of man; in the second essay, prejudice toward minorities is all too prevalent among humans regardless of time or locale; in the third essay, man's response to the printed word is universally recognized; and in "O Christmas Tree," the title alone implies a subject dear to many.

The second preliminary step, the writer's stance, offers another common factor. That each writer stood away from his subject and himself, seeing objectively both his subject and his relationship to it, is disclosed by the attitude that pervades each essay. The author of the first essay explores reflectively, but with amusement, her family background and her growth in procrastination, discovering in the process many positive values from what normally is considered a negative attribute. In "The 1960s," the apparent simplicity of the child's view of the neighbor is really a subtle presentation of a case of prejudice. Throughout the body and the conclusion of the essay, the naive view maintained by the writer creates an ironic effect because she allows the reader to see and understand what the child does not. With quite a different technique that reveals self-perception and self-knowledge, the author of "The Persuasiveness of Print" stages her self-dramatization, a result of her reading, and does so from a humorous perspective. The stance and the subject of the last essay challenge Erma Bombeck. With insight toward himself and his family members, the author writes of the comic conflicts involved in decorating the Christmas tree.

Projecting your audience and stating your purpose is a third preliminary step. As you noticed, each writer has included his audience description and statement of purpose on a separate page preceding the essay. The inclusion, however, offers no proof that, in fact, each writer did relate to his imagined audience or achieve his purpose. But delay the search for proof until you look for common factors in the total effect of each essay.

The Introduction

In the introduction to a familiar essay the writer has three goals. Initially he needs to build a bridge to the reader by stating the subject in terms of the common experience and attitude toward it shared by most readers. Also the writer has to establish his own identity. He does so not merely by using the personal pronoun but by indicating his relationship with the topic or his reason for his interest in the topic. In addition, he must present an unexpected or paradoxical attitude toward the topic or its interpretation. This contrast between the writer's approach and the usual one is one way in which a reader's interest is stimulated. Yet the approach cannot be bizarre because it must be shown in the remainder of the essay to have universal meaning or application.

This unusual attitude or interpretation furnishes the focal point of the essay, just as the central idea does for a deductive and the question does for an inductive. But unlike the statement of the idea or problem in these essays, it is seldom expressed directly in the introduction. More often it is implied, and its implications are revealed fully only as the essay circles from this introductory starting point through the remainder of the essay and back to the starting point. In the introduction, itself, it is the suggestion of something different to come that entices the audience to continue reading.

How do the writers of the sample essays achieve these goals? Reread the introduction to each essay with these three points in mind and then compare your answers with the following comments.

"Procrastination"

1. In "Procrastination," the writer assumes that the reader shares the usual negative attitude toward her subject and does not mention the attitude directly. Yet, by opening the essay with the confession, "Ever since I can remember, I've been a procrastinator," and by referring in the last sentence to the "criticism and mockery" that is applied to procrastinators, she give recognition to the common attitude.

2. She establishes her identity first by indicating her relationship with the topic (she claims that she came "by the quality very naturally," a point she enlarges with reference to her parents, her sister, and her dog) and then by giving the reason for her interest (the assets she has gained).

3. In the last sentence she takes a positive attitude that contrasts with the negative one when she tells the reader that she plans to continue "the family tradition" because "many of my assets were born of my dedication to procrastination." The reader is not surprised by this positive attitude, for throughout the introduction she has treated the topic without apology—even her confession is a mock one. Still, the fact that she has discovered some positive assets arouses the reader's curiosity.

"The 1960s"

1. In "The 1960s," the author opens with a statement of the social and attitudinal upheaval that commonly characterizes the period.
2. She establishes her identity as someone who, though too young at the time to have been a part of or to have understood the events, is now, as an adult, aware of the significance of the period. She implies this understanding by selecting the particular topic and by giving its conspicuous characteristics.

   The identity of the writer in relationship to her subject is of particular interest in this essay. The voice that speaks throughout the essay is that of the adult, but she shifts her perspective from the view she now has of the period to the view she had as a child. This shift in perspective first occurs with the word *strange* in the last sentence of the introduction. Then in the second paragraph of the body of the essay she assumes again the limited view she had as a child. Thus the identity of the writer in this essay is that of an adult who tries to recapture her impressions as a child and to present them as the child saw them.

3. In spite of the fact that she disclaims a direct relationship with the topic because of her age in the 1960s, the childhood memory that she recalls is an incident illustrative of the period. Thus, even though the point of her essay is made indirectly through the anecdote she tells in the remainder of the essay, in the introduction she captures the reader's interest in her memory with the description of the neighbor as "strange." Later in the essay the innocence of her attitude toward prejudice offers a strong contrast with the violent emotions engendered by the social conflicts of the period.

"On the Persuasiveness of Print
or
Why I Appear Schizophrenic"

1. The author presents in the first line of the essay the common attitude toward the subject by quoting the adage "Don't believe everything you read." She reinforces this attitude in line six by recognizing the "insidious persuasiveness of the printed word."

2. In the first line she also gives the reason for her interest in the subject (she is "convinced that the old adage . . . was coined especially for me"), and she builds her identity throughout the introduction as she describes her relationship with the subject—her open-mindedness, her "vulnerability" to the "printed word," and her susceptibility "to the magic of eloquent rhetoric."

3. She does not oppose the common attitude toward the subject: she agrees that one should not believe everything one reads. But her major point, implied in the last three sentences of the introduction, offers a reinterpretation of the adage, extending it beyond the meaning of "Don't accept *as fact* . . . " to "Don't accept *as a philosophy of life* everything you read."

The uniqueness of her approach to the topic lies, therefore, in a fresh interpretation of an old saying, an interpretation that shows, as she says in her statement of purpose, "what happens when life imitates art." However, the full understanding of this difference comes only with reading beyond the introduction. Why then, is a reader enticed to continue with the essay? Her humorous attitude, her insight into herself, and her exuberant treatment of the subject make the reader want to know the results of her vulnerability.

"O Christmas Tree, O Christmas Tree"

1. The title and the couplet composed by the author reveal that the subject will be a Christmas tree and the desire to have a beautiful one. Other than the statement that "Christmas is upon us once again," the opening paragraph does not cite common associations and attitudes. On the other hand, is it really necessary to do so with such a familiar subject? He does engender the joyous mood of Christmas, and, indirectly, that is a recognition of a normal holiday experience. Then he elaborates on activities and attitudes in the second paragraph.

2. The opening paragraph gives clues more to the personality of the author than to his identity in relationship with the topic and in his attitude toward it. He reflects his enthusiasm, his humor, his honesty, his self-knowledge (he admits that he is not adept at writing couplets—though his flair for language suggests that his couplet was deliberately offbeat). But there is no doubt that he has the "Christmas spirit," which, in itself, is an identification with the topic, and that he shares with many readers the ideal of the perfect tree.

3. The focal point of the essay is really expressed directly in the introduction, which states that "I think that I shall never see, / A Christmas tree as lovely as it ought to be!" However, the implications of the statement are disclosed only as the essay progresses. Detailing in the second paragraph the requirements of his family with regard to the shape and height of the tree makes the reader recognize—perhaps for the first time—how some people become perfectionists in

choosing a Christmas tree. And when he explores the conflicting attitudes of his family toward the decorations that enhance the tree, the conflict makes the reader examine his own attitude and the attitude of others toward what makes a Christmas tree beautiful. The reader is carried forward into the essay by the personality of the author and by the zest and comic insight he displays in dramatizing the importance some humans place on achieving the ideal Christmas tree.

The Body

The body of the familiar essay develops the main idea and its implications with illustrations drawn from the author's experience and observations—though the illustrations are not necessarily limited to personal experience. The examples may include observations about the experiences of others, what he has read, and what others have told him—in other words, all of the associations that relate to the topic. He may also use an occasional anecdote to illustrate a point. In doing so, he must remember that the purpose in writing an essay is to discuss an idea and not to tell a story: it is easy to allow anecdotes to get out of hand and become the rudiments of a short story. The author of "The 1960s" avoided the problem by using a single but extended anecdote that focused the idea of the essay.

Because the familiar essay moves by association of idea rather than by logical relationship, the structure is a looser one than that of deductive and inductive essays. The arrangement of ideas in the body is in a sequence that seems natural and that keeps the thought progressing as it explains the implications of the main idea and circles back toward the beginning. Nevertheless, this intuitive arrangement still demands that you connect the thoughts between paragraphs. How these connections are made depends, of course, on the direction the thought is taking.

In the first three essays, the writers use chronological arrangements. In "Procrastination," the author follows her growth in the art of procrastination and the values she gains from her childhood experiences at home, in school, and in later years. Next she reflects on her experiences and the assets produced by them. In "The 1960s," after presenting the family's move to the neighborhood and the reaction of the residents, the author characterizes Mr. Jones, her "strange" neighbor, by describing his breakfast habits (his refusal to mix black coffee with white cream and his tearing the brown crusts from the white bread). Then in writing of trying to deliver his mail some years after he has moved, she follows his trail from one situation to another, each of which illustrates his prejudice against a minority. And the "schizophrenic" writer traces the effect books have had on her through her high school and college years, progressing through her various philosophical stages.

The treatment of "O Christmas Tree," however, does not permit a chronological arrangement. Instead the author sets up the point on which all members of the family agree—the perfection of the Christmas tree in size and shape. He follows this agreement by describing the varying attitudes toward the decoration of the tree—that of the father, the mother, the author, the sister, and the grandmother. Because the father has learned not to involve himself in the decoration of the tree, the grandmother has withdrawn from interest in the tree altogether, and the sister has eased herself out of the conflict by marrying and having her own tree, the battle over tree decorations is fought between the mother and the author. The placement of the father first and the grandmother last serves to heighten the attitudes of the main contestants, which are explored in greater depth than that of other family members.

Once you have an arrangement of associations that is natural and appropriate to your subject and that helps form a circular pattern, check to see that the ideas are related between paragraphs so that the ideas flow smoothly. No pattern exists for you to follow: in the familiar essay you must rely on your own intuition. If you have any difficulty, then study each of the essays to see how each writer achieved the flow of thought.

The Conclusion

The conclusion of the essay fills in the final arc of the curving pattern and brings a reader back to the starting point. Throughout the essay the writer has been drawing on his associations with the topic and carefully selecting those that seem important. Now he must recognize how the arcs fit together and when to stop illustrating the idea. Sometimes the decision to bring the essay to a close is made subconsciously on the basis of a rhythmic pattern and sometimes more consciously by a feeling that enough has been said and more would be redundant. If you have kept the circular shape of the essay in mind, however, and have tried to arrange your material so that the end of the essay completes a circle, your conclusion will be easier to achieve and will appear to be a natural stopping point.

Compare, for example, the conclusion of the last essay. The author has begun to curve his essay toward the conclusion in the preceding paragraph by informing his reader that, again this year, as always, he will choose the tree since he and his mother share the same beliefs about the proper prerequisites for an unadorned tree. But the conflict over the decorations will then begin and, as always, his mother will win. In the conclusion he returns to the idea of his couplet, "I think that I shall never see, / A Christmas tree as lovely as it ought to be!" He tells the reader that "once again on Christmas Eve" he will "go downtown . . . and stare, in utter defeat, at the huge, brightly colored tree high atop the Atlanta Rich's building," vowing that "next year I am going to have icicles on my tree!" But he knows that this vow will not come true: "There will be a tree next year, and that tree will be wearing red. It has always been, and so it will always be."

The Total Effect on the Reader

The total effect on a reader depends to a large extent on the personality of the writer, the special way he views the topic, and his style of writing. It also depends on whether or not he reached his intended audience and achieved his stated purpose—and, by so doing, turned a personal description into one with universal application.

As one would expect, each of the authors of the sample essays has a different personality, a different view of subject, and a different tone. Yet, all write in an informal style, give pleasure to the reader, and bring universal meaning to their topics. For example, the author of "Procrastination" writes reflectively with some touches of humor in a style keyed to probing the effects of her subject on herself. She does reach her audience and achieve her stated purpose because, in pointing out the assets she has gained through procrastination, she makes her reader feel less guilty for all of the times he has "put off until tomorrow what should have been done today." The author of "The 1960s" writes in a low key and in a simple style appropriate to her childhood view of the strange neighbor, the simplicity of the style serving as a contrast with the violence and strong emotions displayed in the 1960s. As she intended, her audience either remembers the period or learns something of the prejudice toward minorities reflected so strongly during the events of the period. By showing her readers the situation through the eyes of an innocent child she makes the reader see the senselessness of prejudice.

Marked differences with the reflective mood of the first and the quiet tone of the second are illustrated by the last two essays. The subjects these authors chose are enhanced by the dramatic quality of the third essay and the liveliness of the fourth. In turn, each writer reached his or her audience and achieved his or her purpose. The author of the third essay indirectly warns all of what can happen when life imitates art, while the author of "O Christmas Tree" probably accomplishes more than he realized. Like Robert Frost, who said of "Stopping by Woods on a Snowy Evening" that he had no idea of the universal applications readers would discover in the poem, so the author of this essay would probably be surprised to learn of his essay's implications. His stated purpose was to "reveal the impact of conflicting standards of tree decorating on one American family"; but to the impact of conflicting standards on a family he has added recognition of how important the Christmas tree is to many people—in their minds, the perfection of its form and the beauty of its decorations remain ideals.

Assignment 1: The Familiar Essay

You should be ready by now to try your skill in writing a familiar essay. Get yourself in a mood keyed to your subject and enjoy letting your personality show as you demonstrate its personal application and universal implication. When you have completed your rough draft, use the checklist below. Then let a friend or a member of your class react to your essay before you revise it and type it in final form.

Checklist for the Familiar Essay

1. Is your subject drawn from common knowledge, experience, attitudes, or relationships—in other words, is it familiar?
2. Have you stood far enough away from yourself and your subject to see objectively both your subject and your relationship to it?
3. Have you projected your audience and stated your purpose?
4. In the introduction have you stated the subject in terms of the common experiences and attitudes shared by most people?
5. Have you written in first person and have you established your identity by indicating your relationship with the topic or the reason for your interest in it?
6. Have you expressed an unexpected or paradoxical attitude toward the topic?
7. Does your introduction entice your audience to continue reading?

8. Is your unexpected attitude developed in the essay?
9. Does the body of your essay use illustrations, examples, and, if appropriate, an occasional anecdote to develop the main idea of the paper?
10. Have you remembered that you are discussing an idea and not telling a story?
11. Have you arranged your illustrations in a natural sequence, connecting the ideas of one paragraph to the next to keep the thoughts flowing?
12. Have you kept in mind the circular pattern of the essay?
13. Does your conclusion complete the circle and bring your essay back to the starting point?
14. Have you shown universal implications in your interpretation of the topic?
15. Have you reached your audience and achieved your purpose?
16. Is your tone appropriate to your topic and to you as author, and is your style informal?
17. Are you tired of questions but pleased with your achievement?

Assignment 2: Familiar Essay #2

Choose another familiar topic and write a second essay (perhaps a third one or more—depending on what your instructor thinks you need or the course time allows). Make this one even better than your first to show that you can really create the personal voice and control the intuitive but circular arrangement of your associations.

CHAPTER VI

Variations and Applications

In the preceding chapters you learned the value of thinking ahead and planning; you explored relationships among writer, reader, and subject; and you became more skillful in shaping ideas while using three different voices and essay forms. Along the way you recognized that in prose the responsibility for communicating is placed on the writer rather than the reader. Now you are ready to increase your writing flexibility by applying to other writing situations the techniques you have gained.

While practicing these techniques, you might have been asking: May I combine the thought flow used in deductive and inductive forms into a single essay? Must I always use objective voice with a deductive essay or personal voice with a familiar? Am I limited to using one voice in an essay, or may I use several different ones? How do I write for an audience that is hostile or neutral to my ideas? This chapter will answer those questions. It also includes a number of selected essays for your reading pleasure and your analysis of structure, voice, and audience.

Structural Variations

Until now you have been choosing your own subject, imagining your audience, and deciding on your purpose, but your assignments dictated how you were to structure your essays. When an instructor gives an essay assignment without specifying that the ideas be arranged deductively, inductively, or by association, you, yourself, must select the thought arrangement that suits your subject and purpose. Do you want to emphasize the results and implications of your main idea? Then you will use the deductive structure, presenting the main idea in your introduction and discussing the divisions of the idea in the body. Do you want to show how you arrived at an idea or an interpretation? Then you will use the inductive structure, raising the question in the introduction, adding the sequence of thoughts in the body, and producing the answer in the conclusion. Do you want informally to reflect your own unique attitude toward a common topic? Then you will move intuitively from one association to the next as you circle from the introductory presentation of the subject back to the initial idea or attitude.

Can structural movements be combined? Yes, if you use discretion. If, for instance, you treated your topic deductively for a paragraph or two and then, for no valid reason, shifted to the inductive mode or vice versa, your reader would not be able to follow your thought. To enable the reader to relate ideas, you will have to remember that you are working with a pattern of thought and that you must maintain a dominant design. Two dominant designs may be combined with one part of the essay devoted to one thought movement and a second to another. Or within a dominant design you may use variations.

In a long essay it is possible to arrive at an answer to a question inductively and then expand the answer deductively to show its implications or applications or both. A scientist, for example, might want to disclose how the pattern of the DNA molecule was discovered and then explain the implications of this pattern to an understanding of human genetics. A marketing consultant might want businessmen to see how he arrived at the conclusion that certain marketing methods are inefficient; then he may deliberately demonstrate the results of this inefficiency. In these examples, part of the essay uses one structure and part uses another, each part functioning according to the purpose of the writer and reflecting a continuing order of thought.

Variations confusing in a short essay may often be used in a longer one. Within the framework of a deductive or inductive arrangement some ideas could be advanced by association, or within the framework of an association arrangement some instances of the deductive or inductive mode could be used. Always it would be necessary to maintain the dominant design and be sure that the reader has been directed so that he does not take a wrong turn and get lost.

But what about varying a single paragraph—using an inductive paragraph in a deductive essay or a deductive paragraph in an inductive essay? When the paragraph serves to point up an idea, then the variation is justified. In fact, in long essays, a brief change in arrangement may be necessary to prevent monotony. Such variations can also serve to emphasize ideas in transitional paragraphs. These brief paragraphs link sections of an essay by interpreting or summarizing previous ideas and anticipating ideas that follow. (In deductive and inductive essays, topics I, II, and III may be developed as separate, transitional paragraphs—see chapter 3, footnote 3.) In long deductive essays, for instance, you might, in a transitional paragraph, anticipate an idea with a question. The question, often used in inductive essays, can serve to involve the reader and simultaneously give emphasis to the thought being developed.

Assignment 1: Analysis of Structure

Read the following essay by E. M. Forster and determine the dominant design and the variations. How does he incorporate the variations within the design so that the reader does not lose his way? Given his subject, what other ways could he have arranged his material? Do you like his choice?

My Wood

E. M. Forster

A few years ago I wrote a book which dealt in part with the difficulties of the English in India. Feeling that they would have had no difficulties in India themselves, the Americans read the book freely. The more they read it the better it made them feel, and a cheque to the author was the result. I bought a wood with the cheque. It is not a large wood—it contains scarcely any trees, and it is intersected, blast it, by a public footpath. Still, it is the first property that I have owned, so it is right that other people should participate in my shame, and should ask themselves, in accents that will vary in horror, this very important question: What is the effect of property upon the character? Don't let's touch economics; the effect of private ownership upon the community as a whole is another question—a more important question, perhaps, but another one. Let's keep to psychology. If you own things, what's their effect on you? What's the effect on me of my wood?

In the first place, it makes me feel heavy. Property does have this effect. Property produces men of weight, and it was a man of weight who failed to

From *Abinger Harvest*, copyright © 1936, 1964 by Edward Morgan Forster. Reprinted by permission of Harcourt Brace Jovanovich, Inc.

get into the Kingdom of Heaven. He was not wicked, that unfortunate millionaire in the parable, he was only stout; he stuck out in front, not to mention
behind, and as he wedged himself this way and that in the crystalline en-
trance and bruised his well-fed flanks, he saw beneath him a comparatively
slim camel passing through the eye of a needle and being woven into the
robe of God. The Gospels all through couple stoutness and slowness. They
point out what is perfectly obvious, yet seldom realized: that if you have a lot
of things you cannot move about a lot, that furniture requires dusting, dust-
ers require servants, servants require insurance stamps, and the whole tan-
gle of them makes you think twice before you accept an invitation to dinner
or go for a bathe in the Jordan. Sometimes the Gospels proceed further and
say with Tolstoy that property is sinful; they approach the difficult ground of
asceticism here, where I cannot follow them. But as to the immediate effects
of property on people, they just show straightforward logic. It produces men
of weight. Men of weight cannot, by definition, move like the lightning from
the East unto the West, and the ascent of a fourteen-stone bishop into a pul-
pit is thus the exact antithesis of the coming of the Son of Man. My wood
makes me feel heavy.

In the second place, it makes me feel it ought to be larger.

The other day I heard a twig snap in it. I was annoyed at first, for I
thought that someone was blackberrying, and depreciating the value of the
undergrowth. On coming nearer, I saw it was not a man who had trodden on
the twig and snapped it, but a bird, and I felt pleased. My bird. The bird was
not equally pleased. Ignoring the relation between us, it took fright as soon
as it saw the shape of my face, and flew straight over the boundary hedge
into a field, the property of Mrs. Henessy, where it sat down with a loud
squawk. It had become Mrs. Henessy's bird. Something seemed grossly
amiss here, something that would not have occurred had the wood been
larger. I could not afford to buy Mrs. Henessy out, I dared not murder her, and
limitations of this sort beset me on every side. Ahab did not want that vine-
yard—he only needed it to round off his property, preparatory to plotting a
new curve—and all the land around my wood has become necessary to me
in order to round off the wood. A boundary protects. But—poor little thing—
the boundary ought in its turn to be protected. Noises on the edge of it. Children throw stones. A little more, and then a little more, until we reach the sea.
Happy Canute! Happier Alexander! And after all, why should even the world
be the limit of possession? A rocket containing a Union Jack will, it is hoped,
be shortly fired at the moon. Mars. Sirius. Beyond which . . . But these im-
mensities ended by saddening me. I could not suppose that my wood was
the destined nucleus of universal dominion—it is so very small and contains
no mineral wealth beyond the blackberries. Nor was I comforted when Mrs.

Henessy's bird took alarm for the second time and flew clean away from us all, under the belief that it belonged to itself.

In the third place, property makes its owner feel that he ought to do something to it. Yet he isn't sure what. A restlessness comes over him, a vague sense that he has a personality to express—the same sense which, without any vagueness, leads the artist to an act of creation. Sometimes I think I will cut down such trees as remain in the wood, at other times I want to fill up the gaps between them with new trees. Both impulses are pretentious and empty. They are not honest movements towards money-making or beauty. They spring from a foolish desire to express myself and from an inability to enjoy what I have got. Creation, property, enjoyment form a sinister trinity in the human mind. Creation and enjoyment are both very, very good, yet they are often unattainable without a material basis, and at such moments property pushes itself in as a substitute, saying, "Accept me instead—I'm good enough for all three." It is not enough. It is, as Shakespeare said of lust, "The expense of spirit in a waste of shame": it is "Before, a joy proposed; behind, a dream." Yet we don't know how to shun it. It is forced on us by our economic system as the alternative to starvation. It is also forced on us by an internal defect in the soul, by the feeling that in property may lie the germs of self-development and of exquisite or heroic deeds. Our life on earth is, and ought to be, material and carnal. But we have not yet learned to manage our materialism and carnality properly; they are still entangled with the desire for ownership, where (in the words of Dante) "Possession is one with loss."

And this brings us to our fourth and final point: the blackberries.

Blackberries are not plentiful in this meager grove, but they are easily seen from the public footpath which traverses it, and all too easily gathered. Foxgloves, too—people will pull up the foxgloves, and ladies of an educational tendency even grub for toadstools to show them on the Monday in class. Other ladies, less educated, roll down the bracken in the arms of their gentlemen friends. There is paper, there are tins. Pray, does my wood belong to me or doesn't it? And, if it does, should I now own it best by allowing no one else to walk there? There is a wood near Lyme Regis, also cursed by a public footpath, where the owner has not hesitated on this point. He had built high stone walls each side of the path, and has spanned it by bridges, so that the public circulate like termites while he gorges on the blackberries unseen. He really does own his wood, this able chap. Dives in Hell did pretty well, but the gulf dividing him from Lazarus could be traversed by vision, and nothing traverses it here. And perhaps I shall come to this in time. I shall wall in and fence out until I really taste the sweets of property. Enormously stout, endlessly avaricious, pseudo-creative, intensely selfish, I shall weave

upon my forehead the quadruple crown of possession until those nasty Bol-
shies come and take it off again and thrust me aside into the outer darkness.

Voice Variations

As you will recall, voice, which reflects the writer's relationship with his subject and with his reader, is the means by which a writer speaks about his subject to his reader. In turn, a writer's stance affects a reader's conception both of the subject and of the writer himself. In your writing thus far you have assumed the objective, the conversational, and the personal voice, using each, respectively, with the deductive, inductive, and familiar essay forms. This limitation was deliberately imposed in order to allow you to develop an understanding of the relationships established by the choice of voice. Nevertheless, voice is promiscuous: it is not wedded to a particular form. Any of these three voices may be used with any of these three essay forms if you decide that the relationship it establishes with subject and reader is appropriate to the purpose. Scientists, for example, often use objective voice with inductive arrangement.

In reading the student inductive and familiar essays used to illustrate the methods involved, you may have discovered an interesting facet of voice. Though each writer used "we" or "I," the voice differed with the personality, attitude, experience, mind, and expression of the writer. The same would be true of various essays written in objective voice by various authors. It would also be true if two people wrote on the same topic with the same purpose and used the same pronouns. Even then they would sound different to a reader. No two people ever sound alike on paper. Thus regardless of what voice you use, that voice will carry your own voice print, will bear your own hallmark.

Moreover, in other forms of writing as well as the essay, you may assume a persona and speak through this created role. You might find it necessary, for example, to write the minutes of a meeting in the role of secretary, to write a report as chairperson of a committee, to write an editorial as a newspaper editor, to explain a process as a teacher or an expert, or to argue a point formally as a debater. In such roles a writer is not being untrue to himself: he is merely masking certain aspects of his personality and using those appropriate to subject and purpose.

As long as one voice is predominant, you may even use other voices in an essay. If speaking to the reader enhances communication, here then is the opportunity of employing the pronoun *you* as direct address (but not to mean *any one*). This pronoun, of course, cannot form a voice by itself: it must always be used in conjunction with the major voice of the essay. For instance, this text combines direct address with the objective voice. However, you must not carelessly use different voices in an essay. You will have to remember (1) that each shift in voice is a shift in the writer's relationship with subject and reader and (2) that the shift in voice clues the reader to a change in this relationship as the direction of thought alters. And you will need to maintain one voice as the major one.

The following essay by X. J. Kennedy, as it moves from the popularity of *King Kong* to the reasons for this popularity, varies the objective voice with the personal and conversational voices (one colloquial phrase also includes the pronoun *you*). Read the essay and notice the shifts in voice (mark them in your book as you read). Then return to the shifts and analyze the reasons for the changes. The comments below may help you:

Paragraph 1	Objective voice	Kennedy identifies and gives significance to the topic. He also sketches the plot of *King Kong*.
Paragraph 2	Objective voice	He gives proof of its continued popularity by citing T.V. results.
Paragraph 3	Objective voice	He gives additional proof of its continued popularity by citing the public's response to movie presentations.
Paragraph 4	Personal Voice	He poses a question and shifts to first person as he ponders the answer.
Paragraph 5	Objective and conversational voices	He begins with objective voice as he identifies Kong with man and shifts to conversational voice as he identifies man with Kong. (Note the effectiveness of the voice here in relating writer and reader as part of humanity.)
Paragraph 6	Conversational voice	He explains how the producers intensify this identification by presenting Kong with sympathy.
Paragraph 7	Objective voice	He discusses *King Kong*'s relevance to the Depression.
Paragraph 8	Objective voice	He continues discussing the relevance of *Kong*—this time to the present.
Paragraph 9	Objective voice	He gives the admirable qualities of Kong.
Paragraph 10	Objective, conversational, and personal voices	He explains the conviction that the script writers desire to leave with the viewer. Then he shifts to conversational voice to identify the reader with the viewer. He includes one shift to personal voice (here he also uses "you") to emphasize his disagreement with the simplicity of the script writers' interpretation. The total response, he thinks, lies in deeper causes.

Paragraph 11   Conversational voice   Once more he underscores the man-ape re-
                                                     lationship, the voice uniting writer and
                                                     reader (viewer) in this tragedy of urban life.

Who Killed
King Kong?

X. J. Kennedy

1   The ordeal and spectacular death of King Kong, the giant ape, undoubtedly have been witnessed by more Americans than have ever seen a
performance of *Hamlet, Iphigenia at Aulis*, or even *Tobacco Road*. Since
RKO-Radio Pictures first released *King Kong* a quarter-century has gone
by; yet year after year, from prints that grow more rain-beaten, from sound
tracks that grow more tinny, ticket-buyers by thousands still pursue Kong's
luckless fight against the forces of technology, tabloid journalism, and the
DAR. They see him chloroformed to sleep, see him whisked from his jungle
isle to New York and placed on show, see him burst his chains to roam the
city (lugging a frightened blonde), at last to plunge from the spire of the Empire State Building, machine-gunned by model airplanes.
2   Though Kong may die, one begins to think his legend unkillable. No
clearer proof of his hold upon the popular imagination may be seen than
what emerged one catastrophic week in March 1955, when New York WOR-
TV programmed *Kong* for seven evenings in a row (a total of sixteen show-
ings). Many a rival network vice-president must have scowled when surveys
showed that *Kong*—the 1933 B-picture—had lured away fat segments of the

From *Dissent* (Spring 1960). Reprinted by permission of *Dissent*.

viewing populace from such powerful competitors as Ed Sullivan, Groucho Marx and Bishop Sheen.

3   But even television has failed to run *King Kong* into oblivion. Coffee-in-the-lobby cinemas still show the old hunk of hokum, with the apology that in its use of composite shots and animated models the film remains technically interesting. And no other monster in movie history has won so devoted a popular audience. None of the plodding mummies, the stultified draculas, the white-coated Lugosis with their shiny pinball-machine laboratories, none of the invisible stranglers, berserk robots, or menaces from Mars has ever enjoyed so many resurrections.

4   Why does the American public refuse to let King Kong rest in peace? It is true, I'll admit, that *Kong* outdid every monster movie before or since in sheer carnage. Producers Cooper and Schoedsack crammed into it dinosaurs, headhunters, riots, aerial battles, bullets, bombs, bloodletting. Heroine Fay Wray, whose function is mainly to scream, shuts her mouth for hardly one uninterrupted minute from first reel to last. It is also true that *Kong* is larded with good healthy sadism, for those whose joy it is to see the frantic girl dangled from cliffs and harried by pterodactyls. But it seems to me that the abiding appeal of the giant ape rests on other foundations.

5   Kong has, first of all, the attraction of being manlike. His simian nature gives him one huge advantage over giant ants and walking vegetables in that an audience may conceivably identify with him. Kong's appeal has the quality that established the Tarzan series as American myth—for what man doesn't secretly image himself a huge hairy howler against whom no other monster has a chance? If Tarzan recalls the ape in us, then Kong may well appeal to that great-granddaddy primordial brute from whose tribe we have all deteriorated.

6   Intentionally or not, the producers of *King Kong* encourage this identification by etching the character of Kong with keen sympathy. For the ape is a figure in a tradition familiar to moviegoers: the tradition of the pitiable monster. We think of Lon Chaney in the role of Quasimodo, of Karloff in the original *Frankenstein*. As we watch the Frankenstein monster's fumbling and disastrous attempts to befriend a flower-picking child, our sympathies are enlisted with the monster in his impenetrable loneliness. And so with Kong. As he roars in his chains, while barkers sell tickets to boobs who gape at him, we perhaps feel something more deep than pathos. We begin to sense something of the problem that engaged Eugene O'Neill in *The Hairy Ape*: the dilemma of a displaced animal spirit forced to live in a jungle built by machines.

7   *King Kong*, it is true, had special relevance in 1933. Landscapes of the depression are glimpsed early in the film when an impresario, seeking some

desperate pretty girl to play the lead in a jungle movie, visits souplines and a Woman's Home Mission. In Fay Wray—who's been caught snitching an apple from a fruitstand—his search is ended. When he gives her a big feed and a movie contract, the girl is magic-carpeted out of the world of the National Recovery Act. And when, in the flim's climax, Kong smashes that very Third Avenue landscape in which Fay had wandered hungry, audiences of 1933 may well have felt a personal satisfaction.

8 What is curious is that audiences of 1960 remain hooked. For in the heart of urban man, one suspects, lurks the impulse to fling a bomb. Though machines speed him to the scene of his daily grind, though IMB comptometers ("freeing the human mind from drudgery") enable him to drudge more efficiently once he arrives, there comes a moment when he wishes to turn upon his machines and kick hell out of them. He wants to hurl his combination radio-alarmclock out the bedroom window and listen to its smash. What subway commuter wouldn't love—just for once—to see the downtown express smack head-on into the uptown local? Such a wish is gratified in that memorable scene in *Kong* that opens with a wide-angle shot: interior of a railway car on the Third Avenue El. Straphangers are nodding, the literate refold their newspapers. Unknown to them, Kong has torn away a section of trestle toward which the train now speeds. The motorman spies Kong up ahead, jams on the brakes. Passengers hurtle together like so many peas in a pail. In a window of the car appear Kong's bloodshot eyes. Women shriek. Kong picks up the railway car as if it were a rat, flips it to the street and ties knots in it, or something. To any commuter the scene must appear one of the most satisfactory pieces of celluloid ever exposed.

9 Yet however violent his acts, Kong remains a gentleman. Remarkable is his sense of chivalry. Whenever a fresh boa constrictor threatens Fay, Kong first sees that the lady is safely parked, then manfully thrashes her attacker. (And she, the ingrate, runs away every time his back is turned.) Atop the Empire State Building, ignoring his pursuers, Kong places Fay on a ledge as tenderly as if she were a dozen eggs. He fondles her, then turns to face the Army Air Force. And Kong is perhaps the most disinterested lover since Cyrano: his attentions to the lady are utterly without hope of reward. After all, between a five-foot blonde and a fifty-foot ape, love can hardly be more than an intellectual flirtation. In his simian way King Kong is the hopelessly yearning lover of Petrarchan convention. His forced exit from his jungle, in chains, results directly from his single-minded pursuit of Fay. He smashes a Broadway theater when the notion enters his dull brain that the flashbulbs of photographers somehow endanger the lady. His perilous shinnying up a skyscraper to pluck Fay from her boudoir is an act of the kindliest of hearts.

He's impossible to discourage even though the love of his life can't lay eyes on him without shrieking murder.

10   The tragedy of King Kong then, is to be the beast who at the end of the fable fails to turn into the handsome prince. This is the conviction that the scriptwriters would leave us with in the film's closing line. As Kong's corpse lies blocking traffic in the street, the entrepreneur who brought Kong to New York turns to the assembled reporters and proclaims: "That's your story, boys—it was Beauty killed the Beast!" But greater forces than those of the screaming Lady have combined to lay Kong low, if you ask me. Kong lives for a time as one of those persecuted near-animal souls bewildered in the middle of an industrial order, whose simple desires are thwarted at every turn. He climbs the Empire State Building because in all New York it's the closet thing he can find to the clifftop of his jungle isle. He dies, a pitiful dolt, and the army brass and publicity-men cackle over him. His death is the only possible outcome to as neat a tragic dilemma as you can ask for. The machineguns do him in, while the manicured human hero (a nice clean Dartmouth boy) carries away Kong's sweetheart to the altar. O, the misery of it all. There's far more truth about upper-middle-class American life in *King Kong* than in the last seven dozen novels of John P. Marquand.

11   Every day in the week on a screen somewhere in the world, King Kong relives his agony. Again and again he expires on the Empire State Building, as audiences of the devout assist his sacrifice. We watch him die, and by extension kill the ape within our bones, but these little deaths of ours occur in prosaic surroundings. We do not die on a tower, New York before our feet, nor do we give our lives to smash a few flying machines. It is not for us to bring to a momentary standstill the civilization in which we move. King Kong does this for us. And so we kill him again and again, in much-spliced celluloid, while the ape in us expires from day to day, obscure, in desperation.

Variations in Subject Treatment

Subject treatment, a nebulous term that an instructor can use to mean many things, refers here to the manner in which the subject is presented. The manner itself is based on an author's purpose and the way he perceives his subject and relates to a reader. It is derived from a number of decisions made by a writer, decisions such as whether to present a subject seriously or lightly, whether to shape the material one way or the other, whether to stand close to the subject or at a distance, whether to speak to the reader about the subject in this way or that.

Obviously, a writer has many options in the way he treats a subject. A story is told that when James Thurber confronted the following exam question in college, "Discuss the international conflict over the fishing rights off of Newfoundland," he discussed the squabble from the point of view of the fish. This angle of vision suddenly elevates the reader from the mundane and promises to delight—if not teach—the reader, but his choice represents only one way the subject might be perceived. No doubt Thurber produced a humorous, informal essay. Someone else might give it a formal, serious treatment. It is a matter of making purposeful choices.

Some writers through practice and experimentation develop a feeling for what will work and what will not; others seem endowed with an intuitive sense of how to treat a subject effectively. That all writers subconsciously make choices illustrates the fact that no one has yet fathomed all the mental processes involved in writing. Everyone has moments when a subject seems to shape itself miraculously before his or her eyes. Everyone has moments when an idea is formed simultaneously as he or she writes, when it seems as though thoughts become words without conscious effort. Call it inspiration until another explanation is found and enjoy the moment of exaltation. But until the time when you have developed a feeling for writing or you can count on those inspired moments, you will need to create an essay by making conscious decisions.

Wide reading of essays and other forms of writing will help you see the possibilities of varying the subject treatment. A number of essays are included at the end of this chapter for your analysis and pleasure.

Assignment 2: Choice Essay #1
You are on your own with this essay assignment. Choose your sub-

ject, decide on your purpose, project your audience, select an appropriate arrangement, and find an appropriate voice (or voices).

Assignment 3: Choice Essay #2

Strengthen your wings with another choice essay. Do not be afraid
to try a new direction: you will learn by experimenting.

The Persuasive Essay

To a certain extent all essays are persuasive. Because the writer wishes
to persuade his reader to read the essay, he is careful in the introduction to
show the reader the significance of the topic. Because the writer wishes to
make the reader trust him, he is conscious of the effect his relationship with
the subject and reader may have on instilling or negating trust. And because
the writer also wants to persuade the reader to respond to his ideas or to his
personality, he tries to present his ideas so that they will be both interesting
and clear.

In selecting a reading audience that, in all likelihood, would be interested in his topic or would relate to his presentation, generally the writer
deliberately ignores those readers who might not react positively. In fact,
the writer directs his essay to readers that he thinks would read the essay
and relate to it. Proof of this fact lies in the questions asked to determine a
reading audience, questions that imply that the writer is seeking an audience to share his interests and attitude. In projecting your audience for the
deductive essay, you posed the following questions:

1. *Who needs or wants to know about the subject I have chosen?* In
   answering this question you considered the sex, age group, educational level, attitudes, and values of the audience.
2. *How do I differ from and what do I have in common with this
   audience?* In answering this question you recognized that the
   way you differed might give a unique perspective to the subject
   and that the way you were alike gave contact with the audience.

Although for the inductive essay, you imaginatively created a person
that you liked and desired to communicate with, in the process you posed
these same questions. With the familiar essay you again returned to the

questions—only this time you were more concerned with the likenesses and differences between yourself and the audience.Here you used your unique perspective to give interest to the topic and to help it achieve universal significance.

In contrast with other essays, the persuasive essay—the essay whose *major* intent is to persuade—presents an idea that may be controversial and chooses an audience that is neutral or even hostile toward the writer's point of view. The writer's purpose in this essay is to persuade the reader to consider the idea objectively, to look at it from a different perspective, to change his attitude if hostile, or to commit himself to a position if neutral. Sometimes the writer's purpose is to go a step further: he may wish to induce his reader to take action.

To effectively communicate to any essay reader, particularly to an antagonistic one, you must first think of him as an intelligent human being whom you respect. With this attitude in mind you will need to search for what you have in common. Do you hold the same basic values? Do you share certain goals? On what can you agree? And you will need to determine where you differ and why you differ. Finally you will need to see how the differences can be adjusted in terms of values and goals.

In this search for likenesses and differences, you will have to know what your position toward the topic is, how your values relate to this position, and what you hope to achieve by writing to an audience that does not share your position or goal. In other words, you must know yourself well—not just your audience. Generally when one is self-motivated to write a persuasive essay, one is excited or emotional about an issue and tempted to dash off a paper to purge oneself of these strong feelings. If doing so helps, then by all means unload your feelings on paper. Afterwards put the paper away and direct your mind in a calm, objective way to analyzing yourself and your audience. Stand at a distance from your topic, yourself, and your reader and ask the following questions:

1. *What attitude or position do I hold toward the topic? What attitude or position does the reader hold toward the topic?*
2. *What reasons can I give for my attitude or position? What reasons might my reader give for his attitude or position?*
3. *What influences helped produce the reasons I give? What influences helped produce the reasons the reader gives?* Consider factors such as custom, prejudice, misunderstanding of the is-

sue, age, sex, education, the need to retain a good self-image, altruism, philosophical tenet, agreement with a person admired. Note: be fair to your reader.

4. *What values do I reflect in my attitude or position? What values does my reader reflect in his attitude or position?*

5. *Are the values the same so that they offer common ground for me to build on?*

6. If not, or in addition, *can I discover a long-range goal that the reader and I share so that my attitude or position can be presented as a step toward achieving this shared future goal?*

By making you examine your relationship and the reader's relationship with the topic, these questions will help you avoid antagonizing the reader. Persuasion is not effective when it threatens a reader's self-esteem and sense of security or robs him of his dignity. To call him names, to say, in effect, that he is an idiot for holding a position or attitude different from your own, only serves to make him defensive. You will have to remember that you are not a debater enjoying the clash of ideas and testing your argumentative ability. You are not standing at a lectern shaking your finger in admonition at your audience or pounding your fist in anger. Aggressive approaches will not produce a happy meeting of minds and goals; they will not encourage your reader to consider another point of view, alter his ideas, or even take action. Ideally any essay should show the reader that you like him, that you are interested in him, and that you believe in what you are saying. In the persuasive essay, this ideal is even more necessary if you are to communicate with a reader who does not share your convictions.

Persuasion calls for understanding and common sense in personal relationships as well as in writing. How many times in your younger days have you reacted to your parents' veto by arguing that your friends were being allowed to do so? Were you able to achieve what you wanted by implying that your parents were strict, or inflexible, or unreasonable—or did you stiffen their resistance? Chances are that only when you realized that they were acting to protect you, sat down with them, and calmly reasoned out the pros and cons of the issue, proving that you had the maturity you claimed to have, were you able to achieve your desire. Or if this experience was not part of your past, you will be able to think of other incidents of failure to persuade someone. Perhaps you did not analyze the other person's attitude and the reason for it or your own attitude and the reason for it. Or perhaps you did not seek grounds on which you could agree.

The following essay by Ted Walker, English poet, broadcaster, and author, does a masterful job of persuasion. With a nostalgic touch he heightens the appreciation of something truly English that is disappearing from the landscape—the English hedgerow. Pictures of "the landscape plotted and pieced" and of the berries, wild flowers, birds, and small animals that find a home in the hedgerow illustrate the essay, published in *Audubon* (September 1972), and add their own appeal. A long essay, it proceeds at a leisurely British pace, a pace that in itself is nonthreatening to the destroyer of hedgerows.

In your first reading, notice the following persuasive aspects. Then read the essay again to discover some of the subtleties of his techniques—how, for example, he creates a belief that the writer is to be trusted.

1. He presents the farmer's situation with understanding so that the farmer, who is removing the hedgerows, will be willing to listen and to maintain or replant hedgerows where possible.
2. His audience includes farmers, parents, teachers, country people, law makers, and all other Englishmen.
3. He appeals to the values of all Englishmen—their sense of history and pride in tradition, their love for what is uniquely English, their practicality, their appreciation of wildlife, their desire to preserve England for future generations.
4. He sets realistic goals for ways in which the hedgerows can be preserved and still allow farmers to use modern methods of cultivation.
5. He persuades farmers to alter their view, others unaware of or unconcerned with the problem to commit themselves, and all to take action.

Bid a sad farewell
to the landscape
plotted and pieced

Ted Walker

I find it almost impossible to visualize an England devoid of hedgerows. Over the centuries they have created the essential Englishness of the English landscape—that patchwork effect of small and often irregularly shaped fields which provide such infinite variety to our countryside, whether hilly or flat. Patchwork, I say, not checkerboard; a bird's-eye view would reveal very few perfectly square fields. The land has been divided into what seems, at first sight, an arbitrary patterning of shapes for which geometry has no names. A three-sided meadow is seldom, properly speaking, a triangle, for while two of its sides might be straight the third is very likely to curve either along some contour of the ground or according to some apparently inexplicable whim of the man who planted it immemorial years ago.

Our forefathers in this way transformed the landscape into a vast and subtly composed artifact of straight lines and curves dividing shape from

From *Audubon* (September 1972). Reprinted by permission of David Higham Associates Limited, author's agent.

shape, arable ground from pasture, color from color. It is as esthetically pleasing, in its unselfconscious and seemingly capricious development, as the most carefully contrived piece of abstract art. Not, of course, that the planters of hedgerows had motives other than the strictly pragmatic ones of separating livestock from crops or establishing the boundaries of their property; but what they created unwittingly was not only the characteristic face of the English pastoral scene but also a world in which so much of our wild flora and fauna could survive and flourish.

It is unthinkable, then, that we should do away with all our hedgerows—England would not be England without them. And yet this is precisely what we are doing, at a rate which frightens and saddens me. For the stern practicality of the English farmer, to which we owe the existence of our huge network of hedges, is now turned toward destroying the creation of centuries. Hedges no longer make economic sense. Modern husbandry doesn't need them. Not only are barbed wire, electric fences, and sheep netting quicker to erect and cheaper to maintain, they also have the extra advantage of being movable. Our hedges, then, and the wildlife they have so unofficially and for so long supported, face a very serious threat indeed.

If I sound unduly pessimistic, I should perhaps state at the outset that my forebodings are based not only on the evidence of my eyes as I walk round my village or drive across Britain, but also on the following plain statistics. Ten years ago it was estimated that there were upwards of 600,000 miles of hedgerows in the whole of Britain. Assuming that the average width of a hedge is two yards, this mileage represents something approaching half a million acres of habitat for birds, small mammals, insects, and flowers—an astonishingly large area which is very much greater than all our national nature reserves put together. And the alarming fact is that we are grubbing up 10,000 miles of hedgerow every year.

If the trend were to continue at the present rate (not that this is likely to happen, of course), it would mean that there would be no hedgerows left at all sixty years from now. The situation is worst in East Anglia, where arable farming has predominated for many years. Here (bearing in mind also that reforestation is overwhelmingly coniferous) it could well be that nine-tenths of the deciduous habitat of plants and creatures will have disappeared within the foreseeable future. One wonders what will happen to the wildlife which depends either wholly or in part upon the hedgerows. Possibly it will diminish in number in some proportion to the decline in hedgerow mileage; probably, with the increased competition, certain species will adapt to other available habitats; certainly the weaker species will become rarer and rarer, maybe to the point of extinction—at any rate locally.

Well, no doubt there will be infinitely worse problems for my children to face during their lifetime than the disappearance of what Gerard Manley Hopkins described as "Landscape plotted and pieced" and the unique community sustained by the hedgerows. However, I would wish them to inherit from us more than just some artificially preserved remnant of the countryside. The not so distant prospect of England as one monotonous prairie relieved only by dead rivers and a thickening network of motorways appalls and saddens me. Also, I consider it a huge responsibility that man should so heedlessly deprive the wild plants and creatures of the living space he himself originally provided.

If now I write with nostalgia of a fast-vanishing scene, I hope that I do so without sentimentality. I see man as part of nature, a creature who can mold his environment according to his will. He has a duty toward his own kind—the future generations—and to the indigenous wildlife of his homeland. While I recognize the exigencies of modern farming methods and accept that land must be made available for housing and roads, and while regretfully, I acknowledge that our life-style is bound to become more and more urbanized on this already overcrowded island, I still believe that with thought and compassion we can achieve a satisfactory compromise of interests.

One of the most disturbing aspects of this change on the farming scene is the very speed at which it is happening. When I was born, in the mid-1930s, the countryside still looked much as it had since before the Great War; indeed, new methods had scarcely altered the face of rural England since the eighteenth century, when with the enclosures and the newly introduced rotational systems more and more hedges were planted to separate grazing from arable land. True, farming was slowly becoming mechanized; but the days of free-cropping (or movable fences), combine-harvesters, battery-houses for chickens, and the like were not yet dreamed of by the ordinary agricultural community. Tractors were few. Such machines as there were generally had to be hauled by a team of horses. Farming still relied overwhelmingly on manpower, both permanent and casual. It was still an activity on a human scale, requiring not only the sweat of heavy labor but also an astonishing number of specialized skills and crafts which were passed on from generation to generation.

The hedger-and-ditcher was still—and seemed likely to remain—one of the most important and revered craftsmen employed by any farmer. Sometimes he was a journeyman laborer, self-employed, who offered various skills nd services according to the season. In autumn he was a familiar sight ong the lanes, working neither fast nor slow but with inexorable steadiness th sickle and hooky-stick, the two simple tools of his trade. It wasn't a job for a fool. What a farmer wanted was a man who understood how to trim and layer a hedge (this involved cutting halfway through the stems and then bending and weaving them together) so that the bush grew thick and dense enough to keep out the winds and keep in the livestock.

Today, less than forty years on, this is a skill that is all but lost; a quaint, bygone craft that seems bound to disappear even from folk memory. Once a year, round the fields near my home in Sussex, a mechanical trimmer hacks its way across the eighteen inches of new growth. It's done peremptorily, with little love or care, as a necessary chore of tidying-up. The process, though cheap and quick, does have its drawbacks, for the mechanical trimmer is indifferent about what it hacks through. Saplings of useful hardwood trees—oak, ash, and elm—are not spared to grow into maturity as once they were. Further, the tractor-drawn buck rake is nowhere near as efficient at picking up thorny trimmings as the old, methodical hedgers used to be; the litter is not only unsightly, but also a hazard to livestock. And when the work is done the hedges, stunted and full of gaps, look like rows of gaunt, savaged sticks until they heal themselves.

It pains me to see this annual brutality, as it pains an old hedger-and-ditcher I know. But, because the hedges no longer perform a useful job and are costly to maintain with the old-fashioned and painstaking methods, this will be the fate of many of them until they are removed altogether. The land they occupy—any farmer will tell you—is worth three or four times what it fetched ten years ago; and hedges not only pay no rent of usefulness, but they also harbor such undesirable lodgers as couch grass and fungus diseases. These days you seldom see a small boy being lectured by a farmer for trying to barge his way through a hedge; it simply doesn't matter anymore.

I learned most of my love and knowledge and understanding of nature from the endless mazes of hedgerows which were as much a habitat for us gangs of marauding boys as they were for chaffinch, shrew, or honeysuckle. Deplorably (one might think now) I spent a good part of every springtime looking for birds' nests and robbing them. My friends and I usually found little more than the big, obvious nests of thrush, blackbird, and starling, which, though they built in the prickliest and most inaccessible corners of the hawthorn, at least did so before the hedge was in full leaf, so we didn't have to look hard. We had an unwritten law that you should never "rag" more than one egg from any one nest. Most of us, I think, obeyed this law; and I like to think that we did so from some crude sense of conservation. We rarely had the patience, or the luck, to find the nests of the less common birds. It seemed like one of nature's commonsensical laws that we had only the eggs of common birds in our collections not simply and obviously because they were common, but also because the less-frequent varieties had a way of not building until the hedgerows were in thick leaf—and even then in crooks and hollows where our eager fingers could never have groped, scratched and bleeding.

From my springtime assaults on the hedgerows I think I picked up some inkling (though of course I couldn't verbalize the theories) of such concepts as natural selection, adaptation to environment, camouflage, the survival of the fittest, and the like. When, years later, I was taught these terms, I remembered my box of eggs—song thrush, starling, blackbird, hedge sparrow, chaffinch, great tit—the eggs that had presented themselves like free gifts. Also, I remembered how we walked the hedgerows in leafless winter to find, exposed and long deserted, the nests (for we could identify them from books) of the rarer birds that had eluded us before: little, delicate nests of buntings and warblers; the curious, bottle-shaped home of the long-tailed tit. Science, when I came to it, merely confirmed for me those mysteries which I had already comprehended, dimly because dumbly, through my own primitive observations and at the expense of bruised limbs and torn jerseys.

Boys with access to the countryside and its hedgerows, I suppose I'm saying, had the makings of natural philosophers before they learned how to read a biology textbook. The hedgerow was a classroom.

All country people considered the hedgerows as a kind of unofficial extension of their gardens, to be harvested freely in due season. Autumn, of course, was the busy time. There were blackberries to be gathered, and hazelnuts to be picked and kept for Christmas; these were, and still are, the commonplace fruits of the hedgerow, and to this day we keep the annual rituals of blackberrying and nutting. But the days are passing, or have already gone, when entire families would make an excursion, of a Sunday afternoon, in quest of the other bounties. There were elderberries for making dark, rich jelly or tart red wine; rose hips for a syrup to keep colds away; sloes from the blackthorn (excruciatingly bitter, though they looked so attractive in their dusky plum bloom) with which to make sloe gin for the old folk; crab apple and wild pears, whose dry acidity was transformed by some alchemy into the most delicious conserve; and this is not to mention the occasional exotic barberry or the various herbs that were gathered and mixed and brewed according to ancient recipes for curing all maladies from swollen ankles to milk fever. Then in spring the versatile elder yielded bushels of its creamy flowers for the making of a violently fizzy dry wine.

All these things were free for the taking, as long as the hedge suffered no damage; they were the wholesome perquisites of country life. From the hedgerow we took so many commodities that it grieves me to think of people paying good money for them today. Nobody ever dreamed of buying bramble jelly or rose-hip syrup or cough mixture; nor would a man ever have to order bean poles from a gardening shop or pay for a walking stick while he could cut them from the nearest hedgerow. The list is unending of what we took: rabbits by the dozen, snared or taken from warrens under the hedgebanks with the help of ferrets or terriers; wild roses, honeysuckle, and trails of hops and bryony for decorating the house, and holly and mistletoe for Christmas. Even the white or pink blossom of the hawthorn (which was called, for a reason that I never understood, bread-and-cheese) produced in summer a berry which, though inedible for humans, made a good bait for chub fishing. Hawthorn, or May blossom (called mother-die in Yorkshire), was by some old superstition considered very unlucky to take indoors; instead, above all at Easter, we gathered great armfuls of catkins and pussy willow (known as "palm") to celebrate Christ's entry into Jerusalem. Every cottage, church, and manor house would be full of it and the inevitable primroses, violets, and wild daffodils picked from under the hedgebanks.

Where should I finish this catalog? Shall I ever forget the nettle soup or salads of dandelion leaves, the bows and arrows and catapults, the acorns, oak apples, and burrs that were the simple yet satisfying playthings for boys who neither had money nor needed it? All this, and so much more, is passing away from rural life as the hedges are torn up. If I regret it, I don't think my regret is entirely mawkish or a soft hankering for the past. The presence of abundant hedgerows betokened a way of life the quality of which has not been adequately replaced. The countryman, until quite recent times, depended on the hedgerow for some of his needs. Like the song thrush, he was a part of nature, and because of his intimacy with the wild creatures and his perpetual awareness of the passing seasons, he became more easily fulfilled and content and endowed with a proper sense of humility in the face of eternal things. Though it is unfashionable to believe in such Wordsworthian notions, I am certain that it won't be long before we come to realize once more that his wisdom—like that of Rousseau, Thoreau, and poets like Edward Thomas and Robert Frost—was neither superficial or spurious or irrelevant to modern life. If we lose the countryside as we know it, and of which the hedgerow is such a predominating feature, we humans are the first to lose. We could even lose the temperate nature of our climate, for the hedgerow network of England acts as a kind of gigantic and complex wind barrier against the blustery weather systems of the northeast Atlantic Ocean.

But while we can be quick to adapt to a worsening situation, buying supermarket jam and deep-frozen Argentinean rabbit and turning to the national parks for our pleasure, the wild creatures to whom we surely owe a living are losing not only their food but also a place to live.

It is not, of course, simply a question of space—for the whole idea of removing hedges from farmland is to make more space. As the plow turns up more and more grassland, indeed, certain species will be favored with the kind of open environment they prefer: the hares will prosper, as will the lapwings and skylarks and the semi-tame pheasant and partridge. But the creatures who are bound to lose, because they need dense cover as a pre-requisite of their way of life, are too numerous to mention. They are the birds, insects, and mammals (as well as the flowers) which, over the centuries, have come to depend entirely on that linear extension of the woodland hab-itat, the hedgerow. One thinks of all the members of the thrush family, in-cluding the blackbird, fieldfare, and redwing, whether or not they breed here; the robins, yellowhammers, whitethroats, and hedge sparrows, and the vast number of more fugitive smaller birds; and, apart from the common rabbit, one thinks of the voles and shrews, the badger and the fox, the stoats, and the weasels, all of whom, to a greater or lesser extent, have made the hedgerows their customary home. It is not as though these birds and ani-mals could find alternative quarters in the roomier, open-plan fields created by the new farming methods; they require a more stable and permanently sheltered surrounding than is offered by the short period of a crop growth, and they simply could not find the means to survive when the land reverts to its winter bareness.

What happens, in fact, is that the hedgerow species simply disappear from country where the hedgerows have been grubbed up. Having lost their cover and privacy, a place to breed and a source of food, they have no al-ternative but to decamp. The arable field—particularly if it contains a cereal crop—does not provide enough of these resources for long enough. Again, one must stress that it is largely a matter of speed. Present-day cultivation is completed at a breakneck speed when compared with the old proce-dures. Plowing, for example, was the slow and steady work of the entire win-ter season when the plow was drawn by horses; today it's all done by the middle of November. There are no longer the rich pickings to be had from the stubble fields. There are fewer weeds and insects; and the chemicals responsible for this are often deadly poison to wild creatures that ingest them.

So far, it has only happened in a few localities like Lincolnshire that the new arable farming methods have produced such a drastic, almost total an-nihilation of the hedgerows. In most other counties, the process is more gradual and is giving the wildlife time to make adaptations. Some recent findings have proved of great interest.

Dr. Max Hooper of the Nature Conservancy discovered that in terrain where hedgerow space was abundant there would be an average of 15 nests to a mile of hedge. What would happen, he wondered, if more than 5,000 miles of hedgerow vanished annually, thus putting 75,000 pairs of birds out of house and home? Would they learn to live in closer communion? The answer was that they would; if available living space was at a high premium, you might find as many as 80 nests to the mile—there would be the same number of birds in a given area, but they would be cramped into a smaller nesting habitat. However, this cramming together was a process that could not continue indefinitely, and Dr. Hooper discovered, as is not surprising, that beyond a certain point the birds simply would not put up with the situation. If too many hedges disappeared, the bird population declined alarmingly. The story is not quite as simple as this, for much depended on the variety of shrub that comprised the hedgerow; a hawthorn, with the thick cover it provides so early in the year, was preferable to the other common hedge bushes.

And so it seems that the birdlife of a hedgerow is not unlike human life in big cities; you can squeeze both birds and humans together up to, and not beyond, a certain level of distress, and the extent to which you can do this will depend on certain variables that can enhance or detract from the quality of life. Perhaps it is possible to lose an annual mileage of hedgerow without doing too much harm. It all depends on how quickly we let the process happen, how extensively we allow it to continue, and how much we bear in mind the relative usefulness of the varieties that make up a mixed hedge. What we need, then, is knowledge as well as patience.

Until fairly recently our knowledge of the hedgerow has been surprisingly scant, having in mind the importance it obviously holds in the scheme of things. Before the invaluable work of men like Max Hooper and Professor W. G. Hoskins of Leicester University, no study in depth had been made either by the scientist or the historian of a feature of England that is disappearing or already vanished. Knowledge, together with public awareness and education, might yet save much of the English hedgerow and the life it supports. Somehow people have got to be told what is happening, their interest must be aroused, and then perhaps their concern (for the majority of Englishmen are at any rate sentimentally fond of nature) might do much to determine the fate of such hedgerows as still remain. Ordinary people can, and do, alter the course of events such as this, once they are aroused; see how they will protect trees from being felled or good old buildings from demolition. We all, when we are young, conceive a lifelong affection for trees. What is needed now is for the schools and parents to instill a similar regard for the hedgerows and the wildlife they support.

Children do worry about the diminution of species, and the pity of it is that whereas the classrooms of English schools are full of posters about the disappearing blue whale and the white rhino, there is little propaganda on behalf of the chaffinch or the blackbird. I should like the younger generation to grow up with a fierce determination to preserve what my generation has been too complacent about; a generation that will be as quick to place a preservation order on a hedgerow as mine is to save a tree or a Victorian railway station.

There is some reason to hope for a legal breakthrough. Under the Town and Country Planning Act of 1962, tree preservation orders have prevented the needless or senseless felling or lopping of trees. And the act has been invoked from time to time recently by local authorities wishing to protect a hedgerow. At Turnworth in Dorset it was argued successfully that a hedgerow did, after all, comprise a line of trees. The trouble is, however, that the law is still nebulous on this point and needs amending to favor the retention of hedges when this is in the public interest and does not seriously incommode the farmer to whom they belong. It is largely a question of creating an urgent sense of awareness. A few simple facts and a little field study could work wonders. I remember being taught how to find the age of a tree by counting rings; I detected a similar sense of wonder in my children when I taught them that you can usually assess the age of a hedge by applying this theory: age in years = (99 x number of tree species) minus 16.

Nobody would suggest that farmers should subsidize the continuance of the English wild flora and fauna by keeping to the agricultural methods of a past age. If they need to create larger, open fields, then we must all accept the fact that the face of the countryside is bound to change. Some farmers in Lincolnshire, where the problem is most acute, have begun a benign policy of providing alternative habitats for wildlife, planting on those patches of ground which exist on all farms and which cannot be used in the large-field system. I believe, however, that it will not be enough to rely on this kind of good will, or on the pious hope that landowners will always want to provide cover for their gamebirds which can be shared by the wild species.

The Crown Estate Commissioners, who manage 155,000 acres of farmland in England, made an encouraging gesture last year when they began a system of payments to tenants for preserving trees—both those newly planted and those spared in trimmed hedgerows—and at the same time ordered that when hedges are removed in the interest of farm efficiency, twice the number of trees thus lost are to be planted elsewhere on the farm. However, what is also needed is strict government legislation to limit the rate at which all other hedgerows are grubbed up and to require alternative and suitable cover to be planted, pro rata, to replace what has been removed. Rural England will, in time, look different from the present patchwork effect;

but it won't necessarily be displeasing, and it is a small price to pay for maintaining the priceless heritage of our wildlife.

Further, I believe that there is any amount of room still left in England where hedgerow habitats could be provided, apart from the odd corners of farms where the large machines don't have room to maneuver efficiently. Municipal and suburban parks could provide more cover than they do, and so could the larger private gardens—it was, after all, the fashion in the eighteenth century for most gardens to maintain a "wilderness" in which nature could take her own course. Above all, I am certain that large public authorities could do much with the considerable acreage of grounds that fall within their jurisdiction. Notably, the ever-increasing mileage of motorways should be bordered along their entire length by thick hedgerows, as a matter of course. I have noticed that certain species—the rook and the kestrel—have adapted well to living on the roadside pickings; the hedgehog, another creature of the hedgerow, has even lost his habit of rolling into a ball at the approach of danger, and instead runs for his life. Motorway hedgerows would be a boon to the driver, for they would soften the drab monotony of his journey; they would therefore be in the true English tradition of being useful as well as gratuitously sustaining wildlife community.

Perhaps, then, there is room for guarded optimism. There is room for us all, and none of us need be the losers; but it will take a sense of urgency, education, planning, and good will—now, before we lose our chance.

In his essay Walker reveals that, before writing, he studied his subject, his readers, and himself. He gives statistics that show the rate hedgerows are disappearing and the influence of this disappearance on bird life. He explains the motives of the farmer: the hedgerows, established by the farmer's ancestors for practical reasons, are now being destroyed for different, yet still practical, reasons. Cognizant of the values that English people share, he finds purposeful, humanitarian, and aesthetic reasons for preserving the hedgerows. And having discovered ways of solving the problem, he presents a compromise that will permit hedgerows to be retained in some places and planted in others. Above all, he has studied himself. He confesses that he writes with nostalgia, but he does not allow nostalgia to move into sentimentality.

Walker's essay also reveals that the persuasive essay shares some features with the argumentative essay. Its premises are based on reason, it views humans as capable of making rational decisions, and its aim is to resolve a conflict. In other ways, however, the persuasive essay differs from the argumentative essay. Like debate, an oral form of argument, the argumentative essay tends to be more formal, marshals its points in a logical sequence, and tries to win its side of the question by stating more telling arguments and citing better evidence. It may not follow all of the conventions of debate such as addressing the opposition as "my honorable opponent" or driving home points with "first," "second," "finally," "therefore," or "in conclusion," but in the fashion of debate the argumentative essay tries to demonstrate that one set of contentions offers stronger proof or evidence than another. In contrast with this underscoring of logic and the implication that the holder of a different opinion is an opponent, the persuasive essay, though based on reason, emphasizes human values, values that may go beyond logic. While it does not neglect the proof and disproof of points, it deliberately avoids the language of debate and tries to establish a warmer, more understanding relationship with the reader. Thus the persuasive essay is often longer than the argumentative one: instead of pushing its advantages, it takes the time to be understanding.

Of course, persuasive techniques can be used to appeal to the weaker side of human nature. Advertisements often do so. So do the Hitlers of the world. Even some psychological theories view humans as animals to be manipulated—ring a bell to make them salivate or wave a carrot in front of them to make them go. But the kind of persuasive essay you are encouraged to write approaches a reader with a belief that human beings can act in an unselfish, reasonable manner and that they will respond to the good if shown the way. Like the movie *E.T.*, this persuasive essay through its understanding of human values appeals to the best in people.

Although you should be aware that the inductive arrangement and the conversational voice lend themselves well to persuasion, the persuasive essay can employ any dominant design or any major voice. Other than choices of arrangement and voice, what you need to concentrate on is knowing your topic, yourself, and your audience. Because you are persuading, avoid the tone and language of argument and debate. Then after you have written the essay, put it aside for a time. Return to it later, imaginatively assume the role of your reader or readers, and try to judge the validity and the psychological impact of your presentation.

Assignment 4: Persuasive Essay #1

Choose a controversial subject, select an audience that is either hostile or neutral to your position, and ask the six questions stated above. When you are satisfied that you have looked at the total relationships involved among your reader, your subject, and yourself, then compose your essay. Take care to make your reader trust you and to build on common values and goals as you seek to persuade.

Assignment 5: Persuasive Essay #2

Choose a different controversial subject and a different audience. Then proceed as you did in the previous assignment. Writing a persuasive essay is a challenge to any author, so bring your mind and all of your skills to bear upon the problem.

Selected Essays
for Reading Pleasure
and Analysis

Needed:
Full Partnership for Women

Margaret Mead

The contemporary Women's Movement has been almost completely a movement of educated, middle-class women rebelling against lives in which their sole function, week after week, year after year, has been the maintenance of households from which husbands have left for work and children for school and marriage. International Women's Year, and especially the more self-conscious inclusion of women and women's concern in the U.N. conferences on Population and Food and Hunger, has changed this culture-bound myopic emphasis and given us a wider view of what women are doing and rebelling against today. The picture that emerges is neither one of oppression—although most women and men have been oppressed since the beginning of civilization—nor of uniformity of second-class citizenship. Rather, what has become evident is the close relationship between the over-all life-style of a society—the way food is produced and human beings are cared for—and the values that the society pursues.

After the age when hunting was done by males and the gathering of vegetables and small animal food by females—always with close coopera-

From *Saturday Review* (14 June 1975). Reprinted by permission of *Saturday Review*.

tion between men and women—the discovery of planting and herding and then of the animal-drawn plow assured a steadier food supply, which underwrote male enterprises: conquest, the building of cities, trade, and the stratification of society. But woman's role continued to be circumscribed by childbearing; whatever a woman did she had to do near home. As men separated out political and economic roles, they left women behind except as companions of the eminent and mothers and household managers. Not until the Industrial Revolution were women cast adrift from the protection and formal supervision of men. And not until the medical revolution, with its lowering of infant mortality and the resulting population explosion, was it possible for society seriously to consider basing the sexual division of labor on considerations other than the production and daily subsistence of the next generation.

Today, the discussions that bring women together from every level of technical development all over the world reveal what women—and the world—have lost. Increasingly centralized, industrialized planning and production steadily reduce women to choosing between the role of housekeeper with mild supplementary activities—in the performance of which she is unprotected and ill paid in the marketplace—or that of educated, but subordinate and unmarried competitor in all the other spheres of life. In the villages, where most of the women of the world still work, contributing their full share to decision making, whether they speak from behind veils or not, women are full partners in local affairs. But as social life has become ever more complicated and decision making is ever further removed from the lives of the people who must live with the decisions made half a world away, woman's role has shrunk, until among the educated, middle-class women of the post-industrial world, it has been reduced to dishwashing and consumerism.

As decision making reached higher levels, half the harvests of the world were bought and sold in political and financial deals which ignored the fact that food was grown to be eaten. Rebellion against the distance between producer and user, planner and planned for, became reinterpreted as a revolt against the exclusion of women as such. Similarly, today's vast war machines, which consume our substance and threaten all life, are visualized, as they were in the earlier feminist movements, as being so inimical to human life that women—the official and historical cherishers of human life—would prevent war if they had the power to do so.

The women who speak may be primitive women who begin to express dissatisfaction with their lot, having sent their sons away to school while their daughters remain uneducated and bound to daily toil. Or they may be suburban women of narrow horizons, bound by an endless round of providing for others through a proliferation of energy-consuming, resource-depleting "labor-saving devices." In both cases, comparison with the life they are living and the life they could be living has bred discontent and a desire for radical change. And this change, which endangers the status quo, causes anxiety in all of those who are not stirred by the prospect of women being freed from lifelong childbearing, freed to use their minds in all the diverse activities of the modern world, freed to contribute as individuals and not only as the mothers of the next generation, freed to act at every level, from the village to the great political decision-making centers of the world.

Women's roles have always been more tightly bound than men's to parenthood, more limited by conceptions of reproduction as mysterious, ritually impure, restricting the development of either mind or soul. As a result, women's rebellion against the simple maintenance role that has been their lot is more vivid than men's. Since the beginning of social life, the performance of men's activities, however tedious, dangerous, or humdrum, has been associated with ideas of achievement that both men and women have often mistaken for innate superiority. If men are conscripted and sent to war without ever being consulted by the distant old men who control the corridors of power, they, too, have no more choice over their lives than women without contraceptives have for preventing an unwanted pregnancy.

In this moment of vision, people caught in one kind of life that they have never questioned are getting a glimpse of the way other peoples live; the current questioning of the status of women is part of the whole process of questioning a social order that no longer meets the newly aroused hopes of the people who live within it. The voices of women are combining with voices all over the world against a new worldwide system of political and economic exploitation of the land, the sea, and the air, and the endangered populations that depend upon them.

But there is a difference between women's voices and the voices of all the others who live meaningless lives within a world where they have no part in decisions made too far away. The revolts of the oppressed—slaves, serfs, peons, peasants, manual workers, white-collar workers—are part of the periodic attempts to correct social systems that are seen as exploitative and unfair. But this is the first time in history when the progress made in the control of disease and reproduction has offered to the female half of the population escape from a lifelong role that was defined for every one of them simply by gender. Having one or two children and rearing them together as parents who have chosen parenthood means for men and women—but most of all for women—permission to participate at every level in our highly complex society.

And it is not only women who gain—society gains. Where once half of the best minds were consumed in the performance of small domestic tasks, society can now draw on them. Where women's experiences—inevitably different from men's because women all had mothers with whom they could identify—have been fenced off from contributing to the high-level planning of the world, they can now be used in the attack on such problems as chaotic abuse of food, resources, human settlements, and the total environment. When women are once more able to participate in decisions and are free to be persons as well as parents, they should be able to contribute basic understandings that are presently lacking in the world. These basic new understandings include the fact that food is meant to be used to feed human beings, not to serve as a weapon or commodity; that towns were meant for generations to live in together, not only as barracks or bedrooms; that education can be used to make life meaningful; that we do live in a world community that is here but is unrecognized, in all its interdependence and need for shared responsibility.

Crane and Hemingway: Anatomy of Trauma

Earle Labor

Recent critics have rightly pointed out that some striking parallels are to be found in the works of Stephen Crane and Ernest Hemingway—particularly in *The Red Badge of Courage* and *A Farewell to Arms*. But more significant, I think, are the remarkable differences between the two novels. The essential contrast between the spiritual orientation of their heroes makes the two works peculiarly representative of the vastly different milieux in which they were written. *The Red Badge* is clearly dated "nineteenth century" by Henry Fleming's ability to resolve a problem which, in little more than a generation, has become virtually insoluble for the archetypal twentieth-century literary hero, Lieutenant Frederick Henry. Quite simply, "the problem" is how to adapt oneself emotionally and spiritually to a world dominated by pain and chaos.

The contrast between the widely divergent conclusions at which the two heroes finally arrive is given ironic emphasis by the parallels between the two novels. Most notable are the basic tonal similarities in the two works: the same attitude of author toward his materials is vividly defined in the opening

From *Renascence* (Summer 1959). Reprinted by permission of *Renascence*.

paragraphs of both. Hemingway's reference to landscape—particularly to the roads, the trees, the distant mountains, and the river—is very much like Crane's. The mutual importance of setting can hardly be over-emphasized. Of both books one is tempted to say that setting not only provides mood and theme but also becomes central character. Certainly there is the similar underplaying of the roles of the human protagonists; we must focus our attention, however, upon the flesh-and-blood heroes. Critics have commonly pointed out how long Crane waits to identify his central character, Henry Fleming, by full name; few have mentioned that, likewise, Hemingway does not disclose Lieutenant Henry's last name until Chapter V, and does not indicate the English spelling of the hero's first name anywhere in the book. Such anonymity is accidental in neither case. Both authors have deliberately subordinated their protagonists to setting in order to emphasize that, like all men in war, their heroes are victims of their surroundings.

Because of such subordination, critics often classify Henry Fleming and Frederick Henry as "passive heroes." Neither is strictly passive, however; both display, on occasion, considerable strength of purpose—distorted though their vision may sometimes be—and both are substantially more active and self-determined than their fellow characters. Perhaps we should call them "realistic" or "victimized" heroes. Private Fleming and Lieutenant Henry have been thrust into a world in which romantic and chivalric concepts no longer seem valid. Their disenchantment concerning such concepts is central to their problem of adjustment to the violence and disorder of war. In the place of Excalibur, they find themselves armed with little more than the fool's cap and bells. Worse, instead of slaying the dragon of evil, the would-be knight has yielded to and been assimilated by the monster; now he is no more than a minute cell within the loathsome serpent itself (note Crane's repeated use of the dragon metaphor in describing the two armies). And battles are fought not only between the forces of good and evil but between vast red-eyed monsters, henchmen for an even more terrifying "red animal—war, the blood-swollen god."

This is the thematic center of both novels: Henry Fleming and Lieutenant Henry are sufficiently sensible to realize that they are being victimized; yet, being idealists, they are ironically still seeking the grail. Each must adjust somehow to a terrible new world of repeated and unreasonable trauma which gives no meaning to his quest. And though this is the central meeting-point for the novels, it is also the point of divergence; for, in the manner of making their adjustments, Fleming and Henry take opposing directions.

For a clearer view of their problem we must examine closely the lives of the two protagonists (especially must we review the personal history of Frederick Henry to understand the reasons underlying the wide difference in their ultimate reactions to war). On the one hand, from beginning to end in *The Red Badge*, Henry Fleming is concerned obviously and deeply with the problem of violence and his reaction to it. He is, in fact, quite overshadowed by the problem. Long before Crane specifies his hero's role in the novel, he points out that Henry "wished to be alone with some new thoughts that had lately come to him," and "He tried mathematically to prove to himself that he could not run from a battle. . . . He felt that in this crisis his laws of life were useless. Whatever he had learned of himself was here of no avail. He was an unknown quantity." This, then, is the youth's first real contact with violence. Crane emphasizes again and again his protagonist's immaturity and na-ïveté: "From his home his youthful eyes had looked upon the war . . . [as] some sort of a play affair." We may infer that such immaturity is due partly to a minimum of suffering: Henry Fleming has led a normally pleasant and pro-tected childhood. The brief but revealing vignette of his mother, added to his own romantic illusions, substantiates this. Every homely allusion to "Ma" Fleming—her cow-milking, her potato-peeling, her sock-knitting—con-vinces us that her son has enjoyed a wholesome, secure home life. She is a wise and practical woman who knows her son much better than he knows himself. Realizing how much he has been shielded until now, she does her best to help him understand his predicament before he leaves home for the war:

"Young fellers in the army get awful careless in their ways, Henry. They're away f'm home and they don't have nobody to look after 'em. I'm 'feard fer yeh about that. Yeh never been used to doing for yourself. . . .

"Yeh must allus remember yer father, too, child, an' remember he never drunk a drop of likker in his life and seldom swore a cross oath."

Also, she tries gently to dispel some of his bloated sense of heroics, knowing that he must ultimately be disabused of them: "Yer jest one little feller an' do what they tell yeh. I know how you are, Henry." Although the youth pays little heed to her advice at the time, he is surely guided by the prudence of his upbringing toward a final resolution of his problem.

Lieutenant Henry has not been so fortunate in his rearing. At the begin-ning of *A Farewell to Arms* he is in several respects already more mature than Henry Fleming is at the end of *The Red Badge*. He is more self-con-trolled, more hardened to violence and cruelty, and less obviously imbued with a sense of heroics and a concern for his personal reaction to battle. The difference in years between his age and Henry Fleming's is not so signifi-cant as the difference in experience. Frederick Henry has had a premature initiation into the society of trauma and disorder. Little of his earlier personal history is disclosed in *A Farewell to Arms*, yet it is almost impossible to com-prehend and to justify his course of action in the novel without knowledge of his childhood and youth (this explains at least partially, I think, the confusing critical disagreements about Lieutenant Henry's character). Such knowledge is conveniently available in Hemingway's earlier portrait of his hero in *In Our Time*. Although the name of the protagonist is different—it is Nick Adams in the earlier work—little stretch of the imagination is required to see that, in essence, the two personalities are the same; the underlying tones of the two books, their themes, the problems confronting the main characters are virtually identical. Especially does the motif of "the separate peace" become more comprehensible when studied in reference to the traumatic baptism of Frederick Henry né Nick Adams in *In Our Time*. The first rites of this excruciating initiation ceremony are conducted in the story "Indian Camp." After being exposed to the horrors of a caesarian operation (performed by Dr. Adams without anesthesia) and the bloody suicide of the Indian woman's invalid husband, Nick asks his father a series of psychologically loaded questions:

> "Why did he kill himself, Daddy?"
> "I don't know, Nick. He couldn't stand things, I guess."
> "Do many men kill themselves, Daddy?"
> "Not very many, Nick."
> . . . .
> "Is dying hard, Daddy?"
> "No, I think it's pretty easy, Nick. It all depends."
> . . . .
> In the early morning on the lake sitting in the stern of the boat
> with his father rowing, he felt quite sure that he would never die.

The child's pathetic innocence in this scene is as touching as anything Hemingway has ever depicted. Nick's sensibility has been doubly violated: first, by his being subjected to an experience with which his young mind is not yet fitted to cope; second, by his father's ineptness in providing some kind of mitigation for the shock. The pathos heightens to tragedy in *A Farewell to Arms* because Lieutenant Henry has never received the "right answers." Unlike Henry Fleming's parents, those of the Hemingway hero have failed to ensure the stability so essential to his subsequent orientation into the multiple experiences of violence. As Frederick Hoffman has pointed out, "The protection given Nick by his parents is insufficient preparation for his move to the world outside, beyond the woods. There is something discernibly unsatisfactory about his mother's Christian Science and her cheerful evasiveness, and his father also proves to be an inadequate protector." The implication of parental inadequacy that recurs throughout *In Our Time* manifests itself subtly in *A Farewell to Arms* through Frederick's refusal to discuss his family with Catherine.

Thus has begun the formation of a kind of psychological and spiritual callus that continues to thicken as the Hemingway hero grows older. Conclusive evidence that it was there long before Frederick Henry went to Italy and joined the ambulance corps may be found in the stories "The End of Something" and "The Three Day Blow." In the latter Nick Adams reflects over the breaking off of the affair with his adolescent sweetheart: "The big thing was that Marjorie was gone and that probably he would never see her again. He had talked to her about how they would go to Italy together and the fun they would have. Places they would be together. It was all gone now. Something gone out of him." That "something gone out of" Nick Adams is to be peculiarly characteristic of the heroes of the great Hemingway trilogy. The stories from *In Our Time* serve to introduce and explain the character of Frederick Henry as he appears to us in *A Farewell to Arms*; also, they provide a context for examining the psychological and spiritual plight of Jake Barnes in *The Sun Also Rises*. Especially revealing, for example, is Chapter VII of *In Our Time*. Under bombardment at Fossalta, Nick prays desperately to Jesus that his life be spared, promising, " 'I believe in you and I'll tell everybody in the world that you are the only thing that matters.' " However, "The next night back at Mestre he did not tell the girl he went upstairs with at the Villa Rossa about Jesus. And he never told anybody." (Note, too, Nick's prayers and his fears of the dark in "Now I Lay Me" from *Men Without Women*.) At any rate, by the time Lieutenant Henry enters the war he has been initiated to the extent that he no longer fears his reaction to violence as Henry Fleming does; however, in the toughening process, his soul has accumulated much dead skin.

An understanding of the nature of this development is vital to an accurate explanation of the reactions of the two young men to war. For the similarities in their predicaments lead us to expect something less widely divergent than are their individual solutions. Henry Fleming has been called an "isolated protagonist." Likewise is Lieutenant Henry alone; more significantly, like Fleming, he is alone with his thoughts. His insistence that he was not made to think, that he fears thinking, serves merely to give weight to the implication that, not unlike Crane's youth, he is a sensitive, reflective individual and a "worrier" (Hemingway's critics too often take his hero's remarks about himself at face value without realizing that few "unthinking" persons are aware of thought's terrors). It is largely this penchant for reflectiveness which makes these two protagonists the outcasts that they are; it also sheds further light upon their common problem: though each is "trapped" within the group, neither is in the strictest sense an integral part of that group—

each is isolated in his sensibility. There is, however, an essential difference between their traps. Henry Fleming is caught in a kind of box (a "blue demonstration"): "He felt carried along by a mob . . . But he instantly saw that it would be impossible for him to escape from the regiment. It inclosed him. And there were iron laws of tradition and law on four sides. He was in a moving box. . . . It was all a trap. . . . They were all going to be sacrificed."

Crane's metaphor implies an order and pattern which must ultimately set a definite limit to Fleming's confusion. There is no such order in the design of Lieutenant Henry's trap. The absence of a defining limit or pattern increases the complexity of his predicament and the difficulty of making a satisfactory adjustment; it is this which finally prompts him to rebel completely and desert the Italian cause: "The killing came suddenly and unreasonably. . . . You had lost your cars and your men as a floorwalker loses the stock of his department in a fire. There was, however, no insurance. You were out of it now. You had no more obligation. If they shot floorwalkers after a fire in the department store because they spoke with an accent they had always had, then certainly the floorwalkers would not be expected to return when the store opened again for business." Had there been any semblance of order or of reasonableness, Lieutenant Henry might have returned to the war; but the initiation code had already taught him the futility of enduring additional pain or death when there was no discernible purpose in the sacrifice.

Conversely, because he still has a clear pattern to guide him, Henry Fleming can return to a path of normal adjustment after he has recovered from his initial disorienting shock. Virtually everything that happens to him in his flight from the battlefield (excepting his grimly humorous encounter with the squirrel) increases his conviction that, to find order out of chaos, he must return to the war as a participant. He cannot escape from the box with its deep grain of tradition. His communion with the dead man in the forest chapel, his observing of Jim Conklin's death rites, his conversation with the tattered soldier, his receiving of the token badge of courage, and, finally, his being led back to the regiment by the nameless good shepherd—all are part of the design of the box. His own perspective of pattern changes almost immediately upon his return to camp. He becomes ineradicably a part of the design. He, too, has been initiated into the fraternity of war, the "mysterious fraternity born of the smoke and danger of death," and with his acceptance of the group comes the relief of the prodigal come home: "He gave a long sigh, snuggled down into his blanket, and in a moment was like his comrades."

Just as Lieutenant Henry's being wounded, his plunge into the river, and his subsequent ride in the flat-car have all been explicated as various forms of death and rebirth, similarly Henry Fleming has emerged into a new world on the morning following his ordeal by terror. Paradoxically, however, the results of Fleming's baptism are very different from those of Lieutenant Henry's. Crane has made this quite clear: "A moral vindication was regarded by the youth as a very important thing." Henry Fleming's vindication began, somewhat hypocritically, with the infliction of his "little red badge of courage." It is virtually fulfilled when he proves himself a worthy member of the fraternity by becoming a real hero. As Arthur Hobson Quinn says, Fleming has been immersed in the "spiritual baptism of fire through which a man is purged of the original sin of cowardice." He is purged also of the immature sense of heroics which prompted his enlistment; he is given in its place a firmer grasp on the meaning of true heroism. Interestingly, he returns to a deep faith in those very abstractions so intensely abhorred by the Hemingway hero:

> He was emerged from his struggles with a large sympathy for the machinery of the universe. With his new eyes, he could see that the secret and open blows which were being dealt about the world with such heavenly lavishness were in truth blessings. It was a deity laying about him with the bludgeon of correction.
>
> His loud mouth against these things had been lost as the storm ceased. He could no more stand upon places high and false and denounce the distant planets. He beheld that he was tiny but not inconsequent to the sun. In the spacewide whirl of events no grain like him would be lost.

Frederick Henry is permitted no such consolation. The thickness of the spiritual callus precludes any such ethereal solace. For example, the contrast between Fleming's concept of the glory attached to "the red badge" and Lieutenant Henry's view is one of the most striking in the two works: "I had seen nothing sacred, and the things that were glorious had no glory and the sacrifices were like the stockyards at Chicago if nothing was done with the meat except to bury it." Unlike Henry Fleming, because he has been "initiated" some years before he receives his "unreasonable wound" at Plava, Lieutenant Henry is never able to return to any kind of secure faith—nor is he able to make any permanent adjustment to a society where such unreasonableness exists. Even after his flight from the war he feels that his solution is temporary and unsatisfactory: "There was no war here. . . . But I did have the feeling that it was really over. I had the feeling of a boy who thinks of what is happening at a certain hour at the schoolhouse from which he has played truant." And his desperate attempt to solve his problems by forming an isolated society of two with Catherine Barkley is the essence of pathos and tragedy. Through the entire Swiss idyll runs an undercurrent of terror, both

lovers sensing the transience of their happiness. The rains bring a culmi-
nation of trauma and chaos for Henry, with the shocking and "unreasonable"
deaths of Catherine and their child. The famous burning-ant metaphor provides a final startling contrast with Henry Fleming's regenerative insight at
the end of *The Red Badge*:

> Once in camp I put a log on top of the fire and it was full of
> ants. As it commenced to burn, the ants swarmed out and went
> first toward the centre where the fire was: then turned back and ran
> toward the end. When there were enough on the end they fell off into
> the fire. Some got out, their bodies burnt and flattened, and went
> off not knowing where they were going. But most of them went to-
> ward the fire and then back toward the end and swarmed on the
> cool end and finally fell off into the fire. I remember thinking at the
> time that it was the end of the world and a splendid chance to be a
> messiah and lift the log off the fire and throw it out where the ants
> could get off onto the ground. But I did not do anything but throw
> a tin cup of water on the log, so that I would have the cup empty to
> put whiskey in before I added water to it. I think the cup of water on
> the burning log only steamed the ants.

Contrary to Henry Fleming's final affirmation, Frederick Henry is left with
nothing at the conclusion of *A Farewell to Arms*—nothing, that is, except a
mass of third-degree psychological burns.

The failure of the Hemingway hero to find a spiritual remedy for the pain
of his wound moves us to pity and sympathy. Certainly his premature initiation to suffering and the lack of family security account considerably for his
inability to make a satisfactory adjustment, but the thing that disturbs us
most deeply is the implication of his dilemma as a universal one. In this respect the contrast between him and the Crane hero is especially instructive.
As I have pointed out, because he is able in the end to find his way back to
spiritual and psychological order, Henry Fleming is clearly representative as
a pre-twentieth-century literary protagonist; his final vision of pattern serves
to give him stature both in his own eyes and in ours. On the other hand, because he can find no order or "reasonableness" in his world—because he
has come to view idealism as no more than a "dirty word" and religion as no
more than "a stiff upper lip"—Frederick Henry is equally representative of
the contemporary fictional hero. As David Daiches describes this type, he
is a character "whose motives are prudential rather than selfless, or who
seeks safety rather than glory." Or, as Sean O'Faolain explains him (he uses
the term "anti-hero"), "Whatever he is, weak or brave, brainy or bewildered,
his one abiding characteristic is that, like his author-creator, he is never able

to see any Pattern in life and rarely its Destination." Perhaps the *reductio ad absurdum* of this type is to be seen in the writings of the Beat Generation. In any case, those of us who are concerned with the absence of spiritual direction in the modern novel may find consoling hope in this: *The Red Badge of Courage* followed *Maggie*, and *The Old Man and the Sea* came after *A Farewell to Arms*—just as the *Four Quartets* grew out of *The Waste Land*.

The Music
of *This* Sphere

Lewis Thomas

————————

It is one of our problems that as we become crowded together, the sounds we make to each other, in our increasingly complex communication systems, become more random-sounding, accidental or incidental, and we have trouble selecting meaningful signals out of the noise. One reason is, of course, that we do not seem able to restrict our communication to information-bearing, relevant signals. Given any new technology for transmitting information, we seem bound to use it for great quantities of small talk. We are only saved by music from being overwhelmed by nonsense.

It is a marginal comfort to know that the relatively new science of bio-acoustics must deal with similar problems in the sounds made by other animals to each other. No matter what sound-making device is placed at their disposal, creatures in general do a great deal of gabbling, and it requires long patience and observation to edit out the parts lacking syntax and

————————

sense. Light social conversation, designed to keep the party going, prevails. Nature abhors a long silence.

Somewhere, underlying all the other signals, is a continual music. Termites make percussive sounds to each other by beating their heads against the floor in the dark, resonating corridors of their nests. The sound has been described as resembling, to the human ear, sand falling on paper, but spectrographic analysis of sound records has recently revealed a high degree of organization in the drumming; the beats occur in regular, rhythmic phrases, differing in duration, like notes for a tympani section.

From time to time, certain termites make a convulsive movement of their mandibles to produce a loud, high-pitched clicking sound, audible ten meters off. So much effort goes into this one note that it must have urgent meaning, at least to the sender. He cannot make it without such a wrench that he is flung one or two centimeters into the air by the recoil.

There is obvious hazard in trying to assign a particular meaning to this special kind of sound, and problems like this exist throughout the field of bioacoustics. One can imagine a woolly-minded Visitor from Outer Space, interested in human beings, discerning on his spectograph the click of that golf ball on the surface of the moon, and trying to account for it as a call of warning (unlikely), a signal of mating (out of the question), or an announcement of territory (could be).

Bats are obliged to make sound almost ceaselessly, to sense, by sonar, all the objects in their surroundings. They can spot with accuracy, on the wing, small insects, and they will home onto things they like with infallibility and speed. With such a system for the equivalent of glancing around, they must live in a world of ultrasonic bat-sound, most of it with an industrial, machinery sound. Still, they communicate with other as well, by clicks and high-pitched greetings. Moreover, they have been heard to produce, while hanging at rest upside down in the depths of woods, strange, solitary, and lovely bell-like notes.

Almost anything that an animal can employ to make a sound is put to use. Drumming, created by beating the feet, is used by prairie hens, rabbits, and mice; the head is banged by woodpeckers and certain other birds; the males of deathwatch beetles make a rapid ticking sound by percussion of a protuberance on the abdomen against the ground; a faint but audible ticking is made by the tiny beetle Lepinotus inquilinus, which is less than two millimeters in length. Fish make sounds by clicking their teeth, blowing air, and drumming with special muscles against tuned inflated air bladders. Solid structures are set to vibrating by toothed bows in crustaceans and insects. The proboscis of the death's-head hawk moth is used as a kind of reed instrument, blown through to make high-pitched, reedy notes.

Gorillas beat their chests for certain kinds of discourse. Animals with loose skeletons rattle them, or, like rattlesnakes, get sounds from externally placed structures. Turtles, alligators, crocodiles, and even snakes make various more or less vocal sounds. Leeches have been heard to tap rhythmically on leaves, engaging the attention of other leeches, which tap back, in synchrony. Even earthworms make sounds, faint staccato notes in regular clusters. Toads sing to each other, and their friends sing back in antiphony.

Birdsong has been so much analyzed for its content of business communication that there seems little time left for music, but it is there. Behind the glossaries of warning calls, alarms, mating messages, pronouncements of territory, calls for recruitment, and demands for dispersal, there is redundant, elegant sound that is unaccountable as part of the working day. The thrush in my backyard sings down his nose in meditative, liquid runs of melody, over and over again, and I have the strongest impression that he does this for his own pleasure. Some of the time he seems to be practicing, like a virtuoso in his apartment. He starts a run, reaches a midpoint in the second bar where there should be a set of complex harmonics, stops, and goes back to begin over, dissatisfied. Sometimes he changes his notation so conspicuously that he seems to be improvising sets of variations. It is a meditative, questioning kind of music, and I cannot believe that he is simply saying, "thrush here."

The robin sings flexible songs, containing a variety of motifs that he rearranges to his liking; the notes in each motif constitute the syntax, and the possibilities for variation produce a considerable repertoire. The meadow lark, with three hundred notes to work with, arranges these in phrases of three to six notes and elaborates fifty types of song. The nightingale has twenty-four basic songs, but gains wild variety by varying the internal arrangement of phrases and the length of pauses. The chaffinch listens to other chaffinches, and incorporates into his memory snatches of their songs.

The need to make music, and to listen to it, is universally expressed by human beings. I cannot imagine, even in our most primitive times, the emergence of talented painters to make cave paintings without there having been, near at hand, equally creative people making song. It is, like speech, a dominant aspect of human biology.

The individual parts played by other instrumentalists—crickets or earthworms, for instance—may not have the sound of music by themselves, but we hear them out of context. If we could listen to them all at once, fully orchestrated, in their immense ensemble, we might become aware of the counterpoint, the balance of tones and timbres and harmonics, the sonorities. The recorded songs of the humpback whale, filled with tensions and resolutions, ambiguities and allusions, incomplete, can be listened to as a *part* of music, like an isolated section of an orchestra. If we had better hearing, and could discern the descants of sea birds, the rhythmic tympani of schools of mollusks, or even the distant harmonics of midges hanging over meadows in the sun, the combined sounds might lift us off our feet.

There are, of course, other ways to account for the songs of whales. They might be simple, down-to-earth statements about navigation, or sources of krill, or limits of territory. But the proof is not in, and until it is shown that these long, convoluted, insistent melodies, repeated by different singers with ornamentations of their own, are the means of sending through several hundred miles of undersea such ordinary information as "whale here," I shall believe otherwise. Now and again, in the intervals between songs, the whales have been seen to breach, leaping clear out of the sea and landing on their backs, awash in the turbulence of their beating flippers. Perhaps they are pleased by the way the piece went, or perhaps it is celebration at hearing one's own song returning after circumnavigation; whatever, it has the look of jubilation.

I suppose that my extraterrestrial Visitor might puzzle over my records in much the same way, on first listening. The 14th Quartet might, for him, be a communication announcing, "Beethoven here," answered, after passage through an undersea of time and submerged currents of human thought, by another long signal a century later, "Bartok here."

If, as I believe, the urge to make a kind of music is as much a characteristic of biology as our other fundamental functions, there ought to be an explanation for it. Having none at hand, I am free to make one up. The rhythmic sounds might be the recapitulation of something else—an earliest memory, a score for the transformation of inanimate, random matter in chaos into the improbable, ordered dance of living forms. Morowitz has presented the case, in thermodynamic terms, for the hypothesis that a steady flow of energy from the inexhaustible source of the sun to the unfillable sink of outer space, by way of the earth, is mathematically destined to cause the organization of matter into an increasingly ordered state. The resulting balancing act involves a ceaseless clustering of bonded atoms into molecules of higher and higher complexity, and the emergence of cycles for the storage and release of energy. In a nonequilibrium steady state, which is postulated, the solar energy would not just flow to the earth and radiate away; it is thermodynamically inevitable that it must rearrange matter into symmetry, away from probability, against entropy, lifting it, so to speak, into a.constantly changing condition of rearrangement and molecular ornamentation. In such a system, the outcome is a chancy kind of order, always on the verge of descending into chaos, held taut against probability by the unremitting, constant surge of energy from the sun.

If there were to be sounds to represent this process, they would have the arrangement of the Brandenburg Concertos for my ear, but I am open to wonder whether the same events are recalled by the rhythms of insects, the long, pulsing runs of birdsong, the descants of whales, the modulated vibrations of a million locusts in migration, the tympani of gorilla breasts, termite heads, drumfish bladders. A "grand canonical ensemble" is, oddly enough, the proper term for a quantitative model system in thermodynamics, borrowed from music by way of mathematics. Borrowed back again, provided with notation, it would do for what I have in mind.

Reflections
on Gandhi

George Orwell

Saints should always be judged guilty until they are proved innocent, but the tests that have to be applied to them are not, of course, the same in all cases. In Gandhi's case the questions one feels inclined to ask are: to what extent was Gandhi moved by vanity—by the consciousness of himself as a humble, naked old man, sitting on a praying-mat and shaking empires by sheer spiritual power—and to what extent did he compromise his own principles by entering into politics, which of their nature are inseparable from coercion and fraud? To give a definite answer one would have to study Gandhi's acts and writings in immense detail, for his whole life was a sort of pilgrimage in which every act was significant. But his partial autobiography, which ends in the nineteen-twenties, is strong evidence in his favor, all the more because it covers what he would have called the unregenerate part of his life and reminds one that inside the saint, or near-saint, there was a very shrewd, able person who could, if he had chosen, have been a brilliant success as a lawyer, an administrator or perhaps even a business man.

At about the time when the autobiography first appeared I remember reading its opening chapters in the ill-printed pages of some Indian newspaper. They made a good impression on me, which Gandhi himself, at that time, did not. The things that one associated with him—homespun cloth, "soul forces" and vegetarianism—were unappealing, and his medievalist program was obviously not viable in a backward, starving, over-populated country. It was also apparent that the British were making use of him, or thought they were making use of him. Strictly speaking, as a Nationalist, he was an enemy, but since in every crisis he would exert himself to prevent violence—which, from the British point of view, meant preventing any effective action whatever—he could be regarded as "our man." In private this was sometimes cynically admitted. The attitude of the Indian millionaires was similar. Gandhi called upon them to repent, and naturally they preferred him to the Socialists and Communists who, given the chance, would actually have taken their money away. How reliable such calculations are in the long run is doubtful; as Gandhi himself says, "in the end deceivers deceive only themselves"; but at any rate the gentleness with which he was nearly always handled was due partly to the feeling that he was useful. The British Conservatives only became really angry with him when, as in 1942, he was in effect turning his non-violence against a different conqueror.

But I could see even then that the British officials who spoke of him with a mixture of amusement and disapproval also genuinely liked and admired him, after a fashion. Nobody ever suggested that he was corrupt, or ambitious in any vulgar way, or that anything he did was actuated by fear or malice. In judging a man like Gandhi one seems instinctively to apply high standards, so that some of his virtues have passed almost unnoticed. For instance, it is clear even from the autobiography that his natural physical courage was quite outstanding: the manner of his death was a later illustration of this, for a public man who attached any value to his own skin would have been more adequately guarded. Again, he seems to have been quite free from that maniacal suspiciousness which, as E. M. Forster rightly says in *A Passage to India*, is the besetting Indian vice, as hypocrisy is the British vice. Although no doubt he was shrewd enough in detecting dishonesty, he seems wherever possible to have believed that other people were acting in good faith and had a better nature through which they could be approached. And though he came of a poor middle-class family, started life rather unfavorably, and was probably of unimpressive physical appearance, he was not afflicted by envy or by the feeling of inferiority. Color feeling, when he first met it in its worst form in South Africa, seems rather to have astonished him. Even when he was fighting what was in effect a color war, he did not think of people in terms of race or status. The governor of a province, a cotton millionaire, a half-starved Dravidian cooly, a British private soldier, were all equally human beings, to be approached in much the same way. It is noticeable that even in the worst possible circumstances, as in South Africa when he was making himself unpopular as the champion of the Indian community, he did not lack European friends.

Written in short lengths for newspaper serialization, the autobiography is not a literary masterpiece, but it is the more impressive because of the commonplaceness of much of its material. It is well to be reminded that Gandhi started out with the normal ambitions of a young Indian student and only adopted his extremist opinions by degrees and, in some cases, rather unwillingly. There was a time, it is interesting to learn, when he wore a top hat, took dancing lessons, studied French and Latin, went up the Eiffel Tower and even tried to learn the violin—all this with the idea of assimilating European civilization as thoroughly as possible. He was not one of those saints who are marked out by their phenomenal piety from childhood onwards, nor one of the other kind who forsake the world after sensational debaucheries. He makes full confession of the misdeeds of his youth, but in fact there is not much to confess. As a frontispiece to the book there is a photograph of Gandhi's possessions at the time of his death. The whole outfit could be purchased for about £ 5, and Gandhi's sins, at least his fleshly sins, would make the same sort of appearance if placed all in one heap. A few cigarettes, a few mouthfuls of meat, a few annas pilfered in childhood from the maidservant, two visits to a brothel (on each occasion he got away without "doing anything"), one narrowly escaped lapse with his landlady in Plymouth, one outburst of temper—that is about the whole collection. Almost from childhood onwards he had a deep earnestness, an attitude ethical rather than religious, but, until he was about thirty, no very definite sense of direction. His first entry into anything describable as public life was made by way of vegetarianism. Underneath his less ordinary qualities one feels all the time the solid middle-class business men who were his ancestors. One feels that even after he had abandoned personal ambition he must have been a resourceful, energetic lawyer and a hardheaded political organizer, careful in keeping down expenses, an adroit handler of committees and an indefatigable chaser of subscriptions. His character was an extraordinarily mixed one, but there was almost nothing in it that you can put your finger on and call bad, and I believe that even Gandhi's worst enemies would admit that he was an interesting and unusual man who enriched the world simply by being alive. Whether he was also a lovable man, and whether his teachings can have much value for those who do not accept the religious beliefs on which they are founded, I have never felt fully certain.

Of late years it has been the fashion to talk about Gandhi as though he were not only sympathetic to the Western leftwing movement, but were even integrally part of it. Anarchists and pacifists, in particular, have claimed him for their own, noticing only that he was opposed to centralism and State violence and ignoring the otherworldly, anti-humanist tendency of his doctrines. But one should, I think, realize that Gandhi's teachings cannot be squared with the belief that Man is the measure of all things and that our job is to make life worth living on this earth, which is the only earth we have. They make sense only on the assumption that God exists and that the world of solid objects is an illusion to be escaped from. It is worth considering the disciplines which Gandhi imposed on himself and which—though he might not insist on every one of his followers observing every detail—he considered indispensable if one wanted to serve either God or humanity. First of all, no meat-eating, and if possible no animal food in any form. (Gandhi himself, for the sake of his health, had to compromise on milk, but seems to have felt this to be a backsliding.) No alcohol or tobacco, and no spices or condiments, even of a vegetable kind, since food should be taken not for its own sake but solely in order to preserve one's strength. Secondly, if possible, no sexual intercourse. If sexual intercourse must happen, then it should be for the sole purpose of begetting children and presumably at long intervals. Gandhi himself, in his middle thirties, took the vow of *bramahcharya*, which means not only complete chastity but the elimination of sexual desire. This condition, it seems, is difficult to attain without a special diet and frequent fasting. One of the dangers of milk-drinking is that it is apt to arouse sexual desire. And finally—this is the cardinal point—for the seeker after goodness there must be no close friendships and no exclusive loves whatever.

Close friendships, Gandhi says, are dangerous, because "friends react on one another" and through loyalty to a friend one can be led into wrong-doing. This in unquestionably true. Moreover, if one is to love God, or to love humanity as a whole, one cannot give one's preference to any individual person. This again is true, and it marks the point at which the humanistic and the religious attitude cease to be reconcilable. To an ordinary human being, love means nothing if it does not mean loving some people more than others. The autobiography leaves it uncertain whether Gandhi behaved in an inconsiderate way to his wife and children, but at any rate it makes clear that on three occasions he was willing to let his wife or a child die rather than administer the animal food prescribed by the doctor. It is true that the threatened death never actually occurred, and also that Gandhi—with, one gathers, a good deal of moral pressure in the opposite direction—

always gave the patient the choice of staying alive at the price of committing a sin: still, if the decision had been solely his own, he would have forbidden the animal food, whatever the risks might be. There must, he says, be some limit to what we will do in order to remain alive, and the limit is well on this side of chicken broth. This attitude is perhaps a noble one, but, in the sense which—I think—most people would give to the word, it is inhuman. The essence of being human is that one does not seek perfection, that one *is* sometimes willing to commit sins for the sake of loyalty, that one does not push asceticism to the point where it makes friendly intercourse impossible, and that one is prepared in the end to be defeated and broken up by life, which is the inevitable price of fastening one's love upon other human individuals. No doubt alcohol, tobacco and so forth are things that a saint must avoid, but sainthood is also a thing that human beings must avoid. There is an obvious retort to this, but one should be wary about making it. In this yogi-ridden age, it is too readily assumed that "non-attachment" is not only better than a full acceptance of earthly life, but that the ordinary man only rejects it because it is too difficult: in other words, that the average human being is a failed saint. It is doubtful whether this is true. Many people genuinely do not wish to be saints, and it is probable that some who achieve or aspire to sainthood have never felt much temptation to be human beings. If one could follow it to its psychological roots, one would, I believe, find that the main motive for "non-attachment" is a desire to escape from the pain of living, and above all from love, which, sexual or non-sexual, is hard work. But it is not necessary here to argue whether the otherworldly or the humanistic idea is "higher." The point is that they are incompatible. One must choose between God and Man, and all "radicals" and "progressives," from the mildest Liberal to the most extreme Anarchist, have in effect chosen Man.

However, Gandhi's pacifism can be separated to some extent from his other teachings. Its motive was religious, but he claimed also for it that it was a definite technique, a method, capable of producing desired political results. Gandhi's attitude was not that of most Western pacifists. *Satyagraha*, first evolved in South Africa, was a sort of non-violent warfare, a way of defeating the enemy without hurting him and without feeling or arousing hatred. It entailed such things as civil disobedience, strikes, lying down in front of railway trains, enduring police charges without running away and without hitting back, and the like. Gandhi objected to "passive resistance" as a translation of *Satyagraha*: in Gujarati, it seems, the word means "firmness in the truth." In his early days Gandhi served as a stretcher-bearer on the British side in the Boer War, and he was prepared to do the same again in the war of 1914-18. Even after he had completely abjured violence he was honest enough to see that in war it is usually necessary to take sides. He did not—indeed, since his whole political life centered round a struggle for national independence, he could not—take the sterile and dishonest line of pretending that in every war both sides are exactly the same and it makes no difference who wins. Nor did he, like most Western pacifists, specialize in avoiding awkward questions. In relation to the late war, one question that every pacifist had a clear obligation to answer was: "What about the Jews? Are you prepared to see them exterminated? If not, how do you propose to save them without resorting to war?" I must say that I have never heard, from any Western pacifist, an honest answer to this question, though I have heard plenty of evasions, usually of the "you're another" type. But it so happens that Gandhi was asked a somewhat similar question in 1938 and that his answer is on record in Mr. Louis Fischer's *Gandhi and Stalin*. According to Mr. Fischer, Gandhi's view was that the German Jews ought to commit collective suicide, which "would have aroused the world and the people of Germany to Hitler's violence." After the war he justified himself: the Jews had been killed anyway, and might as well have died significantly. One has the impression that this attitude staggered even so warm an admirer as Mr. Fischer, but Gandhi was merely being honest. If you are not prepared to take life, you must often be prepared for lives to be lost in some other way. When, in 1942, he urged non-violent resistance against a Japanese invasion, he was ready to admit that it might cost several million deaths.

At the same time there is reason to think that Gandhi, who after all was born in 1869, did not understand the nature of totalitarianism and saw everything in terms of his own struggle against the British government. The important point here is not so much that the British treated him forbearingly as that he was always able to command publicity. As can be seen from the phrase quoted above, he believed in "arousing the world," which is only possible if the world gets a chance to hear what you are doing. It is difficult to see how Gandhi's methods could be applied in a country where opponents of the regime disappear in the middle of the night and are never heard of again. Without a free press and the right of assembly, it is impossible not merely to appeal to outside opinion, but to bring a mass movement into being, or even to make your intentions known to your adversary. Is there a Gandhi in Russia at this moment? And if there is, what is he accomplishing? The Russian masses could only practice civil disobedience if the same idea happened to occur to all of them simultaneously, and even then, to judge by the history of the Ukraine famine, it would make no difference. But let it be granted that non-violent resistance can be effective against one's own government, or against an occupying power: even so, how does one put it into practice internationally? Gandhi's various conflicting statements on the late war seem to show that he felt the difficulty of this. Applied to foreign politics, pacifism either stops being pacifist or becomes appeasement. Moreover the assumption, which served Gandhi so well in dealing with individuals, that all human beings are more or less approachable and will respond to a generous gesture, needs to be seriously questioned. It is not necessarily true, for example, when you are dealing with lunatics. Then the question becomes: Who is sane? Was Hitler sane? And is it not possible for one whole culture to be insane by the standards of another? And, so far as one can gauge the feelings of whole nations, is there any apparent connection between a generous deed and a friendly response? Is gratitude a factor in international politics?

These and kindred questions need discussion, and need it urgently, in the few years left to us before somebody presses the button and the rockets begin to fly. It seems doubtful whether civilization can stand another major war, and it is at least thinkable that the way out lies through non-violence. It is Gandhi's virtue that he would have been ready to give honest consideration to the kind of question that I have raised above; and, indeed, he probably did discuss most of these questions somewhere or other in his innumerable newspaper articles. One feels of him that there was much that he did not understand, but not that there was anything that he was frightened of saying or thinking. I have never been able to feel much liking for Gandhi, but I do not feel sure that as a political thinker he was wrong in the main, nor do I believe that his life was a failure. It is curious that when he was assassinated, many of his warmest admirers exclaimed sorrowfully that he had lived just long enough to see his life work in ruins, because India was engaged in a civil war which had always been foreseen as one of the by-products of the transfer of power. But it was not in trying to smooth down Hindu-Moslem rivalry that Gandhi had spent his life. His main political objective, the peaceful ending of British rule, had after all been attained. As usual, the relevant facts cut across one another. On the one hand, the British did get out of India without fighting, an event which very few observers indeed would have predicted until about a year before it happened. On the other hand, this was done by a Labor government, and it is certain that a Conservative government, especially a government headed by Churchill, would have acted differently. But if, by 1945, there had grown up in Britain a large body of opinion sympathetic to Indian independence, how far was this due to Gandhi's personal influence? And if, as it may happen, India and Britain finally settle down into a decent and friendly relationship, will this be partly because Gandhi, by keeping up his struggle obstinately and without hatred, disinfected the political air? That one even thinks of asking such questions indicates his stature. One may feel, as I do, a sort of aesthetic distaste for Gandhi, one may reject the claims of sainthood made on his behalf (he never made any such claim himself, by the way), one may also reject sainthood as an ideal and therefore feel that Gandhi's basic aims were anti-human and reactionary: but regarded simply as a politician, and compared with the other leading political figures of our time, how clean a smell he has managed to leave behind!

Preface
to a Book of Statistics

Don Marquis

Statistics have always pleased us. They thrill us. There is something romantic about them. They scratch and tickle our imagination till it wakes and yodels. A fact is a fact; an idea is merely an idea. Facts and ideas move on prescribed planes from which they cannot escape. But statistics do not necessarily have any close connection with either facts or ideas.

At will they skip over the boundary into a sort of fourth dimensional land. And there they dance like the motes one sees if one stares at the wind long enough so that the little veins in one's eyes become congested with blood corpuscles. There is always the doubt as to whether the little motes are really flickering and dancing up and down a slanting current of sunlit air or whether they are in the eyes. This doubt makes it a charming occupation to sit and watch them gambol on spring mornings when one should be at work.

It is so with statistics; we like to wonder about them; we look at them and thrill and speculate and doubt and conjecture. But it is no joy to us to know what statistics are about. We do not wish to have them tied down to any specific subject. We love to see them dart and frolic through the pages of great tomes just for the sake of the dance itself.

When we discover that during the first six months of 1912 the United States of America exported 1,395,683, we do not care to know 1,395,683 *what*. It might be codfish, it might be pigs of iron; but what is that to us? Definiteness stops the dance; it gives us images too bold and concrete; it robs us of the fancy of 1,395,683 little motes whirling and swarming as they rise from the coast and fly out across the Atlantic with a pleasant whir and hum of multitudinous wings.

As these 1,395,683 approach the Gulf Stream perhaps they meet 2,965,355 of imports coming westward. It would only ruin the picture if we knew 2,965,355 *what*. It would give us something to think about; we might become convinced of the plausibility of someone's economic theory, perhaps, and our day would be spoiled.

Statistics, for us, fall naturally into various colors. For instance, 7,377,777, whether it stands for imports or exports, is undoubtedly red. But 1,019,901 is a pale, light, cool, grayish blue. And can any one doubt that 525,555,555,555 is of a bright aggressive yellow color, and gives off a high pitched note from the rapid motion of its myriad pinions? There is something querulous and peevish and impatient about 525,555,555,555, too; we shall not admit it into the volume of statistics which we are compiling.

Hitherto there has been a science of statistics, but no art. That is, no avowed art. We suspect that certain advanced statisticians really approach the subject as we do, joyfully and all unshackled. But they pretend to be staid and dry and sober. They have respectable positions in the community to maintain. After compiling several pages of statistics full of sound and color, just for the sheer glee of reveling in sensation, they become cowards and conceal their glee; they write industrial and financial and sociological articles around their lovely tables and twist them into proving something important. They conceal their art, they muffle and smother their finer impulses beneath a repellent cloak of science. They are afraid that their toys will be taken away from them if they play with them frankly, so they affect some sort of useful employment.

We remember reading somewhere, and it was cited as an example of the mental twilight of the Middle Ages, that learned clerks and doctors were accustomed to debate the question as to how many angels could stand on the point of a needle. But these medieval disputants were not stupid at all. They were quite right to be interested in such things. They were wise enough to divorce statistics from reality utterly. Things of every sort—all the arts and philosophies—suffer today because we insist on connecting them with a trivial reality. We try to make them prove something. We try to set them to work. And definite proofs will always be tiresome, and work a thing to be escaped. People are not really enthusiastic about having things proved to them, or about working; they want to have a good time. And they are quite right, too.

Once, in a country town, we heard one of the village loafers make a remark concerning a storekeeper that we have always remembered; it seems to fit in here. It was the custom, in winter time at least, to set a cigar box full of smoking tobacco on the counter near the stove, and those who came in to rest and get warm and wonder if it would be a late spring and tell smutty stories and fry their felt boots before the fire helped themselves to this tobacco without money and without price. The box was always referred to as "the paupers' box." One Mr. Dash, a merchant, put a stop to the paupers' box in his store. Joe Blank, who had been filling his pipe from it for twenty years, arose and remarked from the depths of his outraged being:

"Hennery Dash, your soul is so small that if they was millions and millions of souls the size of yourn put into a flea's belly them souls would be so far apart they couldn't hear each other if they was to holler."

Joe had the mind of a poet. A bungler would have said exactly how many millions of souls, would have stated their exact size and told just how far apart they were; but Joe left it vague and vast and infinitely small. A scientist would have said too much and spoiled it; not so the artist.

Statisticians deal with precious, intangible stuff, with the flecks and atomies of faery—and how few of them dare rise to the full possibilities of their medium! They are merely foolish when they might so readily achieve insanity if they had but the courage to be themselves.

There are, for instance, 1,345 statisticians in this land who would know, if they were laid end to end, that 4,988,898,888 is green in color, a deep, dark green. Yet they are all afraid to stand forth like men and say so; they are afraid of what people will think of them. They are obsessed with the belief that materials are significant, without stopping to reflect that, even were this so, significance would still remain immaterial.

And even now we feel a chill of fear creeping over us—we dare not keep on in this vein any longer or someone will catch us and make a circulation manager for a newspaper out of us.

Which

James Thurber

The relative pronoun "which" can cause more trouble than any other word, if recklessly used. Foolhardy persons sometimes get lost in which-clauses and are never heard of again. My distinguished contemporary, Fowler, cites several tragic cases, of which the following is one: "It was rumored that Beaconsfield intended opening the Conference with a speech in French, his pronunciation of which language leaving everything to be desired . . ." That's as much as Mr. Fowler quotes because, at his age, he was afraid to go any farther. The young man who originally got into that sentence was never found. His fate, however, was not as terrible as that of another adventurer who became involved in a remarkable which-mire. Fowler has followed his devious course as far as he safely could on foot: "Surely what applies to games should also apply to racing, the leaders of which being the very people from whom an example might well be looked for . . ." Not even Henry James could have successfully emerged from a sentence with "which," "whom," and "being" in it. The safest way to avoid such things is to follow in the path of the American author, Ernest Hemingway. In his youth

-----

he was trapped in a which-clause one time and barely escaped with his mind. He was going along on solid ground until he got into this: "It was the one thing of which, being very much afraid—for whom has not been warned to fear such things—he . . ." Being a young and powerfully built man, Hemingway was able to fight his way back to where he had started, and begin again. This time he skirted the treacherous morass in this way: "He was afraid of one thing. This was the one thing. He had been warned to fear such things. Everybody has been warned to fear such things." Today Hemingway is alive and well, and many happy writers are following along the trail he blazed.

What most people don't realize is that one "which" leads to another. Trying to cross a paragraph by leaping from "which" to "which" is like Eliza crossing the ice. The danger is in missing a "which" and falling in. A case in point is this: "He went up to a pew which was in the gallery, which brought him under a colored window which he loved and always quieted his spirit." The writer, worn out, missed the last "which"—the one that should come just before "always" in that sentence. But supposing he had got it in! We would have: "He went up to a pew which was in the gallery, which brought him under a colored window which he loved and which always quieted his spirit." Your inveterate whicher in this way gives the effect of tweeting like a bird or walking with a crutch, and is not welcome in the best company.

It is well to remember that one "which" leads to two and that two "whiches" multiply like rabbits. You should never start out with the idea that you can get by with one "which." Suddenly they are all around you. Take a sentence like this: "It imposes a problem which we either solve, or perish." On a hot night, or after a hard day's work, a man often lets himself get by with a monstrosity like that, but suppose he dictates that sentence bright and early in the morning. It comes to him typed out by his stenographer and he instantly senses that something is the matter with it. He tries to reconstruct the sentence, still clinging to the "which," and gets something like this: "It imposes a problem which we either solve, or which, failing to solve, we must perish on account of." He goes to the water-cooler, gets a drink, sharpens his pencil, and grimly tries again. "It imposes a problem which we either solve or which we don't solve and . . ." He begins once more: "It imposes a problem which we either solve, or which we do not solve, and from which . . ." The more times he does it the more "whiches" he gets. The way out is simple: "We must either solve this problem, or perish." Never monkey with "which." Nothing except getting tangled up in a typewriter ribbon is worse.

What's a Mother For But to Suffer?

Erma Bombeck

Of all the emotions enjoyed by a mother, none makes her feel as wonderfully ignoble as her "What's a Mother For But to Suffer?" period.

It doesn't happen in a day, of course. She has to build up to it through a series of self-inflicted tongue wounds. She observes, for example, "I could be Joan of Arc with the flames licking around my ankles, and Harlow would roast marshmallows." Or, "If I were on the *Titanic* and there was only one seat left in the lifeboat, Merrill would race me for it." Finally, at the peak of her distress, she will sum up her plight thusly, "I could be lying dead in the street and Evelyn would eat a peanut butter sandwich over me."

The image of her own sacrifice and thankless devotion to motherhood grows and grows until finally she is personified in every little old lady who scrubs floors at night to send a son through law school to every snaggle-toothed hag who sells violets in the snow.

Outwardly most women are ashamed of this emotion. They are loathe to admit that a small child, born of love, weaned on innocence, and nurtured with such gentleness could frustrate them to such cornball theatrics. They blame society, the educational system, the government, their mother, their obstetrician, their husband, and Ethel Kennedy for not telling them what motherhood was all about. They weren't prepared and they're probably bungling the whole process of childrearing.

They just took a few of "what Mother always saids" and stirred in a generous portion of "what Daddy always dids" and said a fervent prayer that the kids didn't steal hubcaps while they were trying to figure out what they were going to do.

I've always blamed my shortcomings as a mother on the fact that I studied Child Psychology and Discipline under an unmarried professor whose only experience was in raising a dog. He obviously saw little difference.

At the age of two, my children could fetch and I'd reward them with a biscuit. At the age of four, they could sit, heel, or stay just by listening to the inflection in my voice. They were paper trained by the age of five. It was then that I noted a difference between their aims and goals and mine. So I put away my Child Psychology and Discipline volume and substituted a dog-eared copy of *Crime and Punishment*. I am now the only mother on the block who reaches out to kiss her children and has them flinch and threaten to call their attorneys if I so much as lay a finger on them.

Then a friend told me she had a solution that worked pretty well. It was "Wait until your father gets home." This seemed to be working for me, too. It certainly took away the "acid stomach condition" that had been so bothersome. But one afternoon I heard the children making plans to either give Daddy up for Lent or lend him to a needy boy at Christmas and I felt a twinge of conscience.

We talked it over—their father and I—and finally conceded child-raising was a two-headed job, literally speaking. We would have to share the responsibilities. We have a list of blunders that span Diana Dors twice, not the least being our stab at sex education.

The sex education of a child is a delicate thing. None of us wants to "blow it." I always had a horror of ending up like the woman in the old joke who was asked by her child where he came from and after she explained the technical process in a well-chosen medical vocabulary, he looked at her intently and said, "I just wondered. Mike came from Hartford, Connecticut."

My husband and I talked about it and we figured what better way to explain the beautiful reproduction cycle of life than through the animal kingdom. We bought two pairs of guppies and a small aquarium. We should have bought two pairs of guppies and a small reservoir. Our breakfast conversation eventually assumed a pattern.

"What's new at Peyton Place by the Sea?" my husband would inquire.

"Mrs. Guppy is e-n-c-e-i-n-t-e again," I'd say.

"Put a little salt in the water. That'll cure anything," he mumbled.

"Daddy," said our son. "That means she's pregnant!"

"Again!" Daddy choked. "Can't we organize an intramural volleyball team in there or something?"

The first aquarium begat a second aquarium with no relief in sight.

"Are you getting anything out of your experience with guppies?" I asked my son delicately one afternoon. "Oh yeah," he said, "They're neat."

"I mean, have you watched the male and the female? Do you understand the processes that go into the offspring? The role of the mother in all this?"

"Oh sure," he said. "Listen, how did you know which one of your babies to eat when they were born?"

We added a third aquarium which was promptly filled with salt water and three pairs of sea horses.

"Now, I want you to pay special attention to the female," I instructed. "The chances are it won't take her long to be with child and perhaps you can see her actually give birth."

"The female doesn't give birth, Mom," said my son peeling a banana. (I felt myself smiling, anticipating a trend.) "Ridiculous," I said. "Females always give birth." The male began to take on weight. I thought I saw his ankles swell. He became a mother on the twenty-third of the month.

"That's pretty interesting," observed my son. "I hope when I become a mother, it's on land. I can't tread water that long."

We blew it. We figured we would.

If you want to know the truth, we haven't made out too well in the problem of sibling rivalry either. I think the rumor is that more parents have been driven out of their skulls by sibling rivalry than any other behavior phase. I started the rumor.

In infancy, it's a series of small things. Big sister will stuff a whole banana in the mouth of baby brother with the threat, "Shut your mouth, baby, or out you go." Or big brother will slap his toddler sister off her hobby horse with the reprimand, "Keep that squeak on your side of the room." It eventually reaches a point where they are measuring their cut of meat with a micrometer to see they are getting their fair share as set down by the Geneva Convention, and being represented by legal counsel to see who gets the fruit cocktail with the cherry on top.

The rivalry of each day, however, seems to culminate at the dinner table.

SON: She's doing it again.

FATHER: Doing what?

SON: Humming.

DAUGHTER: I am not humming.

SON: You are so. There, she did it again, Dad. Watch her neck. She's humming so no one can hear her but me. She does it all the time just to make fun of me.

FATHER: I can't hear anything. Eat your dinner.

SON: How come *he* got the bone?

FATHER: What difference does it make? There's no meat on the bone, anyway.

OTHER SON: Then how come *he* got the meat? I got stuck with the bone the last time.

DAUGHTER: I got dibs on the last black olive. *You* got the ice cube in your water after school and *you* got the bike for your birthday, so I get the black olive.

FATHER: What kind of logic is that! I swear it's like eating with the mafia. (*Turning to Mother*) How can you sit there and listen to all this drivel?

MOTHER: I'm under sedation.

This seemed to be the answer until recently, when some dear friends of ours confided in us that they had all but solved their sibling rivalry problems at the dinner table. We listened to them talk of peace, love, and tranquility throughout the meal by engaging in a new game called Category. It worked very simply. Each member of the family was allowed one night at the table where he alone named the Category and led that particular discussion. Hence, everyone had a chance to speak and sooner or later each child could talk about something that interested him.

I had to admit, Category sounded like a better game than we were playing at present called Trials at Nuremberg. This also worked rather simply. We would wait until we were all assembled at the table, then right after the prayer we'd confront the children with crimes they had committed in their playpens up to the present day. We'd touch upon bad manners, bicycles in the driveway, socks under the bed, goofing around with the garbage detail, throwing away their allowances on paraffin teeth and anything else we could document. By the time we reached dessert, we usually had a couple of them sobbing uncontrollably into their mashed potatoes, begging to be sent to an orphanage. We decided to give Category a try.

"Tonight, I'm going to talk about 'Friends,' " said our older son.

"Don't talk with food in your mouth," amended his father.

He swallowed and continued, "My very best, first choice, A-1 top of the list, first class, Cadillac of a friend is Charlie."

"Charlie who?" someone interrupted.

"I don't know his last name," he shrugged. "Just Charlie."

"Well, good grief," I sighed. "You'd certainly think if you had a big, fat Damon and Pythias relationship with a real, live friend you'd get around to last names."

"Who's Damon and Pythias?" asked a small voice.

"Aw, come one," said the speaker. "It's not your turn until tomorrow night. Anyway, today my best friend, Charlie, threw up in school—"

"*Mother*!" screamed a voice. "Do I have to sit here and listen to stories about Charlie up-chucking?"

"Tell us about another friend, son," pleaded his father.

He continued. "Well, my second best B-2, second from the top of the list, Oldsmobile of a friend is Scott. Today Scott went after the janitor to bring the bucket when Charlie threw up and—"

"Please!" the entire table groaned.

"Well, it's my category," he insisted, "and they're my friends. If I have to sit and listen to you talk about your junk, you can listen to me."

"I wish Charlie were here to eat these cold mashed potatoes."

"Yeah, well, when it's your turn to talk I'm going to hum."

"All right, kids," interrupted their father. "While we're on the subject of cold mashed potatoes, who left the red bicycle right in the middle of the driveway tonight? And, as long as we're all together, which one of you lost the nozzle off the garden hose? (*Aside*) Hold up the dessert, Mother, I've got a few things to discuss. Now, about the telephone. I'm getting a little sick and tired of having to shinny up the pole every time I want to call out. . . ."

Very frankly, I don't feel the problem of sibling rivalry will ever be worked out in our time. Especially after reading a recent survey taken among brothers and sisters as to what they liked or disliked about one another. These were some of the reasons for their contempt of one another. "He's my brother." "She says hello to me in front of my friends." "She's a girl." "He's always hanging around the house when I'm there." "She acts big and up-pity." "She's a sloppy beast." "He knows everything." Only one brother said something nice about his sister. He wrote, "Sometimes when she takes a bath, she uses a neat deodorant." I ask you, how are you going to build a quiet meal around that!

The second-largest problem to parents is status. It changes from year to year, beginning with "I'm five years old and *my* mama lets me stay up to watch the late, late show," to "I'm in the sixth grade too and I'm listed in the phone book under my own name."

It gets pretty ridiculous, of course, but it's just another hairshirt in a mother's wardrobe. Another challenge for a mother who must make a decision not to measure her own children's happiness with another mother's yardstick. Just last month, I heard that the latest status symbol around the bridge table is children's dental work. Wild? Not really. The more fillings, the more space maintainers, the more braces, the more status. If the orthodontist says your kid has a bite problem, lady, you're in.

Here's a conversation I overheard illustrating the point.

"You talk about dental work," said a small blonde. "Come here, George. Open your mouth, George." The lights danced on George's metal-filled mouth like Ali Baba's cave. "That," she said emphatically, "is my mink stole. A mother's sacrifice. And is he grateful? He is not."

"Think nothing of it," said her companion. "Come over here, Marcia. Let the lady look at your braces." Marcia mechanically threw back her head and opened wide. The inside of her mouth looked like it was set to go off. "That," she said, "is my trip to Europe. What do you think of that?"

"I think we worry to much about them," said the first one. "Always nagging. 'Brush your teeth, don't eat sweets.' I mean we can't run around after them like those hags on television, can we?"

"Wait till you see what I'm buying George for his mouth this month," the blonde confided. "You'll be dumbfounded. It's very new and expensive and I understand there aren't a half dozen people who have them in their mouths yet. George and I will be one of the first."

"What is it?" asked the first one breathlessly.

"Promise you won't tell anyone?" (*Hushed tone*) "It's a telltale tooth."

"A telltale tooth?"

"Right. They cram six miniature transmitters, twenty-eight other electrical components, and two rechargeable batteries into what looks like an ordinary 'bridge' of a first molar. Then, as they chew, the telltale tooth broadcasts a stream of information to the dentist that tells what the child has eaten and what is causing the breakdown of his teeth."

"A fink tooth! Well, I'll be. I think I'll get one of those for Marcia. Maybe we could hook up her transistor to it and do away with that wire coming out of her ear. Then the music could come from her teeth. Wouldn't that give the kids in her class a jolt!"

"Well, I thought I'd get an antenna for George's. Then maybe he could hook up to that Early Bird channel from Telstar and draw in something from overseas."

"There goes that patio cover you were saving for—but then, what's a mother for, but to sweat in the hot sun."

A mother's suffering—a privilege or a put-upon? Who knows. I only know that when you can no longer evoke any empathy from your children with it, then you must take a firm stance, throw back your head, look determined, and as my old Child Psychology professor advised, "Pull up hard on the leash!"

Old China

Charles Lamb

———————

I have an almost feminine partiality for old china. When I go to see any great house, I inquire for the china-closet, and next for the picture-gallery. I cannot defend the order of preference, but by saying that we have all some taste or other, of too ancient a date to admit of our remembering distinctly that it was an acquired one. I can call to mind the first play, and the first exhibition, that I was taken to; but I am not conscious of a time when china jars and saucers were introduced into my imagination.

I had no repugnance then—why should I now have?—to those little, lawless, azure-tinctured grotesques, that under the notion of men and women, float about, uncircumscribed by any element, in that world before perspective—a china tea cup.

I like to see my old friends—whom distance cannot diminish—figuring up in the air (so they appear to our optics), yet on *terra firma* still—for so we must in courtesy interpret that speck of deeper blue, which the decorous artist, to prevent absurdity, had made to spring up beneath their sandals.

I love the men with women's faces, and the women, if possible, with still more womanish expressions.

Here is a young and courtly Mandarin, handing tea to a lady from a salver—two miles off. See how distance seems to set off respect! And here the same lady, or another—for likeness is identity on tea-cups—is stepping into a little fairy boat, moored on the hither side of this calm garden river, with a dainty mincing foot, which in a right angle of incidence (as angles go in our world) must infallibly land her in the midst of a flowery mead—a furlong off on the other side of the same strange stream!

Farther on—if far or near can be predicated of their world—see horses, trees, pagodas, dancing the hays.

Here—a cow and rabbit couchant, and co-extensive—so objects show, seen through the lucid atmosphere of fine Cathay.

I was pointing out to my cousin last evening, over our Hyson, (which we are old fashioned enough to drink unmixed still of an afternoon) some of these *speciosa miracula* upon a set of extraordinary old blue china (a recent purchase) which we were now for the first time using; and could not help remarking how favourable circumstances had been to us of late years, that we could afford to please the eye sometimes with trifles of this sort—when a passing sentiment seemed to overshade the brows of my companion. I am quick at detecting these summer clouds in Bridget.

"I wish the good old times would come again," she said, "when we were not quite so rich. I do not mean that I want to be poor; but there was a middle state"—so she was pleased to ramble on,—"in which I am sure we were a great deal happier. A purchase is but a purchase, now that you have money enough and to spare. Formerly it used to be a triumph. When we coveted a cheap luxury (and, O!, how much ado I had to get you to consent in those times!)—we were used to have a debate two or three days before, and to weigh the for and against, and think what we might spare it out of, and what saving we could hit upon, that should be an equivalent. A thing was worth buying then, when we felt the money that we paid for it.

"Do you remember the brown suit, which you made to hang upon you, till all your friends cried shame upon you, it grew so thread-bare—and all because of that folio Beaumont and Fletcher, which you dragged home late at night from Barker's in Covent Garden? Do you remember how we eyed it for weeks before we could make up our minds to the purchase, and had not come to a determination till it was near ten o'clock of the Saturday night, when you set off from Islington, fearing you should be too late—and when the old bookseller with some grumbling opened his shop, and by the twinkling taper (for he was setting bedwards) lighted out the relic from his dusty treasures—and when you lugged it home, wishing it were twice as cumbersome—and when you presented it to me—and when we were exploring the perfectness of it (*collating* you called it)—and while I was repairing some of the loose leaves with paste, which your impatience would not suffer to be left till daybreak—was there no pleasure in being a poor man? Or can those neat black clothes which you wear now, and are so careful to keep brushed, since we have become rich and finical, give you half the honest vanity, with which you flaunted it about in that overworn suit—your old cor-beau—for four or five weeks longer than you should have done, to pacify your conscience for the mighty sum of fifteen—or sixteen shillings was it?—a great affair we thought it then—which you had lavished on the old folio. Now you can afford to buy any book that pleases you, but I do not see that you ever bring me home any nice old purchases now.

"When you came home with twenty apologies for laying out a less num-ber of shillings upon that print after Leonardo, which we christened the *Lady Blanch*; when you looked at the purchase, and thought of the money—and thought of the money, and looked again at the picture—was there no plea-sure in being a poor man? Now, you have nothing to do but to walk into Col-naghi's, and buy a wilderness of Leonardos. Yet do you?

"Then, do you remember our pleasant walks to Enfield, and Potter's Bar, and Waltham, when we had a holiday—holidays, and all other fun, are gone, now we are rich—and the little hand-basket in which I used to deposit our day's fare of savoury cold lamb and salad—and how you would pry about at noontime for some decent house, were we might go in, and produce our store—only paying for the ale that you must call for—and speculate upon the looks of the landlady, and whether she was likely to allow us a table-cloth—and wish for such another honest hostess, as Izaak Walton has de-scribed many a one on the pleasant banks of the Lea, when he went a-fish-ing—and sometimes they would prove obliging enough, and sometimes they would look grudgingly upon us—but we had cheerful looks still for one another, and would eat our plain food savourily, scarcely grudging Piscator his Trout Hall? Now, when we go out a day's pleasuring, which is seldom moreover, we ride part of the way—and go into a fine inn, and order the best of dinners, never debating the expense—which, after all, never has half the relish of those chance country snaps, when we were at the mercy of uncer-tain usage, and a precarious welcome.

"You are too proud to see a play anywhere now but in the pit. Do you remember where it was we used to sit, when we saw the *Battle of Hexham*, and the *Surrender of Calais*, and Bannister and Mrs. Bland in the *Children in the Wood*—when we squeezed out our shillings a-piece to sit three or four times in a season in the one-shilling gallery—where you felt all the time that you ought not to have brought me—and more strongly I felt obligation to you for having brought me—and the pleasure was the better for a little shame—and when the curtain drew up, what cared we for our place in the house, or what mattered it where we were sitting, when our thoughts were with Rosalind in Arden, or with Viola at the Court of Illyria? You used to say that the Gallery was the best place of all for enjoying a play socially—that the relish of such exhibitions must be in proportion to the infrequency of going—that the company we met there, not being in general readers of plays, were obliged to attend the more, and did attend, to what was going on on the stage—because a word lost would have been a chasm, which it was impossible for them to fill up. With such reflections we consoled our pride then—and I appeal to you, whether, as a woman, I met generally with less attention and accommodation than I have done since in more expensive situations in the house? The getting in, indeed, and the crowding up those inconvenient staircases was bad enough,—but there was still a law of civility to women recognized to quite as great an extent as we ever found in the other passages—and how a little difficulty overcome heightened the snug seat, and the play, afterwards! Now we can only pay our money and walk in. You cannot see, you say, in the galleries now. I am sure we saw, and heard too, well enough then—but sight, and all, I think, is gone with our poverty.

"There was pleasure in eating strawberries, before they became quite common—in the first dish of peas, while they were yet dear—to have them for a nice supper, a treat. What treat can we have now? If we were to treat ourselves now—that is, to have dainties a little above our means, it would be selfish and wicked. It is the very little more that we allow ourselves beyond what the actual poor can get at, that makes what I call a treat—when two people living together, as we have done, now and then indulge themselves in a cheap luxury, which both like; while each apologizes, and is willing to take both halves of the blame to his single share. I see no harm in people making much of themselves in that sense of the word. It may give them a hint how to make much of others. But now—what I mean by the word—we never do make much of ourselves. None but the poor can do it. I do not mean the veriest poor of all, but persons as we were, just above poverty.

"I know what you were going to say, that it is mighty pleasant at the end of the year to make all meet,—and much ado we used to have every Thirty-first Night of December to account for our exceedings—many a long face did you make over your puzzled accounts, and in contriving to make it out how we had spent so much—or that we had not spent so much—or that it was impossible we should spend so much next year—and still we found our slender capital decreasing—but then, betwixt ways, and projects, and compromises of one sort or another, and talk of curtailing this charge, and doing without that for the future—and the hope that youth brings, and laughing spirits (in which you were never poor till now) we pocketed up our loss, and in conclusion, with 'lusty brimmers' (as you used to quote it out of *hearty cheerful Mr. Cotton*, as you called him), we used to welcome in the 'coming guest.' Now we have no reckoning at all at the end of the old year—no flattering promises about the new year doing better for us."

Bridget is so sparing of her speech on most occasions that when she gets into a rhetorical vein, I am careful how I interrupt it. I could not help, however, smiling at the phantom of wealth which her dear imagination had conjured up out of a clear income of a poor—hundred pounds a year. "It is true we were happier when we were poorer, but we were also younger, my cousin. I am afraid we must put up with the excess, for if we were to shake the superflux into the sea, we should not much mend ourselves. That we had much to struggle with, as we grew up together, we have reason to be most thankful. It strengthened, and knit our compact closer. We could never have been what we have been to each other, if we had always had the sufficiency which you now complain of. The resisting power—those natural dilations of the youthful spirit, which circumstances could not straiten—with us are long since passed away. Competence to age is supplementary youth; a sorry supplement, indeed, but I fear the best that is to be had. We must ride where we formerly walked: live better, and lie softer—and shall be wise to do so—than we had means to do in those good old days you speak of. Yet could those days return—could you and I once more walk our thirty miles a day—could Bannister and Mrs. Bland again be young, and you and I be young to see them—could the good old one-shilling gallery days return—they are dreams, my cousin, now—but could you and I at this moment, instead of this quiet argument, by·our well-carpeted fire-side, sitting on this luxurious sofa—be once more struggling up those inconvenient staircases, pushed about, and squeezed, and elbowed by the poorest rabble of poor gallery scramblers—could I once more hear those anxious shrieks of yours—and the delicious *Thank God, we are safe*, which always followed when the topmost stair, conquered, let in the first light of the whole cheerful theatre down beneath us—I know not the fathom line that ever touched a descent so deep as I would be willing to bury more wealth in than Croesus had, or the great Jew R____ is supposed to have, to purchase it. And now do just look at that merry little Chinese waiter holding an umbrella, big enough for a bed-tester, over the head of that pretty insipid half-Madonna-ish chit of a lady in that very blue summer house."

Once More to the Lake

E. B. White

One summer, along about 1904, my father rented a camp on a lake in Maine and took us all there for the month of August. We all got ringworm from some kittens and had to rub Pond's Extract on our arms and legs night and morning, and my father rolled over in a canoe with all his clothes on; but outside of that the vacation was a success and from then on none of us ever thought there was any place in the world like that lake in Maine. We returned summer after summer—always on August 1st for one month. I have since become a salt-water man, but sometimes in summer there are days when the restlessness of the tides and the fearful cold of the sea water and the incessant wind which blows across the afternoon and into the evening make me wish for the placidity of a lake in the woods. A few weeks ago this feeling got so strong I bought myself a couple of bass hooks and a spinner and returned to the lake where we used to go, for a week's fishing and to revisit old haunts.

I took along my son, who had never had any fresh water up his nose and who had seen lily pads only from train windows. On the journey over to the lake I began to wonder what it would be like. I wondered how time would have marred this unique, this holy spot—the coves and streams, the hills that the sun set behind, the camps and the paths behind the camps. I was sure that the tarred road would have found it out and I wondered in what other ways it would be desolated. It is strange how much you can remember about places like that once you allow your mind to return into the grooves which lead back. You remember one thing, and that suddenly reminds you of another thing. I guess I remembered clearest of all the early mornings, when the lake was cool and motionless, remembered how the bedroom smelled of the lumber it was made of and of the wet woods whose scent entered through the screen. The partitions in the camp were thin and did not extend clear to the top of the rooms, and as I was always the first up I would dress softly so as not to wake the others, and sneak out into the sweet outdoors and start out in the canoe, keeping close along the shore in the long shadows of the pines. I remembered being very careful never to rub my paddle against the gunwale for fear of disturbing the stillness of the cathedral.

The lake had never been what you would call a wild lake. There were cottages sprinkled around the shores, and it was in farming country, although the shores of the lake were quite heavily wooded. Some of the cottages were owned by nearby farmers, and you would live at the shore and eat your meals at the farmhouse. That's what our family did. But although it wasn't wild, it was a fairly large and undisturbed lake and there were places in it which, to a child at least, seemed infinitely remote and primeval.

I was right about the tar: it led to within half a mile of the shore. But when I got back there, with my boy, and we settled into a camp near a farmhouse and into the kind of summertime I had known, I could tell that it was going to be pretty much the same as it had been before—I knew it, lying in bed the first morning, smelling the bedroom, and hearing the boy sneak quietly out and go off along the shore in a boat. I began to sustain the illusion that he was I, and therefore, by simple transposition, that I was my father. This sensation persisted, kept cropping up all the time we were there. It was not an entirely new feeling, but in this setting it grew much stronger. I seemed to be living a dual existence. I would be in the middle of some simple act, I would be picking up a bait box or laying down a table fork, or I would be saying something, and suddenly it would be not I but my father who was saying the words or making the gesture. It gave me a creepy sensation.

We went fishing the first morning. I felt the same damp moss covering the worms in the bait can, and saw the dragonfly alight on the tip of my rod as it hovered a few inches from the surface of the water. It was the arrival of this fly that convinced me beyond any doubt that everything was as it always had been, that the years were a mirage and there had been no years. The small waves were the same, chucking the rowboat under the chin as we fished at anchor, and the boat was the same boat, the same color green and the ribs broken in the same places, and under the floor-boards the same fresh-water leavings and débris—the dead helgramite, the wisps of moss, the rusty discarded fishhook, the dried blood from yesterday's catch. We stared silently at the tips of our rods, at the dragonflies that came and went. I lowered the tip of mine into the water, tentatively, pensively dislodging the fly, which darted two feet away, poised, darted two feet back, and came to rest again a little farther up the rod. There had been no years between the ducking of this dragonfly and the other one—the one that was part of memory. I looked at the boy, who was silently watching his fly, and it was my hands that held his rod, my eyes watching. I felt dizzy and didn't know which rod I was at the end of.

We caught two bass, hauling them in briskly as though they were mackerel, pulling them over the side of the boat in a business-like manner without any landing net, and stunning them with a blow on the back of the head. When we got back for a swim before lunch, the lake was exactly where we had left it, the same number of inches from the dock, and there was only the merest suggestion of a breeze. This seemed an utterly enchanted sea, this lake you could leave to its own devices for a few hours and come back to, and find that it had not stirred, this constant and trustworthy body of water. In the shallows, the dark, water-soaked sticks and twigs, smooth and old, were undulating in clusters on the bottom against the clean ribbed sand, and the track of the mussel was plain. A school of minnows swam by, each minnow with its small individual shadow, doubling the attendance, so clear and sharp in the sunlight. Some of the other campers were in swimming, along the shore, one of them with a cake of soap, and the water felt thin and clear and unsubstantial. Over the years there had been this person with the cake of soap, this cultist, and here he was. There had been no years.

Up to the farmhouse to dinner through the teeming, dusty field, the road under our sneakers was only a two-track road. The middle track was missing, the one with the marks of the hooves and the splotches of dried, flaky manure. There had always been three tracks to choose from in choosing which track to walk in; now the choice was narrowed down to two. For a moment I missed terribly the middle alternative. But the way led past the tennis court, and something about the way it lay there in the sun reassured me; the tape had loosened along the backline, the alleys were green with plantains and other weeds, and the net (installed in June and removed in September) sagged in the dry noon, and the whole place steamed with midday heat and hunger and emptiness. There was a choice of pie for dessert, and one was blueberry and one was apple, and the waitresses were the same country girls, there having been no passage of time, only the illusion of it as in a dropped curtain—the waitresses were still fifteen; their hair had been washed, that was the only difference—they had been to the movies and seen the pretty girls with the clean hair.

Summertime, oh summertime, pattern of life indelible, the fade-proof lake, the woods unshatterable, the pasture with the sweetfern and the juniper forever and ever, summer without end; this was the background, and the life along the shore was the design, the cottagers with their innocent and tranquil design, their tiny docks with the flagpole and the American flag floating against the white clouds in the blue sky, the little paths over the roots of the trees leading from camp to camp and the paths leading back to the outhouses and the can of lime for sprinkling, and at the souvenir counters at the store the miniature birch-bark canoes and the post cards that showed things looking a little better than they looked. This was the American family at play, escaping the city heat, wondering whether the new comers in the camp at the head of the cove were "common" or "nice," wondering whether it was true that the people who drove up for Sunday dinner at the farmhouse were turned away because there wasn't enough chicken.

It seemed to me, as I kept remembering all this, that those times and those summers had been infinitely precious and worth saving. There had been jollity and peace and goodness. The arriving (at the beginning of August) had been so big a business in itself, at the railway station the farm wagon drawn up, the first smell of the pine-laden air, the first glimpse of the smiling farmer, and the great importance of the trunks and your father's enormous authority in such matters, and the feel of the wagon under you for the long ten-mile haul, and at the top of the last long hill catching the first view of the lake after eleven months of not seeing this cherished body of water. The shouts and cries of the other campers when they saw you, and the trunks to be unpacked, to give up their rich burden. (Arriving was less exciting nowadays, when you sneaked up in your car and parked it under a tree near the camp and took out the bags and in five minutes it was all over, no fuss, no loud wonderful fuss about trunks.)

Peace and goodness and jollity. The only thing that was wrong now, really, was the sound of the place, an unfamiliar nervous sound of the outboard motors. This was the note that jarred, the one thing that would sometimes break the illusion and set the years moving. In those other summertimes all motors were inboard; and when they were at a little distance, the noise they made was a sedative, an ingredient of summer sleep. They were one-cylinder and two-cylinder engines, and some were make-

and-break and some were jump-spark, but they all made a sleepy sound across the lake. The one-lungers throbbed and fluttered, and the twin-cylinder ones purred and and purred, and that was a quiet sound too. But now the campers all had outboards. In the daytime, in the hot mornings, these motors made a petulant, irritable sound; at night, in the still evening when the after-glow lit the water, they whined about one's ears like mosquitoes. My boy loved our rented outboard, and his great desire was to achieve single-handed mastery over it, and authority, and he soon learned the trick of choking it a little (but not too much), and the adjustment of the needle valve. Watching him I would remember the things you could do with the old one-cylinder engine with the heavy flywheel, how you could have it eating out of your hand if you got really close to it spiritually. Motor boats in those days didn't have clutches, and you would make a landing by shutting off the motor at the proper time and coasting in with a dead rudder. But there was a way of reversing them, if you learned the trick, by cutting the switch and putting it on again exactly on the final dying revolution of the flywheel, so that it would kick back against compression and begin reversing. Approaching a dock in a strong following breeze, it was difficult to slow up by the ordinary coasting method, and if a boy felt he had complete mastery over his motor, he was tempted to keep it running beyond its time and then reverse it a few feet from the dock. It took a cool nerve, because if you threw the switch a twentieth of a second too soon you would catch the flywheel when it still had speed enough to go past center, and the boat would leap ahead, charging bull-fashion at the dock.

We had a good week at the camp. The bass were biting well and the sun shone endlessly, day after day. We would be tired at night and lie down in the accumulated heat of the little bedrooms after the long hot day and the breeze would stir almost imperceptibly outside and the smell of the swamp drift in through the rusty screens. Sleep would come easily and in the morning the red squirrel would be on the roof, tapping out his gay routine. I kept remembering everything, lying in bed in the mornings—the small steamboat that had a long rounded stern like the lip of a Ubangi, and how quietly she ran on the moonlight sails, when the older boys played their mandolins and the girls sang and we ate doughnuts dipped in sugar, and how sweet the music was on the water in the shining night, and what it had felt like to think about girls then. After breakfast we would go up to the store and the things were in the same place—the minnows in a bottle, the plugs and spinners disarranged and pawed over by the youngsters from the boys' camp, the fig newtons and the Beeman's gum. Outside the road was tarred and cars stood in front of the store. Inside, all was just as it had always been, except there was more Coca-Cola and not so much Moxie and root beer and birch beer and sarsaparilla. We would walk out with a bottle of pop apiece and sometimes the pop would backfire up our noses and hurt. We explored the streams, quietly, where the turtles slid off the sunny logs and dug their way into the soft bottom; and we lay on the town wharf and fed worms to the tame bass. Everywhere we went I had trouble making out which was I, the one walking at my side, the one walking in my pants.

One afternoon while we were there at the lake a thunderstorm came up. It was like the revival of an old melodrama that I had seen long ago with childish awe. The second-act climax of the electrical disturbance over a lake in America had not changed in any important respect. This was the big scene, still the big scene. The whole thing was so familiar, the first feeling of oppression and heat and a general air around camp of not wanting to go very far away. In midafternoon (it was all the same) a curious darkening of the sky, and a lull in everything that had made life tick; and then the way the boats suddenly swung the other way at their moorings with the coming of a breeze out of the new quarter, and the premonitory rumble. Then the kettle drum, then the snare, then the bass drum and cymbals, then crackling light against the dark, and the gods grinning and licking their chops in the hills. Afterward the calm, the rain steadily rustling in the calm lake, the return of light and hope and spirits, and the campers running out in joy and relief to go swimming in the rain, their bright cries perpetuating the deathless joke about how they were getting simply drenched, and the children screaming with delight at the new sensation of bathing in the rain, and the joke about getting drenched linking the generations in a strong indestructible chain. And the comedian who waded in carrying an umbrella.

When the others went swimming my son said he was going in too. He pulled his dripping trunks from the line where they had hung all through the shower, and wrung them out. Languidly, and with no thought of going in, I watched him, his hard little body, skinny and bare, saw him wince slightly as he pulled up around his vitals the small, soggy, icy garment. As he buckled the swollen belt suddenly my groin felt the chill of death.

INDEX

Abstract language
  moving paragraph from abstract to concrete, 63-67
Aesthetic distance
  in writer's stance, illustration, "A Few Writer-Subject-Reader Relationships," 38
  with conversational voice, 37, 91-92
  with objective voice, 37, 39
  with personal voice, 37, 146-48
  with voice variations, 189-90
  see also Voice
Anticlimax, in sentences, 76-77
Association
  illustration, Search, Sort, Select, 16-17
  movement by, 3, 8-9, 13
  narrowing process of, 18
  use with familiar essay, 145, 148, 175-76
Audience
  developing sensitivity towards, 31-32
  identifying, 30-31
  projecting for deductive essay, 30-32, 198-99
  projecting for familiar essay, 149, 198-99

projecting for inductive essay, 91-92, 198-99
projecting for persuasive essay, 199-200
projecting through questions, 30-31
reader's role, 32-33
writer's attitude toward, 29-30
  in persuasion, 199-200
writer's contract in paragraphs, 58-59, 61
  in deductive essay, 90

Bacon, Francis, 78
Benchley, Robert, 150
Bishop, Carole, "Violence and the Young," 51-56
Bombeck, Erma, "What's a Mother For But to Suffer?" 251-56
  referred to, 147, 149, 171
Brooks, Scott, "O Christmas Tree, O Christmas Tree!" 169-70
Cantwell, Mary, "A Childhood of Pegasus," 111-19
Cates, Becky, 66
Checklists
  for deductive essay, rough draft, 48-49
  for familiar essay, 178-79

for inductive essay, see assignment 2, 137, and assignment 3, 142
for inductive sentence outline, 24-25
for paragraph development, 69-70
for sentence variety and emphasis, 78-79
for word choice, 84
Churchill, Winston, 87
Climax, in sentences, 76
Complex sentence, 71-72
as idea signal, 71
Compound sentence, 71-72
as idea signal, 71
overuse, 72
Compound-complex sentence, 72
Contract
in deductive essay, 90
in paragraphs, 58-59, 61
Conversational voice
effect on reader, 34
with inductive essay, 91-92, 134
see also Voice
Crump, Lori, "On the Persuasiveness of Print or Why I Appear Schizophrenic," 163-65

Davidson, Douglas, 73
Deductive essay, 39-57
avoiding static paragraph beginnings, 48
avoiding unnecessary repetition of outline phrasing, 48
body, 45-46
checklist for the rough draft, 48-49
conclusion, 46-47; referred to, 141
format, typed essay, 57
illustration, deductive pattern, 41
introduction, 40-44
outline flexibility, 41
paragraph division, 45n3, 45
polishing rough draft, 47-49
purpose, 39
student essay, 51-56
thought movement, 39
transitions between paragraphs, 45-48
underlining topics, 46
Deductive mode of thought, 3
Deductive paragraphs, 58-70
analyzing the topic sentence, 58-63
building the paragraph, 63-67

checking the paragraph, 67-70
for coherence, 68
for completeness, 68-69
for unity, 67-68
checklist for development, 69-70
division of, according to outline, 45n3, 45
levels of abstraction, 64-65
paragraph traps, 62-63
relationship with essay, 58
steps in development, 65-67
structural patterns, 63
use and arrangement of details, 63-67
variations in arrangement, 66-67
writer's contract, 58-59, 61
DeQuincey, Thomas, 34
Direct address (you), 35n2, 189-90
Dominant design, 183, 214

Editorial we, 34n1, 91
Elbow, Peter, 80
Emert, Pam, 131
End position in sentence, 75-76

Familiar essay, 145-79
the body, 175-76
characteristics, 145-46
checklist, 178-79
choosing a subject, 149-51
circular structure, 145-46, 148, 172, 176-77
the conclusion, 176-77
distinguished from other types of personal essays, 146
effect on reader, 177-78
the introduction, 172-75
intuitive arrangement, 175
the preliminary steps, 171-72
projecting the audience and stating the purpose, 171
selecting a familiar topic, 171
writer's stance, 171
student essays, 153-70
use of association, 145, 148, 175-76
use of Search, Sort, Select with subject, 148
personal voice, 148-49
projecting audience, 149
style, 146, 149
thought arrangement, 145-46, 148
transitions, 175-76

use of question to focus subject, 148
writer's purpose, 146, 148
writer's stance, 146-48, 171
Forster, E. M., "My Wood," 185-86
Frost, Robert, 178

Galloway, Newton, "Beware: Chicken Crossing," 103-109
Garcia, Maria, 85

Henry, Patrick, 78
Henry, Sylvia, "The 1960s," 157-60

Illustration
    Deductive Pattern for Essay of Medium Length, 41
    formats for deductive and inductive outlines, 28
    Inductive Pattern for Essay of Medium Length, 138
    The Search, Sort, Select Process, 16-17
    Voice: A Few Writer-Subject-Reader Relationships, 38
Induction
    as a mode of thought, 3, 90
Inductive essay, 89-143
    achieving reader closeness, 91-92
    body, 137-38
    building inductive paragraphs, 137
    characteristics, 89-90
    checklist, see assignment 2, 137, and assignment 3, 142
    choosing a subject, 92-94, 131
    conclusion, 141-42
    conversational voice, 91-92, 134
    creating the reader, 90-91
    illustration, inductive pattern, 138
    inductive outline, 132-33
    introduction, 133-37
    student essays, 95-130
    transitions, 139-41
Inductive outline
    checklist, 24-25
    formulating inductive sentence, 23-24
    formulating inductive topic, 19-22
    formulating outline for inductive essay, 132-33
Inquiry
    process of, 7-18
    see also Search, Sort, Select

Kennedy, X. J., "Who Killed King Kong?" 193-96

Labor, Earle, "Crane and Hemingway: Anatomy of Trauma," 221-29
Lamb, Charles, "Old China," 257-61
    referred to, 147, 150
Loose sentence, 76

Major voice
    described, 33-35
    variations, 189-90, 214
Marquis, Don, "Preface to a Book of Statistics," 245-47
    referred to, 151
Mead, Margaret, "Needed: Full Partnership for Women," 217-20
Movement-by-association; see Association
Murphy, Kevin W., 36

Notebook, pocket-size, 5, 145, 150
    referred to, 28, 88, 143

Objective voice
    effect on reader, 34-35
    with deductive essay, 37-39
    see also Voice
Ong, Walter J., S.J., 91
Orwell, George, "Reflections on Gandhi," 237-44
Outline
    as an aid to thinking and focusing ideas, 19
    deductive sentence, 25-26
        example, 26
        shifting from inductive to deductive form, 25
    inductive topic
        deriving subtopics and topics, 21-22
        example of, 22
        phrasing question for, 19-21
    inductive sentence
        checklist, 24-25
        example, 23-24
        phrasing, 23
    flexibility, 22, 27, 40, 133
    reason for form used in text, 27

Paragraphs, 58-69
    checklist for development, 69-70
    deductive, 58-69

see also Deductive essay, Deductive paragraph, Familiar essay, Inductive essay
Paralleling equal ideas in sentences, 77
Periodic sentence, 76
Personal voice
    effect on reader, 34
    with familiar essay, 148-49
    see also Voice
Persuasive essay, 198-214
    analyzing writer's and reader's values, goals, and differences, 199-200
    audience, initial attitude toward topic, 199
    avoiding aggressive approach, 200
    compared with argumentative essay, 213
    dominant design, 214
    essay by Ted Walker, 203-12
    purpose, 199
    seeking common ground, 199
    voice, 214
    writer's attitude toward audience, 199
Pope, Alexander, 1, 76-77
Porter, Connie, 33
Position, end, in sentences, 75-76
Pronouns
    as voice, 35
    direct address (you), 35n2, 189-90
    editorial *we*, 34n1, 91
Punctuation, art of, 85-87
Question
    phrasing for inductive outline, 19-21
    to analyze inductive essay introduction, 134
    to analyze topic sentence of paragraph, 59
    to determine values and attitude for writer and reader in persuasion, 199-200
    to find subject for inductive essay, 131, 150
    to focus familiar essay topic, 150
    to project audience of deductive essay, 30-31, 198
    to project audience of familiar essay, 198-99
    to project audience of inductive essay, 198

    to project audience of persuasive essay, 199-200
    to involve reader, 134, 139-40, 183
Relating parts to the whole, 18-28; *see also* Outline
Repetition
    avoiding unnecessary, 48
    of like structures and words, 72, 77-78
Salmon, Keith, "The Braves' Chances in 1982," 121-30
Search, Sort, Select
    as a guide to inquiry, 18
    illustration of process, 16-17
    extension of
        to add outline subtopics, 27, 132-33
        to narrow topic, 15
    relationship of steps, 18
    Search 1, 7-10
        description of, 7-8
        example of, 8-9
        purpose of, 10
    Search 2, 13
    Select 1, 12
    Select 2, 15
    Sort 1, 10-11
    Sort 2, 14
    with familiar essay, 148
    with inductive subject, 92
    used in finding words, 80
Sentences
    anticlimax, 71
    climax, 76
    end position, 75-76
    loose, 76
    parallel ideas in, 77
    periodic, 76
    placing word out of natural order, 77
    repetition of words, 77-78
    variety and emphasis, 71-79
        checklist, 78-79
        external form, 71-75
            form as signal, 71
            sentence length, 72-73
            sentence variety, 72-75
        internal arrangement of words, 75-78
            a few principles of word placement, 75

Shakespeare, William, 78
Shift in voice, 213; *see also* Voice
Simms, Howard, 78
Simpkins, Willie D., "What is Objectivity?" 95-102
Simple sentence, 71-73
    as idea signal, 71
    for emphasis, 72
    overuse of, 72
    varied by modifiers, 72-73
Stevenson, Robert Louis, 150
Stewart, Lisa M., 32-33
Structuring the essay; *see* Deductive essay, Familiar essay, Inductive essay
Subject-first sentence, varying, 73-74
Subject treatment; *see* Variations

Thinking through a topic, 7-18; *see also* Search, Sort, Select
Thomas, Lewis, "The Music of *This* Sphere," 231-35
Thurber, James, "Which," 249-50
    referred to, 150
Tools
    for writing, 4
    used imaginatively, 4
Transitional paragraphs, in long essay, 183
Transitions
    between deductive paragraphs, 45-48; within, 68
    with familiar essay, 175-76
    with inductive essay, 139-41
Turner, Jane, 67

Variations, 181-98
    in paragraph arrangements, 183
    structural, 182-83
    subject treatment, 197
    voice, 189-90
Voice
    conversational, 33-35, 37-39
        with inductive essay, 91-92, 134
    definition of, 33
    direct address (you), 35n2
    editorial *we*, 34n1, 91
    effect on reader, 33-35

function, 33
illustration, 38
initiated by writer's relationships, 35-37
    objective, 33-35, 37-39
    personal, 33-35, 37-39
        with familiar essay, 148-49
    print, 189
    reader trust, 35
    shift in, 189-90
    writer's persona, 36-37, 189
    writer's roles, 36-37, 189
    writer's stance (distance from subject), 37-39, 91-92, 146-47, 189-90

Walker, Ted, "Bid a sad farewell to the landscape plotted and pieced," 200-12
White, E. B., "Once More to the Lake," 263-68
    referred to, 147, 150
Williams, Lib, "Procrastination," 153-56
Word choice, 79-87
    active voice, 81
    checklist, 84
    connotation, 82
    experiencing thoughts, 80-81
    figurative language, 83
    levels of English usage, 83-84
    nouns and verbs, 81
    sensitivity towards, 79-81
    unnecessary words, 82
    verbs and verbals, 81
Word placement
    placed out of natural order, 77
    some principles, 75-78
    see also Word choice
Writer's stance, 37-39, 91-92, 146-47, 189-90; *see also* Voice
Writing
    as an unselfish act, 29-30
    daily, 5
    environment, 4
    to establish a bond with the reader, 29-30